THE BEDSERS

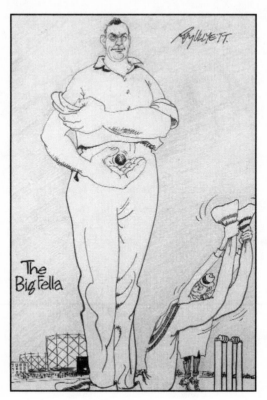

'The Big Fella' – Alec Bedser as visualised
by cartoonist Roy Ulyett.
(Courtesy of Stephen Green, MCC)

The
BEDSERS

TWINNING TRIUMPHS

Alan Hill

MAINSTREAM
PUBLISHING

EDINBURGH AND LONDON

BY THE SAME AUTHOR

The Family Fortune — A Saga of Sussex Cricket
A Chain of Spin Wizards
Hedley Verity — Portrait of a Cricketer
Johnny Wardle — Cricket Conjuror
Les Ames
Herbert Sutcliffe — Cricket Maestro
Bill Edrich
Peter May
Jim Laker

First published in Great Britain in 2001 by
MAINSTREAM PUBLISHING COMPANY (EDINBURGH) LTD
7 Albany Street
Edinburgh EH1 3UG

ISBN 1 84018 314 4

All illustrations supplied by Sir Alec and Eric Bedser, except where stated

A catalogue record for this book is available from the British Library

Typeset in Book Antiqua and Van Dijck
Printed and bound in Great Britain by Butler & Tanner Ltd, Frome and London

Contents

To Mac and Dorothy.

*With affection and gratitude for
memories of winning days at Kennington
and hospitality worthy of champions.*

Foreword

by Rt. Hon. John Major, CH,MP

In all cricket history there has been no partnership to rival that of Alec and Eric Bedser. To know one is to know the other, for they are as identical in mind as they are in form. Often at The Oval or Lord's I have sat with them to hear one express a view about, say, field-placing or a batsman's technique and a few moments later – without any possibility of consultation – to hear the other express a similar sentiment. It was the view of two seasoned professionals with an identical eye.

They have spent a lifetime in cricket. Alec is one of our greatest bowlers: in the line of Sydney Barnes and Maurice Tate came Alec Bedser with, as yet, no successor. For years Alec *was* the England pace attack, toiling so often against the great Australian sides led by Don Bradman and Lindsay Hassett. He bowled hour upon hour, an indefatigable giant, naggingly accurate, inventive and stately as a galleon as he ran up to the wicket. No heart for England was ever stronger or more willing – and few more cunning, for this thinking bowler introduced the leg-cutter to cricket history.

Eric was ever at his side and he was a fine cricketer, too, with both bat and ball. In most decades Eric would have bowled his off-spin for England but fate put Jim Laker, perhaps the greatest of them all, on the pitch at the same time and in the same Surrey team. Even so, Eric played in a Test trial in 1950, only to find the gods frowning on his fortune in that game as Laker took eight wickets for two runs. I can see Eric now, as a batsman, his bulk crouched at the crease, his bat seemingly a toy in his massive hands but one used often enough to good effect for his team.

This book is more than a cricketing biography: it is a unique story of two very special people with values and opinions that do not change with the fashions of the day. They have also a touching love of their country that is as endearing as it is refreshing. England first, always – for Alec and Eric could only be English – but Australia, too, is a great love in their lives. From humble origins through national celebrity to their status today as grand old men of cricket, their story is told by Alan Hill with the affection and insight that was evident in his earlier biographies of their friends and team-mates, Peter May and Jim Laker.

On and off the field, this is a tale worth telling.

Introduction

The celebration dinners, in London and Sydney, accorded recognition of the prestige of the Bedser twins. On their 80th birthday the tributes carried distant echoes of the euphoria which greeted the end of the Second World War. Affection is lasting for sporting heroes who assisted in the healing balm of rehabilitation: 'Cricketing figures, like Alec and Eric, are revered because they played a major part in England's recovery after the war,' says one of their close friends, Doug Insole.

Sir Donald Bradman, Australia's sportsman of the century, paid his own eloquent birthday tribute. He recalled a staunch and true friendship, augmented by the annual visits of the Bedsers to Australia: 'I think their outstanding contribution to cricket and life in general has been their transparent honesty and sincerity. They exude an integrity which is the hallmark of great citizens, and they are examples for young people of all ages to follow.'

Taking a lead from the great Australian, in my own journey of discovery, I can testify to the steadfast qualities of Sir Alec and his inseparable twin brother, Eric. Over the past months we have had many conversations at the Woking home they helped to build with their father nearly 50 years ago. We have ranged over a variety of topics and there has emerged a story of a resolute commitment to a game which has brought so many blessings.

The burden of my work on a long overdue biography has been immeasurably lightened by their unstinting cooperation. Their observations have given substance to my chronicle of their progress from humble origins at Woking to high estate as key members of the Surrey team in the championship years in the 1950s. Michael Barton, one of their first county captains, has referred to Alec's powers of endurance as Surrey's, and England's, bowling standard-bearer in the early post-war years: 'Alec really carried us during that time. There is no question that he was the man who contributed most to our successes.'

The Bedsers parade a beguiling modesty to deflect extravagant claims. They prefer to relate the virtues and rewards of a rigorous apprenticeship on the nursery slopes at The Oval. It was an insistent passage of dialogue in our talks. Any vices, if they can be so described, reveal an implacable realism which places them in dispute with the manners and technical flaws of the modern game. The criticism is considered harsh and unrelenting in some quarters, but the standards set by the Bedsers are imposingly high and should be accepted in the spirit of a challenge by the cricketers of today. Geoffrey Boycott and Ian Botham, with whom Alec had some interesting times as a selector, are cited by him as exemplars of their trade.

The pattern of the lives of the Bedsers is firmly rooted in disciplines bequeathed to them during a strict but kindly upbringing. The twins speak with fervour of a 'wonderful childhood' and the devotion to their parents is manifest and endearing. I have been permitted to eavesdrop on this time and for my sketch of the Woking of their infancy I am also indebted to Ian Wakeford, who allowed me access to his history of the Surrey town.

The recital of the years of acclaim under the adventurous leadership of Stuart Surridge has also been enhanced by the appreciative memories of Surridge's contemporaries, Geoffrey Howard, the former county secretary, Alf Gover, Peter Loader, Raman Subba Row, Dave Fletcher and, notably, Arthur McIntyre – an adept and courageous wicket-keeper who, along with Godfrey Evans at England level, was judged as an influential ally in Alec's progress to stardom. Alec himself generously recalls the benefits of their association: 'Mac was a magnificent keeper who did everything so easily and never made a fuss. He had the most difficult job in English county cricket, standing up to four bowlers.'

I am pleased to acknowledge the recollections of fellow writers, especially the valued help of the late Jim Swanton. Praise must also be given to the courteous assistance of the staffs of the British Newspaper Library at Colindale and the Surrey History Centre at Woking. Special thanks are due to Jeff Hancock, the Surrey CCC librarian, unsparing in his aid and encouragement, and to Stephen Green, the MCC curator at Lord's.

The exploits of Alec and Eric have also elicited telling compliments from contemporary opponents – Peter Richardson, Arthur Milton, Tom Graveney, David Allen, John Dewes, the Rt Rev. David Sheppard, Roy Tattersall and Dennis Brookes. Respectful voices in their favour have also been raised in Yorkshire, Surrey's fierce championship rivals in the 1950s. Bob Appleyard recalls the immense burden shouldered by Alec before the arrival of new England bowling recruits. His testimony is endorsed by one of their numbers, Fred Trueman, whose staggering entry into Test cricket against India in 1952 brought the inestimable rewards of a partnership with a great bowler.

The Bedsers are nowhere more venerated than in Australia. They are now regarded as 'honorary Australians' in this land of warm and hospitable people. Arthur Morris, with whom Alec was poised in combat over four Ashes series, was an engaging spokesman at a breakfast-time interview during the Test at Melbourne in 1998. Ron Archer, another Australian rival and close friend, took the trouble to relay his glowing impressions in a long and detailed fax. Archer's was the wicket at The Oval in 1953 which enabled Alec to achieve a series aggregate of 39 wickets and surpass the previous record held by Maurice Tate. Others aiding my researches on the international front included Walter Hadlee, the former New Zealand captain, who presented his views in typically meticulous fashion in an encouraging letter from Christchurch.

Trevor Bailey, one of the dwindling band of English Test comrades, has confirmed the prevailing view of Alec as the best fast-medium bowler of his time. Bailey recalls the wicked and feared leg-cutter with which Bedser confounded so many opponents. He still winces at the memory of his tussles with the 'big fella'. The most significant feature, says Trevor, was that 'Alec was responsible for bruising the inside of my right hand.' It is a signal tribute to the accuracy of Alec's bowling thrusts: 'He jarred my hand more than any other bowler I faced.'

The knighthood received by Alec in 1997 was the first to be awarded to an England bowler. It reflected not only the esteem in which he is held as a cricketer, but also the service to the game maintained during his record term as chairman of the Test selectors. He was closely associated with a swiftly changing order in cricket during this time. It was his integrity as a former professional which gained him acceptance as a worthy trustee of the game.

The abiding impression which my readers will surely take from an absorbing odyssey is perhaps less concerned with cricket than with the togetherness of the Bedser twins. Theirs is a rare and precious relationship. Peter Richardson provides the happiest of sentiments: 'The joy that Eric has got from Alec's success is so blatant. This is one of the nicest things about them as brothers.'

Alan Hill
Lindfield, Sussex
January 2001

CHAPTER ONE

Playground on the Common

'As like as two Bedsers' may well become the accepted term among cricketers, for no more bewildering similarity between two men could be imagined than that of the Woking twins.

NORMAN PRESTON

The lookalike twins with united voices cherish their comradeship. The cricketing Bedsers began their lives in a rented cottage on a Surrey common. It was there, on the heather- and gorse-covered acres of Horsell, that they forged a regime for endurance. More than 80 years on, they have remained true to this rural domain, stoutly independent in a house built with their bricklayer father in the grounds of the former gentry. It is redolent with memories of devoted parents who first nurtured the blessings of the self-reliance which still informs all the twins' actions today.

Alec and Eric were two homespun country boys who grew up strong and healthy in these peaceful pastures, working on a farm through the long days of summer. As five-year-olds, it is related, they played back-garden cricket with their father. The twins were members of the church choir team. Eric, at seven, competing against boys twice his age, won the prize of a shilling in one match. It was a useful supplement to their quarterly income as choristers.

The lure of cricket for the Bedsers had, at its source, an inner compulsion. The games of their childhood were mostly played without adult supervision and on pitches of doubtful provenance. From their earliest days, Alec and Eric revelled in practice. It was then that they dutifully began to acquire the disciplines of accuracy as bowlers.

As identical twins, Alec and Eric – the senior by ten minutes – were born on 4 July 1918. They weighed in at seven pounds and six and a half pounds respectively. Their arrival, however happy the event, must have caused at least a ripple of concern for their mother, who had been unaware that she was actually carrying twins.

It was expedient that the confinement took place at their grandmother's home in Reading. This was during the last phase of their father's service in the RAF. Therefore, although it is strictly correct that the Bedser brothers shared the same birthplace as future Surrey colleagues Peter May and Ken Barrington, it was only an intermission of a few months before the family returned to Woking. Florence Bedser, their mother, had been in service as a children's nurse before she met her future husband, Arthur, at Woodham. They were married at Christ Church, Woking, on 18 January 1916.

In the beginning, there was one feeding mishap for their newly born sons: it was a moment of confusion, a regular source of bewilderment for others outside the family circle. Eric, to Alec's well-voiced consternation, had a double ration at one session. It did not happen again.

Eric did then have the advantage in weight. It led one aunt to describe them jokingly as 'Tub and Midge'. The pet names faltered in the course of childhood imitation to 'Wub and Nidge'. The boys were thus addressed by their mother and father and other close friends long into their childhood.

The impression of strict but kind parents is one that lingers in the memories of the Bedsers. The years between the two world wars were times of unceasing challenge for Arthur Bedser. His was a precarious livelihood as a bricklayer, working on the local housing estates. He never earned more than £4 a week throughout his working life. Penury was a constant threat, especially in the depression period of the late 1920s.

'Dad used to get the sack on Friday night and then have to find another job on Saturday,' remember Alec and Eric. 'He would cycle all round Woking in search of work.' Arthur Bedser was sometimes in acute pain due to bouts of lumbago. His discomfiture meant that there were times when he had to kneel on the scaffold, laying bricks, so as not to lose money from inaction. On rainy days he wore a wheat sack like a shawl as protection against the worst of the elements.

Bedser senior, in his rare leisure interludes, played 'country house' cricket on the splendid estate of Woodham Hall, which extended over 67 acres. Alec and Eric, as children, worked on the estate each autumn. One of their jobs was sweeping up the mountains of leaves which had fallen on the long looping drive leading up to the mansion. It was, as they say, one of their early aids to fitness.

Their father was always an encouraging influence as a sportsman. Arthur Bedser achieved local renown as a footballer. As a right-winger and semi-professional, he played for Reading Reserves and also represented Woking in the Isthmian League. Woking were four times league champions during their earlier term in the West Surrey League. They also won the Surrey Charity League thrice between 1904 and 1908.

One notable event occurred in the January of the latter year. Woking, with Bedser senior in their ranks, reached the third round of the F.A. Cup. They lost, unsurprisingly, to Bolton Wanderers. The Lancastrians were promoted to the First Division of the Football League at the end of the season. Sporting accomplishments in the Bedser family were also shared by an uncle, Victor Badcock, who played soccer for Maidenhead, Berkshire and Buckinghamshire and cricket for local teams in Reading.

꙰ꙮ ꙰ꙮ ꙰ꙮ

The playground of the Bedsers at Horsell had assumed legendary status before the turn of the last century. It was there, on the sandpits close by their childhood home, that H.G. Wells unleashed his fictional Martians. He described how a devastating heat ray reduced the settlements to 'a heap of fiery ruins'. The story of this episode of destruction was to bring the newly married and aspiring novelist worldwide renown. It was conceived by Wells in his cycling forays from his modest semi-detached villa in Maybury Road. His book, *War of the Worlds*, is today commemorated in Woking by a tile mural featuring the Martians' fighting machine and scenes of the invasion and its terrors.

Another literary figure, George Bernard Shaw, the dramatist and critic, preceded Wells as a Woking resident. His home was only a short distance from Wells's fantasy land of the Martians. Shaw's stay in the Surrey town almost directly coincided with the building of a new church at Woodham. Hidden among the trees near the present busy six-way traffic junction was the All Saints Church. The church celebrated its centenary in 1994.

One former parishioner remembered that they were not allowed to walk on the elegant marble floor of the sanctuary. They had first to change into slippers, a supply of which was kept in the vestry. Sundays were strictly designated as days of religious observance. Attendance for the Bedsers on Sundays involved three journeys to the church for services and school instruction in the afternoon.

The devotions were recalled by another parishioner. She remembered her childhood walks along Woodham Lane to church: 'It was sandy and dusty in the summer and very muddy in the winter.' The lane called for stout footwear and sure strides to negotiate the deep ditches on either side. There were very few houses in her time and no street lighting. 'We used lanterns with candles in them if we had to go out when there was no moon at night.'

Alec and Eric were a contented pair during the happiest of childhoods. Fortitude was, though, needed on those bleak days when the family finances were at a low ebb. Florence Bedser would marshal her young sons into their pram and walk with them into Woking on hopeful shopping expeditions. 'She would only have a shilling in her pocket and was forced to manage until Dad came home with his wages,' recall the brothers.

The Bedsers first lived in two rooms of a property belonging to an aunt at Horsell. The next move was to rented accommodation at Knaphill. There were no cooking or bathroom facilities at this address. All the family meals were prepared on an open fire. In 1920, there was a minor advance when, through the good offices of a friend, the Bedsers were able to rent a cottage. It cost them ten shillings a week, a quarter of Father's wages. Lighting was by oil lamp – later to be replaced, in what seemed an impressive innovation, by gas; and then by electricity.

Household comforts of a kind accepted today were only slowly gained. It was not until Alec and Eric were in their 30s that there was sufficient money to buy the cottage and invest in the luxury of a bathroom. Alec was by then an established Test player. Cricket success brought the change in their fortunes.

Florence Bedser must have been a resourceful manager to meet the challenge of the lusty appetites set by her two sons. Potatoes, bread and ample puddings were among the staple foods supplemented by garden produce. One favourite meal was herring and a special treat was the arrival of chicken on the family menu.

On schooldays, with packages of cheese sandwiches slung across their backs, Alec and Eric polished their soccer footwork with a tennis ball during the mile-and-a-half walk to Maybury Junior School. This preceded their terms as seniors at Monument Hill Central, one of the last of the Victorian schools in the area. The senior school roll in the late 1920s consisted of 280 pupils in 6 (later 7) classes, with an average of 40 children per class.

The Bedsers and their classmates came under the supervision of headmaster Frank Marsh and his staff of five assistant teachers. The curriculum was wide-ranging: apart from the standard subjects, it included garden classes, one seaside outing to Bognor and, on one occasion, a visit to a performance of Shakespeare's *Julius Caesar* at a local theatre.

There was, from the start, evidence of intelligence and the kinship of the Bedser boys. They always shared their distinctions, finishing alternately first and second in the form throughout their schooldays. The consistency of their results prompted one teacher misguidedly to accuse them of cheating in class. He sought to rectify matters by separating them. 'We still came up with the same answers, or made the same mistakes, so we proved him wrong,' say Alec and Eric.

In happier vein were the term reports of Frank Marsh and their form master, Fred Dixon. Eric and Alec were respectively captain and secretary of the Monument Hill School's football and cricket elevens. 'Conscientious and painstaking,' reads one doubtless well-deserved tribute to their industry in these capacities. For Alec, as a 14-year-old, there was the testimony that his standard of behaviour had set an example to the rest of the school. Eric, too, won praise for his general conduct. The hope was expressed that he would represent a model for the younger children.

One day a message was relayed to Frank Marsh by Major May, who had served with the Woking headmaster during the First World War: 'Bright boy wanted as office boy.' May, now a solicitor, had an office at Lincoln's Inn Fields in London. The Bedsers were nominated by Frank Marsh as likely candidates. Eric, as the senior 14-year-old, was recommended and accepted for a probationary period.

Alec's schooldays had another six months to run and he expressed his misgivings about the parting from his brother. He was told: 'If Eric is satisfactory, a place will be found for you when you leave school.' Eric fully measured up to the required standard and Alec was thus able to rejoin his brother. The routine then established was to catch the 8.05 train to London for their day at the office before returning home to further their education with book-keeping and shorthand lessons at evening school.

At 18, Eric and Alec were clerks in the solicitor's office, carrying responsibilities under a senior clerk for estates management and probates. They were paid a weekly salary of 30 shillings each. Articled status was well beyond the means of their parents even though, as time was to prove, their ambitions lay in another direction. A brush with elitism was the catalyst which brought about the change of course. The unwitting intruder was a new entrant at the firm – a Sherborne schoolboy and the son of one of the solicitor's clients.

Alec was entrusted with the tuition of the new employee. At the end of the year there was a rebuff to his esteem. The young man from

Sherborne was given a pay rise of one pound. The Bedsers were rewarded with increases of five shillings each. Not unnaturally, the brothers voiced their protests at the discrepancy. The response from their employer was curt and telling: 'He went to a better school than you did.'

The wheels of fortune can often spin like numbers on a gaming table to come to rest on a winning lifestyle. Alec and Eric did eventually find a happy landing. The call of cricket was shrill and insistent and from their earliest days, lacking special mentors, they were fascinated by the game. Nevertheless it was football, which, without the need for extensive equipment or facilities, first involved them as children. Arsenal in the inter-war period were an illustrious magnet. Eddie Hapgood and George Male, both England internationals, were defenders to admire at Highbury. The Bedsers, growing in forbidding physique and strength, were also full-backs with whom it was probably best not to engage in frequent collision. Their excellence as defenders subsequently brought selection for the Woking and Surrey Boys' teams.

Cricket, however, was to take precedence over soccer ambitions. One exciting adventure was a visit to Lord's in 1932 to watch their first Test match. The historic occasion featured India in their inaugural Test. The Bedsers' chaperone was the Rev. R.T. Jourdain, vicar of All Saints Church at Woodham. This gesture was not forgotten by the brothers and 14 years later, on another auspicious occasion – Alec's début for England, with India again the opposition – the benefactor of the twins' youth was presented with a complimentary ticket to witness the blossoming of a cricketer.

In his autobiography, *Twin Ambitions*, Alec recalled the enthusiasm of the 'kindly old parson' and his – and Eric's – days as members of the Woking Church choir team. Their cricket gear came from jumble sales and one weary-looking and much-repaired bat was the gift of parishioners:

> The games were played on a glorious ground in the Woodham
> Hall estate. On one side were giant rhododendrons, with lovingly
> tended lawns and rose gardens on another. In the background
> stood the stately big house. In such surroundings it was natural
> for a love of cricket and the countryside to be implanted in our
> minds. It was an idyllic environment.

All the Bedsers' school holidays were spent on Horsell Common. From eight in the morning until six at night, punctuated only by a hurried break for lunch, they were invigorated by the sounds of bat and ball. Later, as solicitor's clerks, their summer breaks were organised so as to coincide with cricket at The Oval.

At other times, before the claims of paid employment, they assisted a friend, the son of the bailiff on the Woodham Hall estate. There was no excuse for idleness. Youthful hands were always in demand on the farm; and for the Bedsers there was the glow of good health as well as pleasure in good, honest toil. As Eric recalls, 'Cleaning out animals with the use of a pitchfork made our backs strong.'

Cricket on the common also involved relays of boys in the preparation of wickets for the impromptu games. It was a heavy duty with spades, levelling the earth to make it reasonably playable (this also served as a precaution against too many bruises). One essay in groundsmanship was at the Woodham Cricket Club, then disused and resembling an untended hayfield. The work in restoring the wicket was a long and arduous process. Cans of water, replenished time and time again, were carried from the nearby Basingstoke Canal. The canal, opened in the 1790s, was originally used to carry agricultural goods in horse-drawn barges from Surrey and Hampshire towns and villages to London. Coal and consumer merchandise was the cargo on return journeys. From his time at Woking, H.G. Wells had earlier recalled a 'pretty and rarely used canal amidst the pine woods, a weedy canal upon which one could be happy for hours in a hired canoe'.

The Bedsers and their squads did not have the leisure for such reflections. Herculean labours in pitch watering did eventually yield a surface susceptible to the use of an old roller. Then, as the wicket was pressed into accommodating flatness, it was time to toss up and start play.

Alec and Eric are the third generation of the Bedser family to live in Woking. Indeed, they believe that their own long association with the town can be extended through their forebears to as far back as the eighteenth century. Woking was already a busy commuter town in their youth. There had been a rapid growth in the population after the turn of the twentieth century. By the early 1920s it had reached 23,000. Its inhabitants consisted of small local tradesmen, with the major chain stores beginning to gain a foothold.

The impetus for the development was the coming of the railway in the mid-nineteenth century. By 1859, when the line was extended to Havant in Hampshire, Woking had become an important railway junction. The fanfares at the opening of the service in May 1838 fulsomely described an 'atmosphere serene and clear . . . so smooth and easy was the transit, so utterly undisturbed by even the slightest shock or jar, that if the eyes were closed it was difficult to imagine oneself in motion at all'.

The first journey from London to Woking was accomplished in 45 minutes and subsequently attracted an average of 7,500 passengers a week, four times the anticipated number. By 1862 there were 16 up trains and 12 on the homeward route. You could travel second class on a 'mixed train' for 3s 6d or, for half a crown, as a third-class passenger in the goods train. More luxurious first-class compartments – accommodation only – were available at one pound. The fares of the accompanying servants and livery of these travellers amounted to an extra 13 shillings each.

The enhanced proximity to London brought about a migration of professional people, stockbrokers and bankers, whose lavish retreats ringed the countryside. They were, wrote one local historian, mainly of the middle class rather than those of the upper class with inherited wealth. So Woking was speedily established as a dormitory for commuters; in the 1890s horse-drawn taxis waited at the station to carry them home in the evening.

In the 1920s the Bedsers, based in their rented cottage on Horsell Common, laboured at a sharp remove from the homes of the gentry. Alec and Eric remember the 'toffs' – and their retinues of gardeners, maids and cooks – of their childhood. Loftily stationed amid the kitchen gardens of the district were two particularly imposing residences, one of which occupied eight acres.

As church choristers, by invitation only, the brothers were able to eavesdrop on the luxury when they went carol-singing at Christmas. Even then, or on other occasions, if they lingered too long, there were dangers waiting to snare small boys. Eric recalls: 'We used to shin up the lamp-posts when the dogs chased us.'

The shopping parades of Woking, with their bakers and confectioners, grocers and drapers, flourished in concert with the development of the town. At Christmas time one local pastry cook grandly announced his wares in an advertisement: 'Puddings and mincemeat, iced cakes, bon-bons, crackers and novelties with chocolates in great variety.' The Tipperary Tea Room, opened in Duke Street during the First World War, was a friendly haven for soldiers' wives and their children. For entertainment there was the verve of the latest dancing craze to be enjoyed at the Atalanta Ballroom. Picture-goers had the choice of three cinemas, the Ritz, the Gaumont and the Palace.

One of the most intriguing and bizarre of the nineteenth-century enterprises in Woking was the formation of the London Necropolis and National Mausoleum Company, following a cholera epidemic in London in the 1840s and its consequence of over-crowded graveyards. The company was given parliamentary permission to buy over 2,000 acres of Woking common land at a cost of £34,000. On this site they planned to build a massive cemetery. Only 400 acres – the area of the present Brookwood Cemetery – were actually laid out. Trees were planted and a railway line was constructed, with two stations for parties of the bereaved to travel down from London. Subsequently, the company sold off 230 acres of their land for the building of a prison at Knaphill; a pauper's asylum, later to become Brookwood Hospital; and the Royal Dramatic College at Maybury. The profits from these sales led some cynics to observe that the Necropolis Company was 'a building society masquerading as a burial company'.

The emergence of Woking as a bustling community did reap its rewards for many townspeople. However the Bedsers, in their rural seclusion, had still by the 1930s to enjoy the fruits of their labours. The decision to sever their employment as solicitor's clerks was a gigantic leap into the dark. Alec and Eric had been severely told that they would regret abandoning a secure livelihood. Happily, they were bolstered by the solidarity of understanding parents.

There is little doubt that warnings were expressed in long and earnest debates at home. Their mother, not for the first time, was the rock upon which their hopes brightened. Florence Bedser, a much keener judge and follower of the game of cricket than many of her sex, gave the brothers her full support.

Aiding the family discussions was the knowledge that Alec and Eric had received an offer from Surrey to further their cricket ambitions at The Oval. These days the twins concede the size of their gamble on the future. As county apprentices in 1938, they were paid £2 a week in the summer and £1 in the winter, with little prospect of employment during the close season.

The Bedsers' champion in this uneasy time was the former Surrey all-rounder, Alan Peach. He was the man who recommended Alec and Eric as candidates worthy of attention at The Oval. Alf Gover, another county stalwart, remembers his brief playing association with Peach, who worked as a gamekeeper in the winter months. 'He used to talk about his gentlemen.' Gover recalls a cricketer in the mould of Freddie Brown, the former England captain and all-rounder: 'Alan was a fierce hitter as a batsman and bowled "inners and outers". He would have played for England at a later time.'

Peach crossed the border from Kent to represent Surrey from 1919 until 1931 and scored nearly 9,000 runs in addition to a yield of 795 wickets. He achieved the distinctive feat of taking four wickets in four balls against Sussex at The Oval in 1924. His aggregate of runs included one typically rousing double-century, an innings lasting only two hours, against Northamptonshire at Northampton in 1920. He was appointed Surrey coach in succession to Ernie Hayes in 1935. After his playing days, Peach firstly ran an indoor cricket school at Woking, organising classes at nets erected in a disused section of a local factory. One of his assistants was Harry Baldwin, another former Surrey player and later an outstanding umpire. Baldwin was the official who caused a furore in 1938 when, in the opening match of the Australian tour, he no-balled the Victorian fast bowler Ernie McCormick 19 times in 3 overs. Another umpiring engagement, significant in another context, was at Lord's when he stood in Alec Bedser's first Test match in 1946.

So it was that Woking, where cricket had first weaved its spell for the Bedser twins, was to become the gateway to high estate at Kennington. Alan Peach noted, and was enthused by, their diligence. Alec and Eric did not neglect the opportunity to follow the example of the tutor at the cricket school in the town: 'We were unpaid recruits, practising and learning, as we bowled for hours at his pupils. Alan was our great hero. He became almost a second father to us, and we were his willing helpers. We kept on bowling, all day on Saturdays, for as long as we could stand up.'

The application of the Bedsers, the striving for unnerving accuracy, was to elevate them in stature as cricketers. Those who later duelled with Alec and Eric have often grimaced at the thought that they might well have had to face them as England's opening bowlers. It was not an implausible pairing. The brothers were then both medium-fast bowlers, Alec taking the in-swing route and Eric being the practitioner of out-swingers.

Alan Peach may have to shoulder some of the blame for changing the course of cricket history. Surrey were then well endowed with seam bowlers, and a change for one of the brothers seemed a sensible option. Peach had also noted Eric's ability to spin the ball. He took stock of the bowling situation at The Oval and advised them that one, but not both, should make the bid for honours with the new ball. 'If you want to play in the same side, you will have to bowl differently,' was his verdict.

The ensuing agreement determined that Alec should persevere with his bowling approach. It was decided that Eric, like more than one embyronic fast bowler before him, should begin to fashion a new craft as an off-spinner.

Two elated country boys, with pardonable trepidation, reported for duty at The Oval in April 1938. 'We were impressionable and anxious to please' – that is how they remember their introduction to the ranks of first-class cricket. 'If the future had been revealed on that unforgettable morning,' says Alec, 'I would have scoffed in utter disbelief.'

CHAPTER TWO

Honest Toil at Kennington

With practice and perseverance much can be done. But one thing is particularly essential, and that is the will to learn and go on learning.

SIR ALEC BEDSER

The heroism of bowlers, unless they are in the category of exhilarating speed, often goes unacknowledged. The offence which perturbs Alec Bedser is that the batting gladiators, described by one writer as cricket's darlings, can dominate the sporting headlines. Alec's own fulfilment as an inventive bowler, deploying cunning variations, was only achieved after thousands of overs, in practice and play. Gary Player, a renowned practitioner in another sport, delivered a telling appraisal of his own dedication as a golfer when one observer once accused him of being blessed with luck in his triumphs around the fairways. 'Yes, it is funny,' replied Player, 'the more I practise, the luckier I get.'

The fanaticism which governed the progress of Alec and Eric Bedser, through and beyond their Surrey apprenticeship, was pursued in workaday Kennington. More than 200 years ago, this South London suburb was referred to as 'a little village near Lambeth'. Its name is derived from the Saxon *kyning-tun*, or King's Town, which denotes that the area was once a royal manor. The famous cricket Oval now belies its aristocratic pedigree in an ugly urban sprawl. It was once a market garden, a vast open space, separated from neighbouring Victorian villas only by a trim laurel hedge. Today, the lorries and buses grumble and groan in convoys around the perimeter of the ground and it does require a considerable leap in imagination to accept that in the early fourteenth century the Black Prince's royal palace stood little more than a 100 yards from where now the crowds jostle at the Hobbs Gates.

The great Test arena of The Oval has not only staged cricket but has also accommodated walking contests, poultry shows and pop festivals.

The cries of vendors at Sunday markets have echoed around the Vauxhall End beneath the brooding gasholders. The Oval was the venue for the first F.A. Cup soccer final between the Royal Engineers and the Wanderers in 1872. Charles Alcock was the victorious Wanderers captain and he joined another winning side to reign as secretary of Surrey County Cricket Club for 30 years. Floodlit football was also an innovation during Alcock's time; other events included rugby union and soccer internationals. The first County Championship match against Sussex was staged in 1873 to be followed seven years later by the first Test match against Australia.

The march of time has brought massive investment and changes to the friendly environs of the 'people's ground'. The outlook from the top of the pavilion and the crescent of hospitality suites presents a breathtaking panorama of central London. It is all a far cry from another age when Oval patrons crouched companionably, shoulder to shoulder, on numbing wooden benches. On big match days, when Yorkshire, Kent and Middlesex provided championship opposition, it was often standing room only. If you were lucky, a place might be gained for greater ease on the grassy surrounds of the arena. Others chose not to pay their entrance fees: their vantage point was from the rooftops of a public-house overlooking the ground. Perched on the open-air grandstand, the merriment of this assembly increased with the passing hours. Abuse and advice grew more voluble with the lowering of each pint of beer. The players on the field had to withstand a combined chorus of criticism from the barrackers inside and outside the ground.

One voice soared exultantly above the others. 'Wheel 'em out' was the clarion call of one ardent supporter, a news vendor of the 1930s. He came in to lend his support after selling his morning papers. His special hero was Alf Gover, who needed every encouragement. In those days between the world wars, it was a heartbreaking task to bowl on wickets as unyielding as concrete and overwhelmingly in the batsmen's favour. 'The ground was so hard,' recalls Gover, 'that running up to bowl was akin to running on a hard tarmac road.'

Gover, the genial veteran, was one of the Surrey seniors who gave a cheerful welcome to the Bedser twins when they joined the playing staff at The Oval in April 1938. He remembers how the recruits steeped themselves in cricket disciplines. Alec and Eric were always avid listeners. They soaked up the wisdom of their elders like sponges. Gover's lunchtime ritual on match days was to snatch a quick sandwich and forgo the usual meal. He elected instead to have a brisk rub-down from the

Surrey masseur, Sandy Tait. Then he would change into fresh clothes before resuming his bowling operations after the interval. Alec, as a youngster, would watch this refreshing procedure and ask for an explanation. 'Well, old son,' said Alf, 'you don't want to go out there again and bowl in a sticky shirt and trousers.'

Alan Peach, the Bedsers' mentor at Woking, had by this time taken up his duties as Surrey coach. He helped to break the ice for the two shy country boys. Alec and Eric were ushered into a friendly company of professionals, all of whom exercised, as they say, an almost paternal influence. This contingent included, apart from Gover, such loyal stalwarts as Bob Gregory, Eddie Watts, Tom Barling, Jack Parker and Stan Squires.

The bespectacled Squires was fated to die from leukaemia at the age of 40 in 1950. He was the esteemed senior professional and confidant of Surrey captains before and after the Second World War. Squires was an incorrigible troubadour, strumming away on his ukulele in the style of George Formby. His witty verses helped lessen tensions and kept the Surrey dressing-room in a high state of mirth.

A top-order batsman, Squires was a swift runner between the wickets. He did, though, suffer from short sight and was once involved in a hilarious escapade while batting with Ted Whitfield against Lancashire at The Oval. Whitfield responded to a call for a run after he had glanced the ball behind the wicket. Halfway up the wicket, he looked round to see the ball about to be fielded at leg slip. There was the inevitable moment of hesitation and he collided violently with Squires.

Stan's glasses were swept off in the tangle of their bodies. The act of disengagement was prolonged. Squires was not pleased: 'You bloody fool, Ted, I can't see a damn thing.'

Amid the confusion, the fieldsman asked the umpire, 'Which end do I throw at to get the run out?'

'Please yourself,' said the official. 'By the time these two have sorted themselves out it won't really matter.' A furious Squires was eventually told that his innings was over. Afterwards, in the dressing-room, he regaled his colleagues with his views on the lunacy of his dismissal.

Dave Fletcher, one of the post-war Surrey brigade, remembers the anomalies of the class structure at The Oval. Conduct in an age of respect for the supposed betters was severely regulated. The amateurs always stayed at first-class hotels. 'We used to think that they cost the club much more than we were paid as professionals,' says Fletcher. Even young amateurs, raw in cricketing years, smartly established themselves in the pecking order. They took their places, as by right, at the top of the lunch table.

The professionals, on the other hand, were obliged to meet from their match fees the cost of hotel bills, and to provide their own kit. Herbert Strudwick, then the Surrey scorer, did his best on limited resources to provide at least basic accommodation. Other more prudent seniors established a custom of sharing the duties of hosts with their opponents during home and away matches.

The divide between the amateurs and professionals was strictly enforced by separate dressing-rooms. Alf Gover drolly maintains: 'We preferred it that way. It gave us more independence and it stopped the amateurs, when they were strapped for cash, from coming down to beg a loan.'

The hierarchy of the professionals was imposed in equal measure. Territory was earmarked by the use of pegs in ascending order of seniority. The juniors, such as the Bedsers, were required to change downstairs. Express permission had to be obtained before they were allowed to mingle with the senior capped players.

It was a forbidding, but, in the main, accepted social convention. Alec and Eric remember one conversation with Herbert Strudwick, the doyen of wicket-keepers and a revered figure at The Oval. Strudwick told them how, when he joined the Surrey staff in 1898, he had inadvertently crossed the threshold of the jealously guarded area of his seniors. He was given an austere reception. Tom Hayward, the stylish master batsman and mentor and partner of the young Jack Hobbs, was waiting to greet him. Strudwick was thrust into a kind of despair when asked to give his name. He was sternly rebuked for invading the privileged preserve: 'You have the advantage of me, young man,' barked Hayward. 'Your place is downstairs.'

In later years, even those professional cricketers who had achieved commissioned rank in the Second World War could still find themselves at odds with the authorities. Alf Gover, then a serving Army major, was once refused service in the members' tea-room at The Oval. Only a few weeks before, he had been acceptable as the captain in a wartime game organised by the club.

On his retirement Gover went into sports journalism. He was elected as one of the first professionals to follow Jack Hobbs on to the Surrey committee. He was then presumed to have a conflict of interests and considered untrustworthy by a few senior members of the committee and barred from some meetings.

Another journalist, Hubert Preston, the editor of *Wisden*, expressed his concern at an outdated rule. In a leading article, written in 1943, he called for the cessation of social distinctions in the game. Preston praised the contributions and unbiased leadership of illustrious players, great captains and prudent legislators from the amateur ranks – 'but they are the survivors of an almost lost society of an age that is nearly gone.' Preston added: 'I would welcome the total deletion of all distinctions between professionals and amateurs in first-class cricket. To me at least such questions as the position of a cricketer's initials and the precise gate from which he is to enter the field have long seemed vastly absurd.'

A rigid custom did not immediately expire. The differing status of 'gentlemen and players' was not abandoned until as late as 1962. For Alec and Eric Bedser, in their salad days, the question of equal rights was of little consequence to them. They were furthering their cricket ambitions and too busy to worry about privileges. 'We were proud to be part of Surrey and we certainly did not feel inferior or rebellious.'

Competition for places was a more fearful concern. Demotion from the 1st XI meant a sharp drop in income. Alec and Eric remember the distress of some, including family men, whose livelihoods were at stake and who 'were quite literally in tears'. Their plight was compounded when they had to make way for amateurs in the summer holidays.

Arthur McIntyre was one of the cheerful band of Young Players of Surrey. Little 'Mac', born at Kennington, preceded the Bedsers by four years at The Oval, as a member of the groundstaff. He was recommended as a likely prospect by his teachers at Kennington Road School. They were his first sporting mentors, who enlivened the summers of his boyhood by arranging outings to watch Surrey.

It seems strange that he at first resisted the chance to join the groundstaff. 'I didn't fancy pushing the roller,' he explains. This giant contraption, known as 'Bosser's Pet', might have served to lay a motorway. His mother dismissed the problem and urged her son not to neglect the opportunity. 'Mac', in the event, was allocated the less onerous duties of parking attendant in charge of spectators' bicycles.

McIntyre's early skills as a leg-spinner (he won his 2nd XI cap in this role) were fostered by Percy Fender, the Surrey captain. There were also instructive sessions supervised by another tutor, 'Tich' Freeman, renowned in Kent as an exponent of a fascinating art. 'Mac' was privileged to spend winter months at Freeman's home and attend his cricket school at Maidstone. The promise he displayed as a bowler also enabled 'Mac' to strike up a good relationship with 'Bosser' Martin,

Surrey's head groundsman and a former leg-spinner. Their accord was strengthened when 'Mac' topped the Surrey Young Players' bowling averages in 1934. Martin, his kindly master, thereupon authorised his release from ground duties to allow him to play in schools matches.

An eagerly awaited fixture on the Young Players' calendar was the annual match against the Emanuel School at Wandsworth. One of their opponents was Stuart Surridge, the future Surrey captain. Surridge, strappingly built, was a fierce striker of the ball, even as a boy; but he was confounded by McIntyre's looping spin in one duel between them.

Until his last two years at Emanuel, Surridge had kept wicket. This vigil served as a prelude to his later close-catching renown in Surrey's imposing fielding cordon. He advanced in status when he became a fast bowler by force of circumstances: 'The school hadn't a fast bowler, so I took on the job.' Surridge was always a gambler. The statement exemplified his outlook.

The best of friendships are often formed in youthful exploits. Surridge, while still at school, forged associations which were to be of lasting value during Surrey's great years in the 1950s. Alongside him in the Young Players' ranks were the Bedser twins, McIntyre, Geoff Whittaker and Bernie Constable. 'Mac' recalls Surridge as the ebullient chauffeur at the wheel of a decrepit Ford V8. They were a tight unit in every sense: on some match journeys, Surridge carried 'half the team at a time'.

It was a gruelling apprenticeship for the Surrey triallists. A typical working day, if they were not playing in a match, consisted of net sessions, each lasting two hours, in the morning and afternoon. A rota of boys was then drawn up for another duty – bowling at county members for two hours in the evening. Word-of-mouth intelligence quickly calculated the sum likely to be collected from the members. The goal of the apprentice bowlers was to be engaged by the best of the tippers. One shilling was considered a fair reward for the services. 'There wasn't much of a rush to bowl at the "sixpenny end",' say the Bedsers. There were, however much their tired limbs protested, other rewards in fitness: 'Six hours of bowling a day not only made for accuracy, but also developed the back, shoulder and leg muscles.'

Alec and Eric were first paid £2 a week in the summer plus match money, the latter being negligible sums since they were rarely called into action. The Young Players of Surrey received 5 shillings; promotion to the Club and Ground brought 25 shillings; and the advance to the 2nd XI was sealed by payments of £4 and £6 respectively for home and away games.

The Bedsers' first retainer in the winter of 1938–39 at The Oval was £1 each a week. It did lead to some heart-searchings as to how they might supplement this meagre income. Anxious enquiries at the club did elicit the suggestion that they could be employed on ground reconstruction. Alec and Eric caught the train from Woking to Waterloo at 6.30 each morning. This enabled them to use the workman's rail ticket, costing 1s 1d., and so reduce their travel costs.

The task force at The Oval also included Arthur McIntyre and Geoff Whittaker. Over the long and hard weeks, the boys laboured on the banking at the Vauxhall End. This operation, with pick and shovel, involved bringing in the boundary several yards. Mounds of earth were heaved aside in the digging and then transported in wheelbarrows to the allocated new position. In February, they were grateful to return to cricket and coaching jobs at an indoor school at Kingston run by Andrew Kempton.

Kempton, a close friend of Jack Hobbs, was one of Surrey's influential benefactors. He captained the Surrey Colts in a new venture after the Second World War. His policy, during an impressive stewardship, was to instruct his boys to first master the elementary lessons of cricket. Kempton did inspire a devotion among his pupils. 'They are all very keen,' he once remarked. 'All they require is a little polish.' The raw material was there, he said, but the polish would have to be administered by others who knew their business.

Sparkling on the Surrey fringes as the war drew inexorably closer were the Bedser twins. They won promotion to the 1st XI against the universities, Oxford and Cambridge, at The Oval in June 1939. Their contributions were negligible; but Eric did claim one notable scalp, the wicket of George Mann – a future Middlesex and England captain – in the match against Cambridge.

The credentials of the twins were sound, as *Wisden* noted in its report on their first appearances against Oxford. Eric opened the Surrey innings on his début. His partner was Laurie Fishlock, who had toured Australia under the leadership of Gubby Allen three years earlier. 'Eric created a fine impression while staying for nearly an hour,' commented the *Wisden* correspondent. 'But the pitch afforded Alec no chance of proving his ability as a bowler.' There was, in this game, an early instance of the problem of identification. 'These two tall, dark boys resembled each other so closely that it was impossible to distinguish them, especially when they fielded together in the slips!' reported the observer.

Eric Bedser, during these apprentice years, was privileged to open an innings with Jack Hobbs. One September night in 1938 the twins received a telephone call from the great man. There was an emergency caused by the late withdrawal of two players. Hobbs extended an invitation to the boys to join his XI in the annual Wimbledon charity match. It was to be played at the John Innes Recreation Ground, Merton, on the following day. There must have been a quiver of butterflies when Eric learned that he was to be Hobbs's opening partner. These were eased by smiles of encouragement from his illustrious senior. Eric was able to relax in such company and score a fine half-century.

Alec and Eric were members of the Surrey 2nd XI which won the Minor Counties championship under the captaincy of Dick Eglington in 1939. As champions, Surrey emulated the feat of Buckinghamshire in the previous year, in going through the summer undefeated. Three of their seven victories were by the margin of an innings; two more were obtained against Kent to complete four wins in a row over their rivals from across the border. Lancashire, their nearest rivals, were runners-up for the third year in succession.

The aggressive batting of Geoff Whittaker, the 23-year-old recruit from Peckham, was one of the success stories of Surrey's season. He headed the county and second-class averages with 703 runs at an average of 100.42. His feats gained him the reward of selection for the 1st XI. One of the highlights of the Bedsers' year was Eric's first Minor Counties century – 120 in the five-wicket victory over Kent at The Oval.

The burden of the 2nd XI bowling in 1938 had been shouldered by F.G. Pierpoint, the Bedsers and Stuart Surridge, who between them took 138 wickets. Alec's 42 wickets, at 17.38 runs apiece, placed him at the top of the averages. The succeeding championship year reinforced his promise and the predictions of a great future. Alec took another 41 wickets at a reduced average of 14.29 runs each. He shared the bowling honours with Yorkshire all-rounder Fred Berry, and Bill Nevell from Balham. Berry, who later coached at Wellington College, was a product of the Pennines village of Kirkheaton, the birthplace of George Hirst and Wilfred Rhodes.

Two remarkable veterans, Philip Mead and Bob Relf, continued to prosper in Minor Counties cricket in the pre-war years. Mead, the dour batting accumulator over 31 years with Hampshire, was the coach at Framlington College in Suffolk after his retirement from first-class cricket. One of his batting rituals was to beat a solemn tattoo on his crease at the start of an innings. Bob Wyatt remembered this warning to bowlers and said that the bat seemed twice the normal size. Cecil Parkin, the Lancashire and England bowler, once waggishly remarked that Mead's bat should be taken to a carpenter for a close shave. Both these salutations revealed the stature of the Hampshire champion. His aggregate of 55,061 runs, including 153 hundreds, is only exceeded by Hobbs, Woolley and Hendren.

Mead was in his 51st year when he resumed his career with Suffolk in 1938. The fractious varicose veins, a constant irritant, still hurt him. He would sourly complain about his 'poor old legs'. His eyesight was by then beginning to fail, but it did not prevent him from scoring nearly 900 runs, averaging each time in the 70s, in two seasons with Suffolk.

There must have been an ironic satisfaction for Mead in the century on his début for Suffolk against Surrey seconds at Ipswich in 1938. He was born at Battersea and, as a 15-year-old at the turn of the century, he was on The Oval groundstaff. Not then regarded as a batsman, he was an aspiring slow left-arm bowler. He twice dismissed another triallist, Jack Hobbs, in one match. Surrey, as all the cricket world knows, claimed Hobbs as one of their own. However Mead, had the county been more percipient, could have complemented the artistry of 'The Master' with the weight of his runs. Surrey did not retain his services at the end of the 1903 season. Two weeks later they belatedly decided he might be worth keeping. By then Mead had moved on to fresh and productive pastures in Hampshire.

Alec Bedser was in the Surrey ranks against Suffolk at Ipswich. Mead first shone as a bowler, coming on to break a troublesome partnership and stifle the flow of runs. He took 5 wickets for 69 runs in 26 overs. Surridge, Alec Bedser and Arthur McIntyre were among those who fell to his unfaltering spin. Between the innings, he went into the Surrey dressing-room to announce his intention to score a century. The forecast was fulfilled with typical certainty. Without him Suffolk would have been abject victims. None of the other home batsmen hit more than 30 against Surrey's young professionals. Bedser remembered the poise of the old warrior: 'He didn't run around much, he seemed to strike the ball with no apparent effort. His eyes were going a little, but he hit everything surely in the middle of the bat.'

Another sterling campaigner of yesteryear, Bob Relf, shared the spotlight with Mead in this phase of Minor Counties cricket. Relf, one of three cricketing brothers, had first played for Sussex in 1905. His memories wound back to Edwardian days at Hove and partnerships with the august C.B. Fry.

Cricket coincidences are always intriguing, especially when they connect across the generations. Relf, as a venerable septuagenarian, would later endorse the claims of a great Surrey batsman of the future. He was the first of Peter May's mentors at Leighton Park School, Reading. In his mid-50s, with Berkshire, his bowling skills still made taxing demands of the boys opposing him. Accuracy, grooved over many summers, yielded 80 wickets at a miserly cost in two seasons in a happy swansong to his career.

∽⚬∾ ∽⚬∾ ∽⚬∾

Meanwhile, on the nursery slopes at The Oval, the progress of Alec and Eric Bedser was soon to be checked by the intervention of war. It was a stoppage which linked them with other aspiring young men in sport and many walks of life. The emerging cricketers of 1939, among them the future Test players Godfrey Evans, Jack Robertson, Jack Ikin and Willie Watson, would lose six of their prime years. Those who survived the hazards of a terrible conflict would return maturely fitted to meet the less exacting challenges of cricket. Stirring battles of another kind awaited the Bedsers after their adventures abroad.

CHAPTER THREE

Intelligence at War

Luck was . . . on our side. We avoided the plight of our schoolfriends.
Many of them were . . . taken prisoner at Dunkirk.

ALEC AND ERIC BEDSER

The straggling troops, footsore and forlorn, looked yearningly towards the sea. Across the chasm of the years, this grim image must still haunt those veterans of the retreat from Dunkirk in the spring of 1940. Alec and Eric Bedser were among the beleaguered and helpless forces in flight to the French coast.

The story of their survival was revived for them in a recent unsolicited letter from a Newcastle man. 'Do you remember being at Merville?' asked this correspondent.

The letter vividly evoked the drama of a ferocious machine-gun attack on an RAF airfield near the Belgian border. Alec and Eric recall the perils of this episode. The shout went up: 'German bombers are coming over.' At this warning all the men scattered. The Surrey brothers and another man broke ranks to try to evade the looming assault from the skies. Twisting and turning, they plunged headlong down onto the field. 'The German bomber was about 200 feet up and we were at his mercy,' say the Bedsers. 'We were lucky, the tracer bullets passed between us.'

Amid the turmoil of the attack they could not tell whether the unknown comrade had survived. The letter from him in the late 1990s told them that he, like them, had come through unscathed.

The narrow escape preceded a timely intervention during the trek to Dunkirk. The crowded lanes were teeming with tired men. Alec and Eric were indebted, as they stood by the roadside, to their recognisable twinship. What followed was one of the many miracles of this catastrophic time. They had almost given up hopes of a lift when a van shuddered to a halt. There was a cheerful greeting from the driver, fortuitously, as it turned out, a Surrey member from Wimbledon. 'I can't leave you behind,' he said.

The Bedsers were escorted halfway to the coast before the overworked engine died with a soft sigh of exhaustion. Then, yet another piece of luck: a tow given to the stricken vehicle brought them to the French shores. Alec and Eric spent an anxious night huddled beneath the cliffs south of Dunkirk. Their arrival at the port came a few days before the harrowing bombardment of the troops awaiting rescue on the beaches. Next morning a rescue boat picked them up and carried them on calm seas, as if on a Channel cruise, to England. 'We were not attacked at all,' they remember.

Fortune had also favoured Alec and Eric in a postponed call-up during the lingering peace of the last of their pre-war cricketing summers in 1939. They were aware that university students were exempted from service until the completion of the courses. Accordingly, they considered that, as professional cricketers, this entitlement should apply to them as well. Deferment for them, as Army recruits, was granted until the end of the season. Instructions were then received to report for training with the Royal Artillery in September.

The enlistment was cancelled, but between times they had visited the RAF recruiting office at Mitcham. They were drawn there by the attraction of aircrew duties. Acting as a spur was the example of their father, who had served as a sergeant at first in the Royal Flying Corps, and then in the RAF, in the First World War. The examiner at Mitcham was unable to satisfy the flying ambitions. Looking up at his visitors, he said they would make splendid Guardsmen. His final verdict was that their tall and commanding presence gave them more ideal credentials for the RAF police.

Two weeks after being inducted into the RAF, Alec and Eric again received papers for the Royal Artillery, but it was then too late to change course. 'We were now air force squaddies. Luck was again on our side. We avoided the plight of a number of our schoolfriends. Many of them were later taken prisoner at Dunkirk.'

Cricket during wartime was a pleasant diversion for the Bedsers between attendances on CID security courses arranged under the auspices of the Metropolitan and Yorkshire police forces. The Halton transit camp, their first depot on the return to England, had a fine cricket ground under the supervision of Group Captain (Padre) Cox, the chief chaplain to the RAF. Evidence of his enthusiasm was shown when he arranged 48-hour passes as a concession for the newly arrived cricketers.

It was strictly against regulations, but Alec and Eric were able to travel home to Woking to collect their cricket gear.

The problems of identifying the twins were to surface as light relief on many occasions during the war. At Halton Camp, for instance, the Bedsers devised a scheme to share their guard duties. They both felt that two hours spent on this exercise was unduly prolonged. The decision was taken to do one hour each.

Unfortunately, one night Eric forgot to take the key to the arms cupboard with him when he relieved Alec. He was asked to produce it by the warrant officer. Sharing was second nature to the Bedsers – but this was a double-deal cocking a snook at authority and the trick had misfired. Alec had the key, but it was Eric who was in the guardroom. The senior officer was now aware of the plot, but all was forgiven. Laughter, rather than punishment, was the response to a cunning ruse.

Lord's beckoned Alec Bedser in the intermission before returning to active duties in the RAF Intelligence overseas. Alec appeared in matches arranged by Sir Pelham Warner, an early and influential advocate of the younger Bedser. Warner perceived a burgeoning talent; letters from him to Alec and Eric during their service in Italy were splendid gestures of goodwill.

In 1943, the fourth wartime season, the programme of matches was increased. Sussex, Nottinghamshire and Northamptonshire were in the vanguard with lengthy fixture lists; and service sides all over the country fielded many first-class players. Alec was in an England XI, led by Les Ames, and opposed to a West Indies team captained by Learie Constantine at Lord's in May 1943. The home ranks included other players who were destined to guide England's post-war challenges. Alec was paired for the first time with two allies of later renown, Godfrey Evans and Trevor Bailey. Their colleagues included the Middlesex trio of Denis Compton, Bill Edrich and Jack Robertson; and Harry Halliday, a Yorkshireman from the famed Pudsey cricket nursery.

Trevor Bailey, a 19-year-old Royal Navy officer cadet and former Dulwich School captain, shared the new ball for England. He was later to gain distinction as the outstanding all-rounder of the 1950s. One of his partners was Norman Harding, who, seven years earlier, had achieved a unique feat in Minor Counties championship cricket. For Kent seconds against Wiltshire he took 18 wickets (9 in each innings) for 100 runs.

The sprightly Kent and England veteran, Les Ames, was allied with Jack Robertson in a brisk stand of 134 runs, lasting only 70 minutes, for the fourth wicket against the West Indies. The bowling honours went to Sergeant Alec Bedser, whose figures of 6 wickets for 27 runs in 8 overs, included the hat-trick. *The Cricketer* observed: 'Finely built, he has the necessary stamina, his action is good, and his fast-medium deliveries make haste off the ground.'

The two-day cricket interludes, especially at Lord's, provided stimulating entertainment and at least a hint of a Test match atmosphere. Crowds of over 20,000 watched the games. Alec Bedser supplemented his haul of wartime wickets in an exciting victory by eight runs over the Dominions at the headquarters. Ames struck an exuberant hundred and Denis Compton twirled his bat for fifty, while Bedser, partnered by Bailey, took seven wickets in a high-scoring match.

Alec had ample reason to be pleased with his work. His victims included Keith Miller, Learie Constantine and Stewart Dempster. Dempster was acknowledged as one of the finest of New Zealand batsmen and had captained Leicestershire during the 1930s. His century for the Dominions set up a grandstand finale at Lord's.

'None of those present on the second evening,' reported *The Cricketer*, 'will forget the thrilling finish when C.B. Clarke, of the West Indies, and Stan Sismey [the New South Wales wicket-keeper] very nearly won the match for the Dominions against great odds by adding 108 runs for the eighth wicket.'

Major Alf Gover, then in hospital near Cape Town, had listened to the radio broadcasts of the big games at Lord's. In a letter home he offered his congratulations and noted: 'I was very interested and not surprised to hear that young Bedser took some wickets.'

Alec Bedser claimed another hat-trick in his nine wickets for the Royal Air Force in the match against the Metropolitan Police at Westcliff in 1943. His most startling analysis had, though, been achieved at Hove in the previous year. The feat was recorded for the RAF against the Police in a Sussex Services tournament match. Alec dismissed 9 batsmen for 3 runs, 8 of them bowled, in 23 deliveries.

Eric Bedser also starred in wartime cricket beside the seaside. At Hove, in 1943, he took 13 wickets at 10 runs apiece; a year earlier his off-spin had been rewarded with two hat-tricks at the same venue. He was complimented in a *Cricketer* article by Sir Home Gordon, who appealed for more bowling opportunities to be given to Bedser: 'The bowling ability of the "batting Bedser", as he is often described, remains much under-rated.

This is not just because I once saw him take eight wickets and catch out the other two. I have watched him many times since I first came across him in 1938. I am convinced of his skill in the control of the ball.'

⁊⁊⁊ ⁊⁊⁊ ⁊⁊⁊

The luxuries of cricket were withdrawn from the Bedsers when they were posted overseas in the autumn of 1943. Nearly three years were to elapse before they seriously took bat and ball in hand again. They sailed from Greenock on the Clyde aboard a Dutch ship, one of a large convoy, to Algiers. This was followed by a journey of 500 miles in a rickety cattle truck to Tunis. 'I'll never forget that journey,' wrote Alec in *Twin Ambitions*. 'It lasted for seven days. There was no water for a wash, and we scrounged hot water from the driver to brew tea. It was so uncomfortable and utterly crazy that we spent most of the time laughing.'

Alec and Eric were members of the War Crimes Intelligence Branch in Italy during the last phase of the conflict. As they recall, the brief took them into a dark maze of events, with the menace of a thriller written by Graham Greene.

Security was a high priority as the Allied Forces reached the crossroads of the war. Political agitation carried constant perils. Naples, volatile at the best of times, was a dangerous city. One of the Bedsers' investigations involved the murder of three RAF servicemen who had been seized and attacked while on leave in Naples.

In Naples, Alec and Eric witnessed the last eruption in modern times of the 'double-humped old monster', Vesuvius, in March 1944. One eye-witness said the whole horizon was plunged into an abyss of fire. The raging explosion blew about 200 feet off the top of the mountain. The Bedsers, along with other servicemen, assisted in the evacuation of people from surrounding villages.

'The lava came shooting down,' remember Alec and Eric. 'You couldn't get within 100 yards of it.' The ash from the volcano, about 12 miles away, was two feet deep. In the Bay of Naples two American liberty ships were thrown up onto the beach. An Allied airfield was brought to a standstill on the east slope of the mountain. At Turzigno, where the ash grains were up to an inch long, a British unit had to be evacuated because of the lava flow. Afterwards, when the Bedsers moved to Bari, 160 miles away on the opposite coast, they were told that the succeeding rains there had been laden with mud.

The Vesuvius eruption, the first for 38 years, began on 12 March and lasted until the 29th day of the month. Another observer, a young infantry subaltern, had arrived in bomb-scarred Naples shortly before the event. He recalled that the Allies had dropped at least 150 bombs on the Pompeii ruins in the belief that the Germans were using it as an ammunition dump. The writer missed the actual eruption, but he said that when he returned in June he noticed that Vesuvius had lost its shape. Previously the cone could easily be seen from Naples; now the top was flat – indeed, the whole mountain appeared lower and lopsided.

One description of the eruption was related by a sister at Nocera General Hospital, 13 miles away from the volcano. 'When we awoke on the morning of the blow-off it was extremely dark like a foggy winter morning, and at first we thought it was going to snow. When we got downstairs there was a group of women who used to come every day to collect the laundry, all wailing, "Vesuvio! Vesuvio!".'

This last eruption of the century was mild and not followed by the vast mudflow which had submerged another Roman site, that at Herculaneum, in AD 79. The toll of casualties in 1944 was happily slight, reduced by the intervention of strong winds, which meant that the ash was well dispersed. At Nocera, where bulldozers worked to make the village habitable, nothing could be done about the thick carpet of ash. For over a year, said the villagers, it was like living in a coal mine.

᧯᧯᧯᧯ ᧯᧯᧯᧯ ᧯᧯᧯᧯

The salvoes of war were now charged in the offensive which took the Bedsers up the spine of Italy. On the journey north, Eric was taken ill with jaundice and became a patient in a military hospital in Perugia. Alec had first contracted the sickness. In less than brotherly fashion, he passed on the symptoms to Eric. He did, as he thought, try to make amends by visiting his stricken twin: 'I went walking down the hospital corridor and a very stern ward sister tore me off a strip for being out of bed.' She remonstrated with him for being so disobedient: 'Get back to bed this instant.'

The irate nurse was about to move on, but then hesitated and took a closer look at Alec. 'Good heavens, he's lost his colour,' she exclaimed. Alec explained that she was talking to the recovered Bedser. But she remained unconvinced until reaching Eric's bedside. Then, at last, she was able to compare the two shades of Bedser. Her confusion was the joke of the ward for weeks.

Alec and Eric undoubtedly were bolstered by their togetherness amid the trials of war. They were never separated. In 1943, they had both been promoted to warrant officer. It was the rule, however, that only one of this rank could be allocated to the same unit – so Eric accepted the promotion and Alec remained a flight sergeant. (They did, of course, share the extra pay.) The decision also enabled the Bedsers to take advantage of another Air Force regulation. Eric, as the elder, could claim the younger Alec in the spirit of a guardian. Towards the end of the war they received a posting notice which stated, 'One not to proceed without the other.'

As the war entered its last phase, the claims of cricket could be addressed with greater freedom. Celebrity cricketers from the distant lands of the Commonwealth came together in the fields of Italy. Arthur McIntyre, while at a convalescent depot in Salerno, was visited by the Bedsers. It was at this reunion of three of Surrey's young cricketers that Alec and Eric first broached a new cricketing direction for McIntyre. Their recommendation was that he should seriously consider taking on the role of wicket-keeper when they returned home. The advice was to prove immensely beneficial in the years ahead.

Cricket in Italy was not without early teething problems. The difficulties of ground preparation in the country – not a land of flat meadows – were enormous. Appeals to various service departments did find willing acceptance; and in a comparatively short time, grounds of first-class order were brought into use throughout the country.

Arthur McIntyre, who had been wounded in the Anzio landings, was then recuperating at a convalescent home near Bari on the east coast. He remembers the cricket zeal of another companion, Harry Secombe, in Italy, and the effervescence of this well-loved entertainer in raising the morale of the troops. Cricket – and the presence of distinguished players in this theatre of war – was also designed to assist rehabilitation. McIntyre, engaged in remedial work in a new position of Army physical training instructor, was one of those who helped to establish one of the service grounds at Bari. One observer described this as one of the best of wartime cricket settings: it was 'perfectly situated' by the Adriatic and the outfield, 'being of plain earth, was large, very true and flat after the efforts of a bulldozer and a heavy roller. The wicket was of concrete, with a mat stretched over it.'

The organisation at Bari was precise in its military efficiency. All the paraphernalia associated with first-class cricket was set in place. Sightscreens and scoreboxes were made and erected, and the arena was roped off and surrounded with seating accommodation for several hundred spectators. Marquees lined the field, some for dispensing refreshments while others served as dressing-rooms. Loudspeakers provided a running commentary and scorecards, showing the latest match details, were freely available. Arthur McIntyre remembers the enthusiasm of another cricket devotee, Colonel Malam, at Bari. At his direction the lunches were of the convivial variety, happily complementing the vigour out in the middle.

Sergeant McIntyre did have some misgivings about the aggression displayed by one opponent, Jack Martin. Martin played most of his cricket for Catford Wanderers, representing Kent only during holidays from the Legal and General Assurance Society. The dearth of fast bowlers after the war did allow the distinction of his one and only Test appearance against South Africa at Trent Bridge in 1947.

McIntyre's duel with Martin occurred during the match between East and West at Bari in July 1945. He had scored 115 for Western Italy before he was compelled to retire hurt. A fast and rising delivery from Martin caught him unawares and fractured his nose. He was fractionally late in his counter. 'I went for the hook and missed it,' recalls McIntyre.

The element of service discipline imposed on cricket arrangements in Italy was reflected at other centres. In Naples a ground was produced on the city racecourse, while in Rome, the venue for many big games at the time, a wicket was carved out at the football stadium. At all these grounds, commented one English officer, the administration and hospitality were on a par with any experienced on a first-class ground in England.

One of the most distinguished and historic settings was in the grounds of the Royal Palace at Caserta, 16 miles inland from Naples. It was to Caserta that the German General von Vietinghoff flew to surrender the German forces in Italy. Around this time, the Bedsers were among the first to make a pilgrimage there to the grave of Hedley Verity. The revered Yorkshire and England cricketer had died from wounds received while leading an infantry attack on the plain of Catania in Sicily. He was first laid to rest in a cemetery situated above Caserta and off a peaceful country lane. The Bedsers – along with Frank Smailes, one of Verity's pre-war colleagues – arranged with a local mason to erect a marble headstone to the grave. A photograph was taken and sent to Verity's widow.

In June 1945, Alec Bedser again demonstrated his increasing prowess on the Caserta Palace ground. Bowling in tandem with the pre-war Somerset and England stalwart Arthur Wellard, he took 5 wickets for 42 runs in a closely contested challenge match. Six-hitting was an exhilarating feature of Wellard's county batting assaults. Earlier in the war, playing for London Counties, he had struck a fifty, including seven sixes, in eight minutes in one match. He was only slightly slower in another outing for London Counties, his half-century on that occasion occupying 19 minutes; Bill Merritt, the New Zealand leg-spinner, was hit for seven sixes. It is not recorded whether Wellard swaggered again with the bat at Caserta, but Grahame Parker, another West Country representative, did dictate in his own style to score a century.

∿ ∿ ∿

Alec and Eric Bedser were demobilised in March 1946. A scene of devastation had greeted them on their earlier return to The Oval. The cricket acres of Kennington had served as a forbidding fortress during the Second World War. They had been prepared as a major prisoner-of-war camp for Germans who might have been captured during an airborne invasion of London. The hallowed turf had been desecrated by stakes and caged with barbed wire.

In the Battle of Britain, weary Londoners were in the front line. Night by night, enemy aircraft unloaded deadly cargoes of incendiary bombs to set the capital ablaze. Searchlights ringed The Oval and anti-aircraft guns were raised defiantly in defence against the onslaught. The camp was never used, although the legend persists that a German bomber pilot baled out over Kennington and spent the rest of one wartime night at The Oval.

The reversion to cricket after the ravages of war must count as one of the miracles of groundsmanship. The newly appointed Bert Lock was given the monumental task of restoring The Oval in Surrey's centenary year. The great clear-up began in October 1945. The preliminaries involved the removal of mounds of accumulated debris. Concrete posts were dismantled and holes filled in. Then scythes and sickles were deployed to uncover the cricket square. Lock organised transport and laid 45,000 turves brought from Hoo marshes in Kent.

Alec Bedser is unstinting in his admiration of Lock's stamina over many arduous months.

> Starting at 8 a.m., and working until he could no longer see the pitch, he and his makeshift staff somehow got the ground into playable shape. The practice nets had been gnawed by rats. Bert

sat in the east stand, often in freezing winds, repairing the nets to
have them ready for the new season in early April 1946. I have
often thought of him as an unsung hero.

This epic feat coincided with other heroic endeavours in the first post-
war season. Three years earlier, the editor of *The Cricketer* had advanced
the England claims of Alec Bedser: 'He improves with every match he
plays, he is physically strong, knows the value of length and with added
experience should develop into a fast-medium bowler after the manner of
Maurice Tate.'

In 1946, the advance was confirmed. All who watched him in a
remarkable Test début against India revelled in the emergence of a great
bowler. From this auspicious beginning, Alec Bedser was to stand alone in
his undisputed command. Like a famous London theatre, observed A.A.
Thomson, his battling effort never closed.

CHAPTER FOUR

Calling Cards for Australia

The next four years will be Bedser's testing time. Meanwhile, England may be thankful that she has him. He will serve her faithfully.

JOHN ARLOTT

'What a lot of nonsense,' thought Florence Bedser in later years, as she dusted the silverware on the mantlepiece. 'All for bowling a cricket ball.' She was always intent on keeping the feet of her sons firmly on the ground. The good times were beginning for Alec Bedser: a remarkable Test début in 1946 would be followed by other accomplishments to strike a chord of pride. Amid all his triumphs, the 'wonderful mother' would quietly acknowledge the congratulations. Then, with a smile to signal her pleasure, she would add: 'Well, of course, that's his job!'

The reticence was there to defuse excessive praise; discretion was the keynote of an undemonstrative family. As if in accord with this reserve, the headlines were muted during Alec's summer of success in 1946. Austerity held the nation in its grasp. Newsprint was not excluded from the strict post-war rationing. Four daily pages was the allotment for news items, good and bad. Spectacular sporting feats were tucked away in the margins. Alec was deprived of column inches which, in other times, would have carried the message of his exploits in glowing terms.

The Indian tourists were in spirited mood when they came to The Oval in May 1946 at the start of a summer of slate skies and peevish rains. Surrey were forced to follow on after the visitors had gained unexpected prosperity with a record-breaking last-wicket stand. Merchant and Gul Mahomed had shared a century partnership for the third wicket.

This preceded a major collapse: the Indians lost 9 men for 209 runs before their recovery. Surrey could not make the final thrust. Their bowling resources were depleted by the absence of the veteran, Alf

Gover, who had strained a tendon in his heel and bowled only seven overs in the match. Another factor was the fumble of the erring Mobey, who missed a stumping off Parker at the outset of the Indian rally. The reprieved batsman, Sarwate, along with his partner, Banerjee, stood firm for over three hours. Their stand started at 4.03 on the Saturday and did not end until 12.27 on the Monday. There was no trace of last-wicket anxiety. Both scored centuries, the first time this had been achieved by No. 10 and No. 11 batsmen. Their partnership of 249 runs was the highest ever recorded for the last wicket in England. In world cricket it has only been superseded by two Australians, Kippax and Hooker, who scored 307 for New South Wales against Victoria at Melbourne in 1928–29.

Alec Bedser, while acknowledging the assured strokeplay of Sarwate and Banerjee at The Oval, does point out that neither were duffers as batsmen. They had both opened for their states, respectively Holkar and Bihar, in India. Sarwate, in particular, was a genuine all-rounder. His leg-spin gave him a yield of nearly 500 wickets; he also scored 7,430 runs in first-class cricket. Earlier in 1946, while representing Holkar against Mysore at Indore in the semi-final of the Ranji Trophy tournament, he had scored a century. Holkar declared at 912 for 8 and Sarwate then took 9 wickets for 61 runs, his best-ever bowling analysis.

The extravagant spin of Nayudu, who claimed a hat-trick, confounded all but Fishlock in Surrey's first innings at The Oval. A century stand between Gregory and Fishlock summoned greater resistance in the second innings. Sarwate, who did not bowl in the first innings, took five wickets, and India were able to coast to a victory by nine wickets. Sarwate was promoted to open the Indian innings with Merchant. Alec Bedser, having bowled 47 overs for his 5 wickets in India's first innings, gained some recompense for his earlier punishment when he dismissed Sarwate for one.

Reverses can have a beneficial effect and this springtime mishap only briefly checked the progress of Bedser. He was awarded his county cap on 12 June and was then selected to play in his first Test after only 11 first-class matches and with only 46 wickets behind him. Destiny might ultimately have brought Alec his England colours; but he gave it a mighty heave when he ignored a painful thigh injury to play for The Rest against an England XI in the Test trial at Lord's in early June.

He stoically maintained a strict silence. 'I didn't tell anyone,' he says. Away from the dressing-room he found a quiet, unattended corner where he could heavily bandage his thigh. It was another instance of an awareness of the practicalities of cricket, first learnt as an apprentice at The Oval: 'If you didn't play, you didn't get paid.' At Lord's, Alec spurned the handicap to earn Test recognition. 'Had I cried off there, I might never have played for England.'

Jack Martin, of Kent, was the first of Alec's representative match bowling partners in the Test trial. There were two prized and eminent names, Len Hutton and Wally Hammond, to insert in Alec's wicket-taking collection at Lord's. Along with Joe Hardstaff and Jack Ikin in the opposing ranks, Bedser won the commendation of Crawford White in the *News Chronicle*:

> Alec Bedser was impressive until he tired late in the day. On an easy pitch he had Hutton and Hammond tied down for six successive maiden overs and finally got both their wickets, with the aid of catches by Martin and Edrich. Six feet three and 15 stone, Bedser puts plenty of body in his bowling. He makes the ball move both ways and gets remarkable pace off the pitch.

Ten days later, Alec mingled with the spectators carrying their picnic hampers down St John's Wood Road. His own burden was a big leather bag containing flannels and shirts, all devotedly washed by his mother in the kitchen copper back home at Woking. Alec laconically describes his journey into cricket fame. On the day of his Test début against India he had caught the train to Waterloo, then strap-hanged on the underground train to Baker Street. 'I took the bus up to St. John's Wood church, walked along to Lord's and went in to play.' It was the same routine, to and from home, for each day of the match. For his travelling and cricket labours he received third-class rail fares and a match fee of £45.

The enigmatic Wally Hammond resumed his England captaincy in the three-match series against India. Alec remembers the perfunctory greeting he received on entering the dressing-room at Lord's. 'Hammond was never a man to enthuse; he hardly ever spoke to you. All he said to me was, "Welcome. Hope you have a good game" – and that was it.'

Bill Bowes, the first of Alec's Test partners, was at the other end to scrutinise the England débutant. The wise old campaigner looked on eagerly, offering welcome advice. His eyes were refreshed by the promise of the Surrey recruit. Bowes, the bowling broadsword of Yorkshire's great years in the 1930s, must have known that he was eavesdropping on the blossoming challenge of a contender equal to himself.

Beyond the boundary there were cautious words of praise from the

Manchester Guardian correspondent. His compliments were not rash and none the worse for that. The judgement was accorded to a raw and relatively unknown newcomer: 'Bedser is not a heaven-sent opening bowler, but like the British private soldier he gives of his best and will bowl with Tom Richardson spirit until his heart bursts.'

The blueprint for magnificence was, though, first drawn up in a spectacular entry at Lord's. Alec Bedser, immediately brought into the fray, took 7 wickets for 49 runs in 29.1 overs in India's first innings. They included seasoned opponents in Hazare, Amarnath and the Indian captain, the Nawab of Pataudi. (The only cricketer to play for both England and India, Pataudi had earlier emulated his fellow Indian princes, Ranjitsinhji and Duleepsinhji in scoring a century in his first Test against Australia on the 1932–33 tour.)

The first of Alec's wickets was that of Vijay Merchant, caught on the leg side by Paul Gibb who was attentively standing up in the manner to be followed by other wicket-keeping allies. Alec remembers: 'Luckily for me, I was in the thick of the action right away. I was able to bowl from the Nursery End, my favourite end at Lord's, as I could make the ball go away with the slope and also swing in against it to the batsmen.'

The eclipse of Merchant gave an added buoyancy to Bedser's stride. It was a major conquest. Dudley Carew, the *Times* correspondent, watching Merchant in this first post-war season, thought of him as a batsman equipped to play in a representative world XI. John Arlott was another to pay tribute to the smooth, never-violent technique of the Indian: 'An innings by Merchant sprouts no exotic blooms but its construction is perfect to the last detail.' Arlott likened Merchant to Herbert Sutcliffe: 'No brutishness of the wicket, no pace or spin or swing can disconcert him.' Merchant was the first Indian to score 2,000 runs on a tour, averaging 74.53 in all first-class matches and 49 in five Test innings. He hit seven hundreds, with a highest score of 242, and exceeded 50 in 20 out of his 41 innings. His 128 in the third Test at The Oval was the highest ever played for his country against England. A signal indication of Merchant's mastery is that his first-class career average of 71.22 is second only to that of Don Bradman.

At Lord's, commented one writer, Alec Bedser revealed to the selectors what they most wanted to know – that he had the heart as well as the action of a great bowler. A packed assembly of nearly 30,000 people watched the resumption of Test cricket in June 1946 and they were heartened by an exceptional début, one to arouse high expectations. The verdict of *Wisden* underlined the threat of the débutant: 'Bedser maintained an admirable length at fast-medium pace, with swerve or spin, which often turned the ball appreciably on the sodden turf.'

Out in the country at Guildford, there was another deeply interested partisan. Eric Bedser, playing for Surrey against Oxford University, spent every available moment listening to a radio broadcast of the match in the house of the groundsman, Jack Patterson. There must have been at least a ripple of elation at the news of the events at Lord's.

Brother Alec followed his seven wickets in India's first innings with four more in the second innings. His match figures of 11 wickets for 145 runs on a début are not without parallels. Fred ('Nutty') Martin, the Kent left-arm fast-medium bowler, holds the English record of 12 for 102. This was achieved, as deputy for Bobby Peel, in his only Test against Australia at The Oval in 1890. Another Kent man, leg-spinner C.S. Marriott, took 11 wickets (for 96) against the West Indies at The Oval in 1933; and Clarrie Grimmett also displayed his spinning arts to take 11 for 85 against England at Sydney in the 1924–25 series.

In more recent times there have been more telling analyses of 16 wickets by Massie (Australia) and Hirwani (India) on their first appearances. None of these bowlers, however, was able to match the sustained excellence of Alec Bedser against India. He followed his feat at Lord's by taking another 11 wickets in the second drawn match at Manchester. Such was his accuracy that his 22 wickets in two Tests cost him less than 11 runs apiece. Alec headed the England bowling averages against India with 24 wickets at 12.41 runs each.

England completed a ten-wicket victory over India at Lord's by 1.30 on the third day. As he enjoyed a relaxed lunch, Bedser knew that the spotlight thrown upon him heightened his responsibilities. At 28, he was accounted the best young pace bowler in the country. His apprenticeship had been suspended, but there was the gain in mature strength. Mentally, too, he was philosophically attuned as a cricketer. Along with other returning professionals after six years of war, he had been subjected to far worse pressures than would ever assail him in cricket.

Discerning critics, while acknowledging Bedser as a welcome discovery, insisted that his cricket career was still in the making. 'The next four years,' wrote John Arlott, 'will be his testing time. Meanwhile, England may be thankful that she has him. He will serve her faithfully.'

Alec, at Lord's, also demonstrated a batting ability which was to serve England well on other occasions. It might have been more freely expressed but for the burden he carried as a bowler. England lost four wickets – those of Hutton; Compton, bowled first ball by Amarnath;

Washbrook; and Hammond – for 70 runs. Then Hardstaff and Gibb were associated in a match-winning stand of 182 runs for the fifth wicket. Smailes and Bedser also flourished in Hardstaff's company.

The artistry of Hardstaff's unbeaten double-century was unfurled in a stay of five and a quarter hours. The design of the innings matched his immaculate bearing. Before the Second World War he had teetered on the brink of greatness. Trevor Bailey presents an impressive claim for an England quartet of that time. He has ranked Hardstaff, Hutton, Compton and Edrich as the best professional batsmen to grace the stage in this brief pre-war interlude.

There was another glimpse of Hardstaff's grandeur at Lord's. As his – and England's – total soared, so did dejection shroud the Indians. Unruffled and bareheaded, as usual, he kept a watchful vigil and Crawford White, in the *News Chronicle*, commented:

> On Saturday, when England were faltering against the attack of Amarnath, it was Hardstaff who stopped the rot. While wickets fell at the other end, Hardstaff seldom seemed troubled. He made square-cuts, cover drives, and forcing shots off his legs with equal ease. By comparison, valuable though they were, the efforts of his colleagues bordered on the rural.

Alec Bedser, as one of these batting courtiers, remembers his modest 30 in a partnership of 70 runs with Hardstaff: 'He scored 205 with such elegance that I was grateful not to have been bowling against him.' Alec's bowling feat at Lord's elicited the fulfilled prophecy from Hardstaff that he had booked his passage to Australia for the following winter. The kindly words preceded another splendid gesture. One of Alec's most treasured souvenirs of his opening Test is the England cap he received from his Nottinghamshire-based senior. 'Take this home,' said Joe, 'and give it to your mother.'

At 43, Wally Hammond was the oldest cricketer to captain England when the MCC side toured Australia in the winter of 1946–47. Although in retrospect it was shown to be a sad mistake, his appointment was a formality. In the previous English summer he had topped the first-class averages with 1,783 runs at an average of 84.90. The tally of hundreds, seven in all, included two double-centuries. Hammond had shown, reported *Wisden*, 'the batting form that made him almost the terror of bowlers'.

Charles Barnett has testified to Hammond's dominance in his heyday between the two world wars. 'It was an education to bat with him,' recalled the former Gloucestershire opening batsman. 'But you were lucky to get two balls in an over if he was in the mood to plunder the bowling. With the lightest of strides, he could make a good-length ball into an overpitched one.'

Hammond, recalled Barnett, had a demoralising effect on bowlers. One esteemed opponent, Tommy Mitchell (the Derbyshire and England leg-spinner) always took fright at the appearance of Hammond. 'Poor Tommy couldn't stay on the field. He would make some excuse and retire to the pavilion until Hammond was out.' Barnett confirmed the view of Hammond as a great athlete and considered that his strength lay in his eyesight. As a supreme first slip, Hammond would observe bowlers: 'Wally had the talent to use his assessment of them to advantage as a batsman.'

Alec Bedser was still an enthusiastic and tireless learner under the leadership of Hammond in England and Australia. Hammond had been his – and Eric's – idol during their boyhood. They had once cycled to Chobham, a neighbouring Surrey village, to watch and admire the great man in action. The Bedsers looked on with envy as Hammond strolled around the ground in his England blazer. The hero-worship receded, though, when Alec himself achieved England status. 'I found him to be below my ideal as a captain. I was still inexperienced and would have appreciated some words of advice and encouragement.'

The feud between Charles Barnett and Hammond is well known in cricket circles. Barnett lived in the same Gloucestershire valley as Hammond. Their association, in cricket terms, was substantial: 'Ours was a "convenience friendship" – we had our understandings and disagreements,' quietly observed Barnett. They travelled many miles together on cricket journeys. 'Sometimes Wally wouldn't utter a word; at other times he could be charming and we would chat amicably together.'

Barnett, as an astute and congenial West Countryman, usually forbore malice, but he did endorse Bedser's opinion of Hammond as a captain. His explanation puts the flaws of an exalted champion under a searching microscope: 'Wally had spent 14 years of his life as an army sergeant's son. It was a difficult upbringing. He had to do as he was told. So when he became a cricketer he expected people to carry out his orders without question.'

Barnett conveyed the image of a charmless captain lacking tactical acumen. He had first noted the deficiencies when Hammond turned amateur to succeed to the England captaincy in 1938. 'Wally wasn't an influence for good; he hadn't got a kind streak. Gloucestershire's young bowlers suffered. They were too frightened of making mistakes which could have been avoided if he had been more approachable.'

The arrogance was, in Barnett's judgement, indefensible. 'All successes in life can be achieved with the word "please". It is such an easy thing to say. Cricket can be tough, but still a gentleman's game. If it isn't, it's hardly worth playing.' Hammond's chameleon character and unpredictable moods rendered him a lonely man on his majestic plateau. 'He had many acquaintances, but very few friends' – that was Barnett's sad view of his old batting partner.

❧ ❧ ❧

There were premature expressions of optimism about the challenge facing the MCC party on the hastily arranged tour of Australia in 1946–47. Jim Swanton sagely warned of waiting perils. 'Cricketers of talent and strong fibre seem to fall from trees in this country,' he said.

Australia's cricketers, as Alec Bedser points out, were younger and in practice. They had emerged relatively unscathed, in sporting terms, from the war. By contrast, England were reliant on an old guard whose best years were behind them. Hammond, Voce, Hardstaff and Fishlock were the only players previously to have toured Australia. Only four of the party were under 30, with Godfrey Evans, one of the finds of the tour, at 26 the youngest member. The intervention of war had disturbed the momentum of other tourists who had been approaching their prime time. Among them were Len Hutton (whose prowess, however, was happily not to be dimmed by a severe wartime injury), Denis Compton, Bill Edrich and Doug Wright.

The conditions of austerity in Britain were not entirely forgotten aboard the RMS *Stirling Castle*, which set sail for Australia in August 1946. The ship carried wartime brides and fiancées of Australian servicemen as well as the England cricketers. Only Hammond was allocated really congenial surroundings and players recalled invitations to his cabin suite for drinks. Gerald Howat observed: 'What was not the least reminiscent of wartime was the food. Menus which gourmets on desert islands dreamed of were set before those used to spam, snoek and reconstituted egg.' There was, understandably, little resistance offered to the temptations by those who had long existed on meagre rations. Waistlines expanded alarmingly. Remedial deck games had scant impact and agility, naturally on the ebb among so many veterans, further declined with the mounting weight.

Alec Bedser, the raw newcomer in the 1946–47 series, now enjoys the status of an 'honorary Australian'. The affection with which he and Eric are greeted in that hospitable country is a continuing source of happiness and it was sealed by a dinner commemorating their 80th birthdays at Parliament House, Sydney, in 1998.

The old colonial Anglo-Australian relationship persisted on the first post-war tour (as it still does, on the evidence of recent polls). Jim Swanton remembered one instance of the rapport between the two peoples on his own first tour of Australia as a journalist. The driver of a taxicab in Perth regaled him with vivid descriptions of the manifold attractions and delights of Australia. He ended his recital with bluff words of welcome: 'Yeah, it's a great country. Remember, it's yours as well as ours – and if you don't enjoy yourself here, it'll be your own ruddy fault.'

Alec and Eric Bedser were also enthralled by the atmosphere of good fellowship. Having grown up in a rigid social climate – and cricket under the imperious rule of amateurs – prevailing in pre-war England, the impact was staggering. They were able to cast aside the deferential attitudes of their youth. The release from the stress on privilege was a refreshing bonus. 'From the beginning,' says Alec, 'I thought Australia was a great place. I liked the people, so friendly and approachable. They accept you for what you are.' Entertainment, generous and unstinting, rewards those who gain the respect of Australian hosts. 'They always make a fuss of you, which is nice.'

Friendships, established in 1946, are still maintained today on the Bedsers' regular winter holidays in Australia. While other players preferred to stay in cities, Alec and Eric enjoyed relaxing interludes on sheep farms in New South Wales and Victoria. In the immediate post-war touring days, with less frenetic schedules, there was time to build up an accord with people in country districts.

Many of these associations were forged on voyages carrying Australian graziers and their families on the same ships as those bearing the Bedsers to cricket duties in Australia. These were times when vast fortunes were being made in wool: 'Prices were so good that the traders could afford to come to England on holiday. This was how we met most of them. They would be returning to Australia at the same time as us.' An agreeable instance of the Bedsers' social links with Australia is that they now stay with the grandchildren of friends they first met in 1946.

Good fortune of another kind aided the Bedsers at the outset of the first Australian tour. A separation loomed until, quite 'out of the blue', the pools promoter Alfie Cope offered to pay Eric's expenses to join his twin abroad. This gesture did have a publicity motive, but the gift of £500 was a substantial sum. Eric travelled to Australia via Cape Town on a cargo ship. He was reunited with Alec during the match against Victoria at Melbourne in October.

Wally Hammond revealed the better side of his nature in recognising the importance of Eric as a rallying companion on Alec's first tour. 'My brother introduced me to Hammond and he said, "Just feel yourself one of the party."' As the Bedsers explain, this was a rare concession in days when pavilion privacy was strictly maintained. Eric was able to express his gratitude by assisting Bill Ferguson, the MCC baggage-master, with his duties. It is also instructive to recall that the only other official accompanying the tour party was Major Rupert Howard, the manager. An Australian masseur was recruited at Perth to complete the back-up team.

The pattern of the series was shaped by the calamities of the first Test at Brisbane in December. The course of the match was put irretrievably beyond England's grasp by the denial of Bradman's wicket. The great Australian was struggling to regain his pre-war powers. He survived a much debated and controversial decision while his innings was still in its infancy. He had scored only 28 when a catch was disallowed.

The escape is less certainly verified by the Bedsers. They both consider that there was room for doubt. 'Bill Voce bowled a full half-volley and the ball flew, pretty fast and straight, to Jack Ikin at second slip. It was one of those incidents for which they would ask for the camera today. Don was convinced that he had pinched the ball into the ground.'

Most observers, including Hammond, thought it was an unjust reprieve. Norman Yardley, fielding in the gully, commented: 'Bradman attempted one of his favourite strokes, a drive just wide of cover point. The ball went from the top edge of the bat towards Ikin, who caught it beautifully'. Bradman himself said the point at issue was whether the ball finished its downward course before making contact with the bat. In his opinion, the ball had touched the bottom of his bat just before hitting the ground and therefore was not a catch.

Scott Borwick, the umpire, was so far unconvinced that he did not consult his colleague at square leg. 'Had he done so, the result would have been the same,' said Bradman. Borwick, in an article written after the series, confirmed his verdict: 'It was a bump ball. It hit the ground a few inches from Bradman's bat.'

The aborted dismissal was, in the event, a pyschological reverse of severe dimensions for England. Bradman went on to score 187 before being bowled by Edrich. He shared a third-wicket record stand of 276 with Hassett. The plunder was reinforced by Test débutants Keith Miller and Colin McCool, who capitalised on the advantage with further century partnerships. Australia went on to score 645, their highest total at home, before a tropical storm engulfed the Wooloongabba ground.

The violence of that storm, which twice waterlogged the arena within 24 hours, was unparalleled in Brisbane's history. It signalled the unforgiving terrors of a bowler's pitch. The winds reached a velocity of 79 mph. In half an hour, '250 points of rain fell,' according to the *Sydney Morning Herald*; transport services were disrupted and power lines torn down; city buildings and roads were flooded; and a barrage of hailstones left a trail of wreckage (surfers at a nearby seaside resort, wounded by the jagged pieces of ice, had to be treated for head injuries). Don Bradman also recalled the ferocity of the downpour:

> In half an hour one could have sailed a boat across the oval. The stumps, which had been left in the middle, floated away. One sightscreen had been blown over the fence by the cyclonic wind, and the hailstones on the roof sounded like machine-gun fire. We were marooned in the dressing-room.

The ensuing treachery of the wicket duplicated the conditions in which England had overwhelmed the hapless Australians ten years earlier. Australia, this time, were the avengers. Neville Cardus, in his vivid imagery, said a description of the perils would have taxed the language of the Old Testament and Joseph Conrad: 'The atmosphere was greedy for the Englishmen's ruin; the fieldsmen stood on tiptoe, and in the feverish vision of the batsmen they would surely have appeared each to have many hungry arms to stretch, seize and throw up into the air without pity.'

England could point to the injustice and futility of being asked to offer any sort of a counter in such conditions. The events at Brisbane proved to be a catalyst for the introduction of covered wickets throughout the world. Gallantry of the highest order was displayed by Hammond and Edrich before the inevitable innings defeat at Brisbane.

Wally Hammond did provide one last glimpse of his batting majesty in an unequal struggle. 'If I had never seen Hammond play some of the liveliest innings of all creation, I would remember him for the classical innings he played on the Brisbane gluepot,' wrote Jack Fingleton. 'In such circumstances, the scoresheet is a fraud and a humbug.'

Another Australian, Bill O'Reilly, considered that Hammond had no peer as an all-weather player. 'He is second to none in playing the "dead bat" at the lifting ball. He played it so well that one might have been excused for thinking that his right arm was either broken or made of jelly, so little pressure did he place on the bat.'

Cardus reported that Hammond was given a royal welcome in England's first innings as he slowly walked out to the hazardous field: 'He used his bat like a Roman centurion's shield, a spectacle of dignity in the surrounding turbulence.' Hammond had a plucky partner in Bill Edrich; but it was the captain's near-miraculous 32 which won undivided attention. It vied with his noble poise on another malicious pitch at Melbourne in 1936. The evidence of his skill was shown afterwards to the admiration of players in the England dressing-room. 'Hammond didn't have a mark on him, while Bill was black and blue and covered in bruises,' recalls Alec Bedser.

A heroic cameo did, thankfully, enable Hammond to salvage some pride in his last Test series. His decline saddened those with memories of his great years. There were mitigating factors. His domestic affairs were in tatters and the news of his divorce was made public before the tour began. He scored only 168 runs in 8 innings before he finally acknowledged the crippling pain of fibrositis. Yardley took over as captain in the final Test at Sydney.

Hammond's captaincy, never his strong suit, also wavered in Australia. It came under intense scrutiny. One Australian writer, generally sympathetic to Hammond, thought it lacked 'intelligence, thought and inspiration'. The remoteness of the introspective man was also intensified amid England's reverses. Jack Fingleton observed: 'He sailed like a schooner from slip to slip anchorage with hardly a consultation.'

The demons which bedevilled Hammond apparently produced a state of insecurity. When his batting command deteriorated, as it did in Australia, he was unsure of himself. Joe Hardstaff looked on sympathetically: 'There was a worried look on his face when he failed. I thought it was a big mistake to make him captain: it was more than he could take.'

Australia's triumphs, two by an innings at Brisbane and Sydney, were a salutary reminder of the buoyancy of youth over age. It was also a demonstration of their all-round strengths, which would lift them to a plateau of eminence in the 1940s. Three of their leading bowlers, Miller, Lindwall and McCool, scored centuries.

England, for their part, were consoled by the burgeoning talents of Godfrey Evans, Alec Bedser and Cyril Washbrook, who had made his début for England against New Zealand at The Oval in 1937. They did achieve commendable draws at Melbourne and Adelaide. Denis Compton, in a welcome purple patch, led the recovery with two centuries at Adelaide. In the final Test at Sydney, where Australia won by five wickets, Hutton was stricken by tonsillitis after scoring a century and did not bat in the second innings.

Wally Hammond paid generous tribute to the Australian victors after a tour which, however reluctantly undertaken so soon after the war, did give an enormous fillip to the game of cricket in both countries. Vast crowds, totalling 850,000, watched the series. At Melbourne, for the third Test in January, the official aggregate attendance was 343,675 and the receipts of £44,063 were a world record for a cricket match. 'I revelled in the sight of Australia's dauntless, picturesque, and happy youth, giving to the game we love something we older players could no longer offer it,' wrote Hammond.

For Alec Bedser, then at the learning stage, the tour of Australia marked an important step in his cricket education. His prodigious burden then, as in the future, would have been immeasurably lightened by another bowler of similar heart and strength at the other end. It meant that he emerged from the series having bowled in the Tests 246 (eight-ball) overs – more than twice the amount of bowling done by each of the Australian opening pair, Lindwall and Miller.

Alec proudly reflects on his stamina which enabled him to go through an onerous tour, lasting eight months, without once breaking down. Lesser men would surely have quailed amid the stifling heat which prevailed during the fourth Test at Adelaide. Matters there were made worse by the high humidity in a city where dry heat was the norm. Mount Lofty on the skyline shimmered in temperatures, which, on four out of the six days of the match, exceeded 100 degrees. Bedser remembers the unrelenting conditions: 'The temperature on the field was 134 and it only subsided to 90 after dark. There was no air-conditioning, so I sweated all day and sweated all night.'

In the circumstances, it was not surprising that Alec succumbed to sickness at one stage during the match. That day, he bowled 22 eight-ball overs. The drain on energy was further increased by the attire of heavy woollen flannels, which became as heavy as lead when drenched with perspiration. Alec recalls: 'I retired to the dressing-room and was as sick as a dog under the shower.' His team-mates looked on in consternation when he re-emerged to continue bowling. They said he was as 'white as a sheet'.

Bill Edrich, Alec's bowling partner, was also afflicted by the heat. It was so hot that he was unable to breathe properly as he ran in to the wicket. Drinks intervals were restricted to three in the playing sessions throughout the day. Alec was so dehydrated that he had lost six pounds by the close of play. It was said that Eric, occupied less strenuously bowling in the nets at Adelaide, was so concerned by his brother's misfortune that his own weight fell by the equivalent amount by the end of what was a horrendous day.

~~~

Billy Griffith would, in due course, reflect on an unnerving delivery first discovered by chance by Alec Bedser in Australia. It was described, less than accurately, as a leg-cutter. The former MCC secretary, in an article in *The Cricketer*, wrote:

> Bedser cuts the ball from leg using his long fingers to impart spin exactly as the face of the racket is used in tennis. When he bowls it – and herein lies the immense skill – he pitches on a length and invariably makes the batsman play.
>
> The ball's value as a wicket-taker is multiplied since it is wonderfully effective, particularly when the more orthodox spinner can turn it yards but too slowly to be of much use . . . No one in my time has achieved, to anything like the same degree, such a combination of pace, accuracy, and length as has Bedser with this particular ball.

It was an attacking ploy which would produce woe and despair. But for those who sought to emulate the method, as Griffith and Alec himself says, the leg-cutter didn't just happen. It was only fully mastered after two years of diligent application. The delivery was first unveiled in the second Test at Sydney in December 1946. Bedser was bowling to Sid Barnes, the Australian opener, on a perfect batting wicket. 'Barnes was very powerful off his legs, so I didn't want to swing the ball in that area,' says Bedser. 'Alan Peach, my old Surrey coach, had told me, "If you want to stop the ball swinging, hold it across the seam like a leg-spinner.'"

Experimentally, as Peach had advised, Alec held the ball's seam horizontally: 'I ran up and bowled and the ball went across the wicket like a leg-spinner, so I'd obviously spun it.' Peter Smith, fielding at mid-on, gasped in disbelief: 'You can't bowl with a new ball like that.' Alec was undeterred by the rebuke and replied, 'I've just seen something happen and I want to do it again.' Barnes, hitherto at ease, would have preferred the tactic to be abandoned. 'What the hell's going on here?' he grumbled.

A great deed would follow this intriguing episode. A few weeks later, at Adelaide, Don Bradman came in to bat, ten minutes before the end of play, on a February evening. Jim Swanton described this as a red-letter day. He had received an invitation to dinner at Bradman's home. Along with Jessie Bradman and her son, John, he elected to escape the rush by leaving an over before the close. They were beneath the stand when there was a tremendous uproar from above. 'That'll be Dad,' said John happily. And he was right. Bedser had bowled his father for nought.

Bradman would later announce that the ball which defeated him was the finest ever to take his wicket: 'It must have come three-quarters of the way straight on my off stump, then suddenly dipped to pitch on the leg-stump, only to turn off the pitch and hit the middle and off stumps.'

The delivery which overthrew Bradman at Adelaide was 'spun at speed'. The effect was a genuine leg-break and Bedser later said that it was the turning-point in his career. In the years to come he was to bring that magnificent ball under almost sure command.

CHAPTER FIVE

England's Standard-Bearer

Alec was deadly accurate. He was literally bowling fast leg-breaks.
WALTER HADLEE

A merger of Surrey lionhearts was affirmed when Alec Bedser was installed in an illustrious triumvirate at The Oval. Shepherding him through two post-war seasons was the veteran, Alf Gover, whose own monumental efforts in the 1930s cast him in the lineage of the Victorian stalwart Tom Richardson. In 1936 and 1937, Gover bowled 2,379 overs and twice took 200 wickets to become the first English fast bowler to achieve this feat since Richardson in 1897.

Alec Bedser would summon his powers of endurance, as he singlehandedly held sway before Surrey's years of plenty. Michael Barton, his captain from 1948 to 1951, readily accepts that Bedser was overbowled in his formative seasons: 'Alec really carried us during that time. There is no question that he was the man who contributed most to our successes. Alec was a very hard worker, with great stamina, and he was a brilliant bowler, particularly on a bad wicket.'

Testimony to Bedser's workload is indelibly contained in the statistical lists. The figures almost crush belief. Between April 1946 and September 1947 – two English seasons and one overseas tour – he bowled 17,395 balls. In five summers on Test and county duties at home, he busily accumulated an aggregate of 5,636 overs, well over 1,000 each season. Throughout the long haul of post-war summers, Alec was unflaggingly both wicket-taker and stock bowler.

The 'huge, quick, lifting leg-spinners', as one contemporary described them, would ultimately divide Bedser from the rest of his breed as incomparably a world-class bowler. The ascent to greatness was accomplished without a settled partner. Fast bowlers traditionally hunt in complementary pairs. Bedser, however, was called upon to shoulder his burden unaccompanied until the arrival of Bailey, Trueman and

Statham – all companions of the requisite steel.

Juggling their meagre resources, the England selectors discovered and discarded a variable contingent of new-ball allies, 17 in all, through Alec's Test career. These included Bill Bowes, Bill Voce, Dick Pollard and Alf Gover in 1946; Bill Edrich, Jack Martin, George Pope, Cliff Gladwin, Alec Coxon, Allan Watkins, Derek Shackleton, Freddie Brown, John Warr and Frank Tyson.

❧ ❧ ❧

The platform was established for the ensuing great years at The Oval during the stewardship of Michael Barton. He had taken over the captaincy from Errol Holmes midway through the 1948 season. Glamorgan, with 172 points, won the championship for the first time. Surrey finished second, only four points in arrears. It was their best position since 1925, when they were runners-up to Yorkshire. In an exciting finale, Glamorgan, Surrey and Yorkshire were all in contention less than a fortnight from the end of the season.

Eric Bedser and Jim Laker had earlier helped to orchestrate two thrilling back-to-back wins over Gloucestershire and Lancashire at The Oval. The first was a one-day affair after rain had prevented play on the Saturday and Monday. Goddard and Cook bowled out Surrey for 133. Tom Barling, on the verge of retirement and coaching duties at Harrow School, was top scorer with 45. The Gloucestershire innings was also dominated by one batsman, Jack Crapp, who hit 65 in the battle for the lead. Laker, at his most venomous on a spiteful pitch, took eight wickets, and Surrey won by two runs in the last over.

The nerves of the Surrey partisans tingled again in the following match against Lancashire. Laurie Fishlock and Dave Fletcher shared a century partnership and Lancashire narrowly avoided the follow-on. Ken Cranston, with seven wickets, produced tremors of anxiety. These were reinforced when Winston Place scored a century to take the visitors within sight of their target of 248 runs.

Eric Bedser was the saviour in the winning cause. He brought his match tally to eight wickets, taking three of the last four in a rousing conclusion. Only two minutes remained when Fishlock, out in the deep, held on to a steepling catch off Bedser. The relief of the Surrey men matched the prolonged sighs of the spectators. Victory by one run left everyone struggling for breath.

Surrey's title challenge in 1948 foundered in Stan Squires's benefit match against Middlesex in August at The Oval. Laurie Fishlock hit 82 out of 156 when George Mann put Surrey in to bat. His duel with the wily left-hander, Jack Young, who took 14 wickets in the match, was a lesson in faultless strokeplay. The mastery of Fishlock, then in his 40s, showed why he had twice toured Australia in 1936–37 and 1946–47. Fractures of identical fingers on both tours deprived another audience of a glimpse of his talents.

Fishlock's career aggregate of 25,376 runs included 56 centuries. The fervour of his batting did not waver in the post-war years leading up to Surrey's renaissance. His was the blade which provided the cutting edge in many victories. In his benefit year of 1950, he displayed remarkable form. In 16 innings he hit 908 runs, including four centuries, at an average of nearly 65. He was sturdily resistant against the all-conquering Australians in 1948. His 81 out of a Surrey total of 141, was a display to remember.

Alec Bedser and Jim Laker seemed to have countered the Middlesex advance at The Oval in 1948. They shared seven wickets, as the visitors trailed by 38 runs on the first innings. Middlesex required 142 to win and lost half their wickets for 39. Mann and Robins then scattered the pigeons with exhilarating strokes. They put on 62 in half an hour. Jim Sims caught the mood of adventure and scored 36 in an unbroken last-wicket stand of 41 runs. He was dropped when only 10 runs separated the teams.

Laker was the culprit, failing to hold on to a return catch. 'Jim never said very much, but he was silent that day. He was obviously deeply upset at the lapse,' recalls Michael Barton. In 1949, however, Sims was permitted no second chance. Laker, this time, took a brilliant one-handed catch as the ball was struck fiercely back at him. 'One year too late,' he said – a droll aside couched in self-rebuke.

The long years of waiting ended in 1950 when Surrey tied with Lancashire to gain their first championship since 1914. It was the second year in succession that the title had been shared. Yorkshire and Middlesex were linked at the head of the table in 1949. Surrey ended their season of triumph with a flush of seven successive victories, one first-innings lead and another win in their last nine championship matches.

Lancashire, for their part, seemed assured of winning the championship outright until rain interfered with their game against Warwickshire. The necessary four points eluded them in a crucial and wary encounter at The Oval. The zeal of the 20-year-old Peter May confounded the Lancastrians. His innings of 92 was rewarded with the county cap. Just as importantly, it nudged Surrey towards the title goal.

Michael Barton recalls his exhortation to Alec Bedser in the following decisive match against Leicestershire, when the intervention of rain had effectively reduced the duration of the match to two days: 'Alec had become a little stale towards the end of this season. I said, "Now, I know I've bowled you too much, but I want a real effort."' Barton remembers the defiant heave of Alec's shoulders at his unintended slight. 'Alec was annoyed but my only thought was to provide a stimulus.'

The audacity of the Surrey captain produced a devastating counter. Alec swung the ball ever more sharply into the leg trap to take 8 wickets for 53 runs in Leicestershire's first innings. His match tally was increased by 4 in the second innings. In 54 overs his 12 wickets cost him only 8 runs apiece.

One of the assets of any captain worth his salt is to know when and how to direct the conductor's baton. 'If we've any hope at all, it will have to be you to get them out' is a well-proven gambit. Barton did not quite address Alec in such terms. But the intention of the command was the same, and the trick worked.

Surrey, bolstered by a first innings century by Fishlock, did, in the end, need only one ball to win by 10 wickets. It was a gentle half-volley, bowled in a pre-arranged 'scene' to Barton by his opposing captain, Charles Palmer.

Other 'enthusiastic scenes', laconically reported *Wisden*, greeted the long-delayed championship honour. A straightforward victory did first have to disable the resistance of Leicestershire opening batsman, Les Berry. Neither was it helped by fielding confusion, which gave the redoubtable Berry a prolonged stay at the wicket. Barton recalls: 'Les Berry got going in the second innings and it looked as if Leicestershire might save the match. He hit a skier off Tony Lock which went straight towards Laurie Fishlock fielding at mid-off.' In the custom of the time, Barton called out the surname of his intended catcher to distinguish him from others with identical Christian names. Fishlock failed to respond to the appeal: he was rather deaf and he only heard the word 'Lock'. The ball fell harmlessly between him and the bowler.

Alec Bedser has often thought it unfair that the fruits of his – and Eric's – endeavours should have fallen to him alone. It might have been supposed that Alec's superiority as a cricketer would lead to friction, even an estrangement between the brothers. Not the least remarkable feature of their relationship is that each of them took the utmost pleasure in their respective achievements. Criticism was not withheld in their many post-match cricket conversations. Stressful occasions brought sympathy. At all times, both lean and bountiful, they took comfort in each other's counsel. 'I was always more concerned at what Alec was doing than with my own performances,' insists Eric.

A more vexed point at issue is the situation in which the senior Bedser twin was placed in the Surrey ranks. Eric had, as related earlier, opted for off-spin in order to marshal different bowling resources to those of his brother. As events were to prove, it set him in opposition to Jim Laker. The consequence was restricted opportunity to demonstrate his worth. Brother Alec, in *Twin Ambitions*, presented this ruling:

> I have no doubt that, had Eric not been destined to compete with the genius of Laker, his reputation would have been much higher. He had to be content with being a fine all-rounder, getting the most of his opportunities when Jim was away playing for England or when batting conditions were good.

The respective merits of both bowlers have been acknowledged in Surrey quarters and elsewhere in cricket. Temperamentally, Laker was judged to be suspect in certain circumstances. Peter Walker, the former Glamorgan all-rounder and a later broadcasting colleague, vigorously responds to those critics who seek to present Laker as a bowler who was quick to surrender: 'Any bowler with an ego which he had would have always tried. If you gave him a wicket to bowl on, and he didn't take five or six wickets, you could sense that he had let himself down, never mind the team. There was no question that luck had not gone with him.'

It is undoubtedly true that the phlegmatic Yorkshireman, for all his superior gifts, was regarded as someone who received preferential treatment as a Surrey bowler. Getting the right end, as with all great bowlers, was a prime requirement. It was a matter of consequence for leading batsmen, too. They would want to dominate the strike in propitious circumstances.

Eric Bedser, as his figures show, generally bowled better when Laker was not in the Surrey team. Brother Alec confirms this and says that Eric would then have first use of responsive wickets. On other occasions, in the same prevailing conditions and when Laker was also on county duty, Eric very often would not even get a bowl.

The advantage did markedly accrue to the elder Bedser in two periods – from 1947 to 1952 and again from 1956 to 1959. Test calls for Laker allowed Eric greater scope; he was then granted a choice of ends. Given a fairer crack of the whip, he outbowled Laker in 1951 and in 1956, when his colleague was preoccupied with other remarkable deeds for England.

Jim Laker has been derided as a member of the awkward squad. His austere demeanour masked a highly emotional man. If the prima-donna allegations are true, it does need to be emphasised that he was not alone in this category in a highly combative team led by Stuart Surridge in the 1950s. His rapid promotion to the first team did, as he himself admitted, usurp the spinning role earmarked for the elder Bedser. He was not without sympathy: 'Eric was forced to take a back seat because of my involvement. On helpful pitches he held a watching brief, and on good wickets one could easily imagine what went through his mind when he was tossed the ball after the rest of us had toiled in vain. With his enormous hands, Eric could spin the ball like a top.'

Geoffrey Howard, the former Surrey and Lancashire secretary. remembers one conversation at the outset of the careers of Bedser and Laker. His companion was Bob Gregory, the Surrey batsman, who was a member of the MCC party which toured India under the captaincy of Douglas Jardine in 1933–34. 'If I had been captain,' said Gregory, 'Laker would not have got into the Surrey team.' Gregory considered that Eric Bedser possessed spinning attributes which could have matched those of the Gloucestershire maestro, Tom Goddard.

Peter Richardson, the former Worcestershire, Kent and England batsman, is another supporter of Bedser's claims. He takes the view that his old Surrey rival should never be underestimated: 'Eric was a high-class bowler. If Jim wasn't playing, you didn't actually jump in the air with delight.' Richardson, in his assessment, says that Eric has to be judged on the role – often as an 'odd-jobbing' bowler – that he was given and his opportunities within the Surrey team. He tellingly adds: 'Eric was a bowler who batted, not a batsman who bowled.'

Trevor Bailey is also sympathetic in expressing concern at Bedser's misfortune. 'Eric,' he says, 'was a good all-round cricketer who was unlucky to be an off-spinner at a time when we had two great bowlers, Jim Laker and Tony Lock, with their contrasting spins. There really wasn't a place for him, either as an all-rounder, or as a spinner at the highest level.' Bailey subscribes to the general view that in other eras, and especially at the present time, Bedser would have been an automatic choice as an England player.

Michael Barton is another key eye-witness in an intriguing debate. Eric Bedser was strongly advocated as a candidate to tour Australia in 1950–51. In 1949 he scored 1,749 runs and took 88 wickets. It was a season of high achievement in which his all-round talents were acknowledged by the *Wisden* correspondent: 'Bedser's batting has improved beyond all recognition, and besides imparting considerable off-spin he flighted the ball skilfully.'

The Bedser twins were linked as batsmen and bowlers in the victory by 52 runs over Middlesex at Lord's. It was Surrey's second win in a fortnight over their rivals from across the river. Eric shared a century opening stand with Fishlock and then dismissed the first five Middlesex batsmen – Robertson, Brown, Edrich, Compton and Sims – for 59 runs. Middlesex were set a target of 147; rain on the last day rendered 'batting more a matter of chance than ability'; and Alec did not spurn the opportunity. He took 8 wickets for 42 runs as Middlesex were routed for 94 in 105 minutes.

Jim Swanton recalled a pitch of the most sinister order at Lord's upon which, he related with some glee, Australia would not have made a hundred:

> Bedser bowled as well as I've seen him since the war. He hurled the ball down on a tantalising length and it lifted, moved both ways off the seam and, just to complete the programme, occasionally squatted as well. In 6 hours Bedser sent down 38 overs, nearly a third of the total bowled.

In his final conclusive spell, Alec took charge of one end for 1¾ hours. 'The batsmen were forced involuntarily into blind strokes which gave catch after catch either at slip or short leg,' reported Swanton.

Walter Hadlee was the New Zealand captain in 1949 and is now a Surrey life member. The Oval, he says, has special memories for him, not least because he played what he considers the best innings of his career there. The match was between Surrey and the New Zealanders in May. Hadlee's unbeaten 119 was largely responsible for the victory by 149 runs.

Hadlee recalls a rare hoar frost which carpeted the ground on his arrival at The Oval: 'A hot sun under clear skies soon removed all signs of frost. But it also brought to the surface the preparation moisture.' The consequence was a dry pitch and difficult batting conditions. 'By the time we batted in the second innings, the top had broken off the wicket.

Alec and Jim Laker were not easy to score from. Alec was deadly accurate. He was literally bowling fast leg-breaks and beat the bat repeatedly.'

An indication of the sternness of the contest was Bedser's figures in the innings. He bowled 36 overs for 37 runs, including 16 maidens, and took 3 wickets. 'I was fortunate to survive,' continues Hadlee, 'but it was mentally draining and physically demanding. Jim, at the pavilion end, spun his off-breaks prodigiously. I put my survival against him down to taking a stance three or so inches outside the leg stump. I could not bat that way against Alec, as he was so much quicker.'

Laurie Fishlock, ever reliant in his final seasons, scored 2,426 runs despite being dismissed five times in the 90s. Eric Bedser, as his opening partner, enjoyed his association with the veteran: 'Laurie was a fine player of spin and a good attacking batsman.' They shared a stand of 260 in 3 hours and 40 minutes against Somerset in July. Eric's contribution of 154 was then his highest score; but he went on to surpass this with 163 in another sparkling century overture with Fishlock against Nottinghamshire. E.M. Wellings, in the *London Evening News*, commented that 'this was further evidence of Bedser's approach towards Test class as an all-rounder'. The *Sunday Times* correspondent praised a 'sturdy, patient innings transformed by strokes of power and polish too long held in check'. Eric's last 50 runs were scored in under an hour.

❧ ❧ ❧

The events of the one-sided Test trial in the intimate sporting basin of Park Avenue, Bradford, thrust Jim Laker into the national spotlight in 1950. On a wicket left open to heavy rain 24 hours before the match, he took 8 wickets for 2 runs. The Rest included the Cambridge trio of Hubert Doggart, Peter May and David Sheppard.

Eric Bedser was also in The Rest's ranks at Bradford. One of the runs conceded by Laker was off a full toss charitably wheeled up to his Surrey colleague. Alex Bannister jokingly reflected that this was probably the only favour ever granted by Laker to his fellow bowler at The Oval. Trevor Bailey provided a delicious memory of Jim's dry humour at Park Avenue. Amid the compliments on his remarkable figures, he produced the deadpan reply: 'Well, they would have been less expensive if I hadn't given Eric one to get off the mark.' Eric did not need any assistance in the second innings. He was top scorer, with 30 out of the total of 113.

A long understanding between the Bedsers never to compete against each other had to be disregarded at Bradford. Alec was opposed to Eric, being a member of the England XI. It was one of the rare occasions when Alec and Eric changed in different dressing-rooms. Eventually Alec was obliged to bowl to Eric, which prompted Tom Pearce, one of the Test selectors, to remark: 'This is the first time I have ever seen a man bowling to himself.'

Michael Barton has confessed his puzzlement at the decline of Eric Bedser in 1950 after his exploits in the previous season. The defence, offered by brother Alec, is that Eric was not given the opportunities to consolidate his position. The sad facts are that Eric scored only 97 runs in 20 championship matches and took only 8 wickets in the 130 overs allotted to him. As *Wisden* reported, he displayed such inconsistency that towards the end of the programme he lost his place in the Surrey team.

Barton can offer no explanation for Bedser's depressing blip in form, something which can affect the best of cricketers. Eric, he once said, could be linked with Percy Fender as one of the finest all-rounders in Surrey's history. In 1950 there was the chance for Eric to bolster this claim: 'I was very sorry for Eric because this was a crucial season for him. Unfortunately, his form [with bat and ball] completely disintegrated. Another season at the same level as in 1949, and he would have gone to Australia. The opportunity never occurred again. Time went on and Jim Laker came into his own.'

Eric Bedser did overcome his disappointment to become a vital component in Surrey's successes in the 1950s. In 1956, Surrey's fifth championship year, he was deprived of the double by the weather. He regularly bowled in tandem with Laker and Lock. His figures of 804 runs and 92 wickets were acknowledged by the compliment of his captain, Stuart Surridge. 'Without Eric in the side,' said Surridge, 'Surrey might not have retained the title.'

The adamant verdict of Michael Barton, gleaned from his years of leadership, is that Eric Bedser was an all-rounder of sufficient quality to have played for Surrey either as a batsman or bowler. 'He did spin the ball, but not as violently as Laker did. But for Jim's mastery, Eric would have done the double year after year. He might well then have won a further chance to advance his England claims.' A player with such skills could have gained distinction with another county. Loyalty, in Eric's time, counted for much more than today; and, in any event, separation from Alec would have trounced such thoughts.

Stealing the show at The Oval did not confer on Jim Laker the coveted prize of a tour of Australia under Freddie Brown's captaincy in 1950–51. His omission from the MCC party, after taking 166 wickets at a little over 15 runs apiece, was among the many follies of selection. Another deposed Yorkshireman, Johnny Wardle, had also enjoyed a magnificent season. His marathon bowling spells, exceeding 1,600 overs, had yielded 174 wickets at 16.71 runs each. The selectors turned instead to another left-hander, Bob Berry, of Lancashire. An astonishing choice almost prompted an irate Wardle to sever his connection with first-class cricket and take up a lucrative offer from a league club.

Selection also eluded Roy Tattersall, one of Laker's off-spinning rivals. Tattersall headed the national averages with 193 wickets in his finest summer. He was belatedly called upon, along with Lancashire colleague, Brian Statham, as an emergency replacement. Jim Swanton, in his pre-tour notes, lamented the disregard of obvious candidates for the tour: 'It is an unusual if inevitable mix of the pre-war young and the newly fledged.' Swanton found it hard to explain the absences of Edrich, Wardle and Laker. 'These last two, together with Tattersall, were easily the biggest wicket-takers of the English season.'

Perhaps the biggest travesty of all was the decision to exclude Les Jackson, the Derbyshire fast bowler. Jackson and Alec Bedser were twinned as the most dangerous bowlers in England at this time. Yet Jackson played in only two Tests: against New Zealand at Old Trafford in 1949; and 12 years later against Australia at Headingley. Donald Carr, his Derbyshire captain, said, 'Les was the linchpin of any success we had. He was a matchwinner and a marvellous fellow to captain. He never let you down.' In Carr's opinion, he moved the ball off the seam better than any bowler of his generation.

Trevor Bailey remembers the consternation of the Derbyshire players at the non-selection of Les Jackson. Essex were playing Derbyshire at Southend when the last two names, Washbrook and John Warr, were announced for the tour of Australia. Expressions of disbelief greeted the news that Warr, of Middlesex, had been preferred to Jackson. 'What on earth is happening?' went up the cry in a post-match drinks session at the Southend Pier Hotel.

'Les just quietly sat in a corner, sank his pint, and never said a word,' recalls Bailey, who was sympathetic and as mystified as the rest of the party. 'Les was in a different class to Warr. His slinging-type action was reminiscent of another Derbyshire bowler, Bill Copson, who had toured Australia before the Second World War. On a green wicket, Les was a tremendous bowler. He bowled a beautiful line and length and begrudged giving runs away.'

Alec Bedser has since lamented the accent on unproven youth on the Australian tour and the decision to leave more experienced campaigners kicking their heels at home. John Dewes, one of the favoured younger members, believes, however inadvisedly, it had to be a calculated gamble: 'The pre-war players were ten years older and we hadn't yet bred others of the right calibre.'

The divergence in strengths was pronounced, but the picture was distorted in the outcome of the series. England were beaten 4–1, but two of the defeats were by the slender margins of 70 and 28 runs. A major regret was a lack of stability in the batting. The experience of Bill Edrich, as Trevor Bailey indicates, might have tipped the scales in England's favour.

Freddie Brown was the third-choice captain in Australia after Norman Yardley and George Mann had made it known that they were unable to tour because of business commitments. Wilfred Wooller, the combative Glamorgan captain, also withdrew as a candidate after heading one newspaper's captaincy poll. Brown, nearing his 40th birthday, was deemed an unlikely tourist; but he enhanced his credentials and sealed his appointment with a barnstorming century for the Gentlemen against the Players at Lord's.

'Ginger for pluck' was the admiring compliment accorded to Brown in Australia. The insignia of his silk neckerchief fluttered around his neck and his ruddy complexion intensified in colour amid his labours. Australian crowds admired the resolution of the veteran. A significant tribute was paid by a vegetable barrowman on Sydney Quay: 'Fine lettuce,' he yelled. 'All for ninepence . . . with hearts like Freddie Brown's.'

CHAPTER SIX

Mighty Swings Down Under

Alec Bedser's accurate and lively bowling meant more than any other
single factor. He was the man who kept giving England a chance.

RAY ROBINSON

The Union Jack fluttered defiantly on the grandstand in the Melbourne twilight on the eve of England's first victory over Australia for 13 years, in February 1951. It had taken 15 post-war Tests to bring the coming great day, one more than the number required after the First World War. On the ground where his team beat the Australians in 1925, Arthur Gilligan kept a watching brief from the broadcasting box. 'What do you think, Arthur?' was a familiar sally. Gilligan, the commentator, would not have been stumped for words to express his joy at the long-awaited success.

Alec Bedser was in the vanguard of this notable conquest. The novice of four years earlier was now a feared opponent. Facing him was Arthur Morris, the left-handed marauder who had headed the Australian batting averages in England in his finest season in 1948. Encounters between the two men assumed a special significance in 1950–51. As Ray Robinson wrote, 'Morris's eyes would have vanished amid their puckering laugh-wrinkles had a teacup reader told him he would meet a tall dark man and go on a long journey back to the pavilion time and again.'

Sickness had at first threatened to remove Alec Bedser from the fray. He contracted influenza while bowling into the wintry breezes at Perth. Jim Swanton reported that Bedser appeared listless on his return against New South Wales at Sydney: 'His reputation among the Australians is such that it seemed especially important for him to strike form.'

When the big man was restored to fitness his action, in the words of Lindsay Hassett, the Australian captain, combined a 'weighty and explosive harmony'. This was a series of cruelly deflating close calls. Alec demonstrated his renewed strength in bowling 195 overs (1,558 balls) and taking 30 wickets at 16.06 runs each. He was the first to achieve this distinction in an Anglo-Australian rubber since Harold Larwood 18 years earlier.

Neville Cardus voiced his appreciation of Bedser's efforts in the second Test at Melbourne when Australia were dismissed for 194 in a day: 'For the connoisseur, there was nothing better in the cricket than Bedser's bowling. After an hour of unrelieved effort, after the new ball had lost its shine, Bedser was still on the spot, dangerous and straining the batsman's nerve and eyesight.' Throughout the series, wrote another observer, no Australian batsman wholly mastered the late swerve, the accuracy of direction, and the stinging pace from the pitch: 'His [Bedser's] was a double task, to quell runs and to take wickets.'

It was largely due to Bedser that only once in Australia's nine innings did the first wicket survive the twenties, and only one century innings was played by their opening batsmen. 'Sometimes he cut the ball off the pitch like a quick leg-break. Then he was totally unplayable,' enthused Ray Robinson. Alec, forewarned after his first trip to Australia, had wisely assessed the need to conserve his energy. He reduced his speed and settled into a rhythmical run-up, which was so steadily repetitive that it appeared mechanical. 'His air of round-faced simplicity concealed the working of a brain of a bowling genius,' observed Robinson.

Gloomy overtures preceded the first Test at Brisbane. Charles Bray, in the *Daily Herald*, was among the pessimists: 'The odds against our winning one Test, let alone the series, are insultingly high.' Australia were installed as 5–1 favourites. Before Brisbane the criticism had soared into a crescendo of despair. England were described as 'apathetic in spirit' and monstrously culpable in wayward fielding. It was estimated that as many as 27 catches, some of them difficult but the majority ridiculously easy, had been dropped.

Jack Fingleton wrote: 'Those who missed their chances with bat and ball, and spilling innumerable catches in the field, were mostly youngsters upon whom England was relying for its cricket revival.' Jim Swanton dwelt on the 'science of field-placings': 'There was not sufficient appreciation of the importance of finding specialists for key places in the field. Too often the field switches round so that the man occupies the nearest position.'

The clouds of uncertainty parted in an astonishing transformation at Brisbane. England's four-man attack of Bedser, Bailey, Brown and Wright bowled out Australia for 228. Godfrey Evans was at his inspirational best. Fingleton had thought Evans had been 'playing to the gallery' against

Australia in England in 1948 and his form had suffered as a result; but 'here,' he said, 'his mind was hard on the game. Darting here and there behind the stumps, he was like a leaping and live electricity wire that had been broken. He threatened danger in all directions.'

Freddie Brown believed that his ill-luck with the toss was one explanation for England's reverses in 1950–51. None were more important than his lost call at Brisbane, where the rains once again disadvantaged England. Bill Bowes described the ensuing conditions on a 'crazy, unreal Test day': 'Great batsmen were reduced to wild slogging. The ball, when it pitched, performed antics which the batsmen could not anticipate, or for which the bowlers were not responsible.' He added, 'England were beaten by a treacherous pitch, not by Australian supremacy.' For John Dewes, one of the affronted English batsmen, it was not a fair test because 'it was just like batting on plasticine'.

The Australian view, as expressed by Jack Fingleton, was less severe: 'It was a nasty wicket. The ball took any amount of turn and sometimes it kicked high. But I do not think it was as cantankerous as the one for the Test four years ago when England made 141 and 172.'

A selectorial misjudgement was a factor in England's plight. Len Hutton was, in an attempt to preserve his skills, relegated to third wicket down in the batting order. The demotion left him undefeated in the match. He scored 8 in the first innings and 62 in the second innings. Fingleton railed against the perpetrators: 'Hutton must never again go in other than first because England cannot afford to lose a minute of him. The "brains trust" that suggested sending him in lower down should be sacked immediately, and without a reference.'

Hutton himself remembered the burden he and Washbrook shared as England's opening batsmen in this lean period. 'Do you realise,' he wryly said many years later, 'when Cyril and me go out to bat, we are like a couple of window cleaners set to work on the top floor of a skyscraper? Only some silly so-and-so has whipped the ladder away.'

Twenty wickets fell for 130 runs in a curtailed day when the rains relented at Brisbane. England struggled to 68 for 7 in their first innings. Australia, at one stage 0 for 3, finally declared at 32 for 7. England were set a target of 193 and were betrayed by madcap batting. They tottered to 30 for 6, and 3 of the wickets went down for 7 runs in 10 minutes before the close of play. 'All the nightwatchmen had failed Brown,' commented Fingleton. 'It was rather like a real nightwatchman putting his keys in the warehouse door and then going for a stroll around the block.'

Arthur McIntyre, Evans's deputy, was selected as a batsman at Brisbane. He was one of the anxious victims in the collapse, thrown out by Don Tallon, the Australian wicket-keeper, while attempting a fourth run:

> I was batting with Godfrey. We were tearing up and down the wicket like a couple of whippets. Bill Johnston was way out on the boundary; he'd just managed to hold the ball up. I called Godfrey for the fourth run. Bill's throw was fairly wide and Tallon had to stretch some distance and gather the return before putting down the wicket. He had only one stump to aim at, and he hit it.
>
> It was a gloomy night and we'd already appealed against the light. I did feel terrible, but there were no excuses.

'Mac' dejectedly made his way back to the pavilion, well aware of the reception awaiting him: 'I would have chosen another gate for my return had it been possible.'

Len Hutton was given the near-impossible task of nursing England towards salvation on the final day. The squandering of wickets on the previous evening seemed wanton now on a pitch rendered placid by the heavy roller. 'It was like a man the day after an alcoholic fling, full of remorse and respectability,' commented one writer.

Neville Cardus, while applauding Hutton's mastery in a lost cause, lamented the lack of a supporting cast. The imperturbable Yorkshireman was the bulwark of England's batting, shouldering the burden almost unaided in some of the tour's darkest hours. Cardus observed: 'Hutton, in this team, travels a long furrow of responsibility. I cannot recall an instance in Test cricket when any batsman has had Hutton's reason to believe that he and nobody else was the spinal column of an innings.'

Hutton revelled in his lone command at Brisbane. His purpose did not falter even after the first-ball dismissal of Denis Compton. Compton was the fallen cavalier caught in a web of indecision throughout the series. In other happier times, there would have been the comradely pursuit of winning runs. As it was, the last-wicket partnership of 45 runs between Hutton and Wright only served to delay Australia's victory by 70 runs.

Compton's decline should perhaps have been expected. He had had a cartilage removed in the spring of 1950 and missed most of the English season. The state of his knee aroused much speculation and came under intense scrutiny before the tour. Medical experts who knew its full history were more inclined to praise Compton for his bravery rather than

73

to disown him as a liability in Australia.

In fact, he finished second in the tour averages to Hutton. He was deeply upset by his form in the Tests in which he scored only 53 runs at an average of 7.57. It must be regarded as one of the worst series ever for a batsman of his stature. A writer in the *Sporting Globe* interviewed Compton following his century against Western Australia at Perth in October. The troublesome knee, he learned, was the legacy of a pre-war soccer injury. In 1947, Compton had suffered another knock without any visible reaction during his wonderful summer against the South African tourists. Three years later the condition had worsened to the extent that the bones in his right knee joint had begun to scale and chip.

The restorative qualities of warm sunshine in Australia did at first give rise to optimism. The century at Perth was an exercise in the familiar freedom as one observer commented:

> Compton bats with the same pristine delight . . . He still rips the textbook to shreds. He spins and sweeps the ball late off his heels to the fence. He moves yards down the pitch to anticipate the bowler's length before the ball is actually delivered. Yesterday he cut, drove, hooked or glanced to his heart's delight.

The bowling of Doug Wright – at 36, the second oldest of the MCC party in Australia – reached its nadir in the low-scoring second Test at Melbourne. Wright was a finely tuned artist whose leg-breaks veered between the unplayable and the wildly erratic. The wayward side of his bowling unhappily surfaced at Melbourne. He conceded 105 runs, including 63 off 8 overs in Australia's first innings. It was, as the margin of defeat showed, a concession too luxurious for the batsmen to overcome.

Fluctuations in fortune tended to diminish Wright's renown. Some considered him a magnificent but unlucky bowler. That his majestic days far exceeded his mediocre ones are shown by his career figures of over 2,000 wickets, including 108 in 34 Tests against Australia and South Africa. His figures included seven hat-tricks.

Trevor Bailey refers to one cameo illustrating the bewildering spin of his England colleague in 1950–51. The match was against Western Australia at Perth. Wright's extravagant spin was this time allied to unwavering length. Bailey recalls: 'Doug's bowling there, before he was stricken by fibrositis, was the best leg-break bowling I've ever seen. No one apart from Godfrey [Wright's Kent wicket-keeper] knew where the ball was going.' Wright's rhythm was well under control at Perth. He took seven wickets, including six with his mesmeric googlies.

❧ ❧ ❧

'Look here,' said big Jake Iverson, in conversation with an Australian writer. 'You must have seen a fellow throw away a smoked cigarette. He gives it a flick from the back of his finger and away it flies. In a different way that is exactly what I do. My longer finger just flicks the ball out, spinning as it does so.'

Iverson, then aged 35, was described as the rawest of Test débutants against England. Yet this bowler with the freak grip enjoyed remarkable success against the tourists. Sid Barnes, excluded from the Australian ranks in the series, related the view of one Englishman that Iverson's deliveries had more curves than in a six-day bike race. This was the Victorian's finest hour. But he would soon be stunned into submission by more adventurous batsmanship and depart from first-class cricket.

His curious grip was the result of wartime experiments, flicking table tennis balls down the table at fellow servicemen in New Guinea. 'I take the ball between my thumb and second finger,' said Iverson. 'My index and third fingers do not touch the ball. So the grip is solely between the ball of the thumb and the side of the long finger. When I deliver the ball I never twist or turn my wrist; the knuckles are facing the batsman when the ball leaves my fingers.' By changing the position of the thumb he could deliver a leg-break, an off-break, or a googly, with little discernable change of action.

Iverson headed the Australian bowling averages against England. His 21 wickets cost him only 15.23 runs each. Twice he confounded Hutton in the series, once in the third Test at Sydney where his sharp spin and bounce earned him a second-innings analysis of 6 for 27. In his first 7 overs he took 3 wickets and, after a rest, 3 more in 10 balls. England were dismissed for 123 and Australia won by an innings to retain the Ashes.

Magnificent bowling by Alec Bedser and Trevor Bailey deserved a better reward in the second Test at Melbourne. The pitch was fast and the atmosphere heavy, and the stage was set for an unnerving bowling performance. 'Alec,' wrote Keith Miller, 'seems to have that extra devil in his bowling that extracts increased venom from a slightly inferior batting wicket.'

'Uplifted by the swift capture of Morris's wicket, Bedser opened with a spell of sustained hostility lasting two and a half hours,' commented *Wisden*. 'Twice more he returned to hurl himself into the attack with life, lift and swing. No batsman played him with anything approaching relish. For once, the adjective "great" carried no exaggeration.' Bedser and Bailey shared 8 wickets, including 4 in the last 10 minutes, as Australia tumbled to 194 all out at the end of a dramatic day.

An umpiring decision to rank with the Bradman incident at Brisbane in 1946 turned the tide against England. At Melbourne, it was Len Hutton who was controversially given out to a catch by Tallon off Iverson. Keith Miller related how Hutton appeared set for a big score: 'Len had been tied down by Iverson in the previous over. So in the next over he moved down the wicket to drive one away. The ball dropped just shorter than he expected. Hutton realised the situation and pulled his bat away.'

There was some confusion as the ball rebounded from Hutton's pad and flew into the air. Tallon did not evince any enthusiasm as he casually stepped from behind the wicket to take a simple catch. He did not appeal, but Iverson and Hassett did, winning the umpire's approval. Hutton walked sadly away. Players, including Miller, who was fielding at short mid-on, shook their heads at the decision. 'I do not think Hutton went within inches of the ball,' wrote Miller. 'There was only a dull thud of the ball striking the pad.'

Hutton, said Miller, looked at him with a startled look usually seen at a horror movie. 'He blanched a little and made some remark in his Yorkshire dialect that I didn't quite catch. He walked out in bewilderment rather than in annoyance.'

England, in the end, required 178 to win and the result was exasperatingly close. Australia, with Lindwall and Johnston as their spearheads, won by 28 runs. Excessive caution by the England batsmen played into their hands. 'The impression could not be avoided,' observed *Wisden*, 'that if England had been left with three or four hours to make the runs instead of three whole days they would have adopted different, and probably, more successful methods.'

The gracious city of Adelaide was shrouded in a haze of smoke swept in from surrounding bush fires when the MCC party arrived there for the fourth Test in February. They found some respite from the torrid heat in quarters at Glenelg, the neighbouring bay resort. Before the days of air-conditioning, successive England teams had suffered in the extreme night-time temperatures. In other days there had been constant queues for showers in the early hours of the morning. 'One just grumbled and stewed while those monsters of the night, the mosquitoes, indulged themselves in interminable dive-bombing,' remembered Jack Fingleton. 'On such nights, the Adelaide folk took an undersheet and slept on the beaches, or on their home lawns.'

Keith Miller was moved to extol the mastery of Len Hutton in Australia. For such a dauntless rival, his endorsement reflected not only his appreciation but also his sportsmanship. 'He is one player you can watch without monotony, even if it is your own bowling he is hitting around the oval.' The 'high-class technician', as is the way of greatness, always controlled and commanded without fuss.

At Adelaide Hutton once again bestrode his kingdom. In the previous English season, he had resisted the wiles of the West Indian spinners Ramadhin and Valentine in scoring 202 not out at Kennington Oval. He repeated this single-handed exercise in carrying his bat for 156 (out of a total of 272) at Adelaide. The only other Englishman to survive the fall of all ten wickets in a Test between the two countries was Bobby Abel at Sydney in the 1891–92 series. Hutton batted for six hours and ten minutes. His only supporter was, as at Brisbane, Doug Wright, who resisted for over an hour in a last-wicket stand of 53 runs.

❧ ❧ ❧

The reception which greeted England's victory by eight wickets at Melbourne could not have been bettered at Kennington Oval. There was a sense – even among the Australian partisans – that England, narrowly denied on other occasions during the series, deserved to carry the day. There were another ten wickets for Alec Bedser to place alongside Hutton's winning runs. These gave the Yorkshireman a series aggregate of 533 runs at an average of 88.83.

The batting challenge at Melbourne did not this time rest with Hutton alone. Reg Simpson, on his 31st birthday, was undefeated on 156 in England's first innings. 'Late, but not too late, he found his own high artistry of stroke-play,' was the compliment of one writer. 'He put away the pedestrian accuracy of a mere workman and turned a position of doubt into one of lively hope.'

The acclamation at the end of the series demonstrated the appeal of

Freddie Brown. His valour in adversity established him as one of the heroes of the season. Keith Miller considered the England captain to be the 'surprise packet' of the team. At Melbourne, in the second Test, Brown took 5 wickets and scored 62 runs. 'He did not let the occasion upset his main batting asset – an ability to hit hard and often,' wrote Miller. 'This day at Melbourne he lofted shots over the cover fieldsmen and slammed an occasional glorious drive with a power and timing worthy of Hutton. He took the game by the scruff of the neck, chanced his luck, and succeeded.'

Brown had first toured Australia as a 22-year-old leg-spinner under the leadership of Douglas Jardine in 1932–33. At The Leys School, he had regularly opened the attack, bowling at brisk medium-pace. Then, at the instigation of Aubrey Faulkner, he had reverted to leg-spin before going on to win his blue at Cambridge. His leg-breaks were seldom used in the 1950–51 series; injuries to Bailey and Wright forced him to enter the quick bowling lists more often than he had intended. The transition was surprisingly effective and was reflected in the yield of wickets.

Alec Bedser was once asked to describe the bowling of his captain in Australia. 'He just holds the ball seam-up and bowls with a good action,' was the reply. Determination was the keynote of an ebullient leader. Twice he took five or more wickets in a Test, on both occasions at Melbourne, and his 18 wickets in the series showed him to be an indispensable member of the team.

Captains come in many shades of character. Freddie Brown was cast in the traditional mould of the amateur. The iron fist was rarely concealed, especially where the professionals were concerned. Prejudices often distorted his judgement although Roy Tattersall, a late replacement in Australia, strongly defends Brown and remembers his guidance and help in adjusting to alien conditions.

Brown could, though, be bossy and brusque – then as a captain and later as an MCC manager. John Dewes refers to the gulf between the 'officers' (amateurs) and the 'men' (professionals) which was only beginning to narrow in the post-war years. Relationships forged between the two ranks in the war marked a change towards a new awareness. As Dewes observes: 'We had both fought and we had both won.' Freddie Brown, however, still kept his foot firmly jammed on the barrier in Australia. 'To those of us who were young and amateurs, he was friendly and fatherly,' recalls Dewes. 'For others, I suspect, he adopted a different manner.'

There was a rousing reception to greet Alec Bedser, Woking's sporting ambassador, on his return home from Australia. The news of his feats – and the descriptions praising him as 'the best bowler in the world' – prompted the Surrey townspeople to establish a testimonial fund as a gesture of appreciation. In April 1951, Alec was the guest of honour at a public reception in Christ Church Hall followed by a dinner at the Albion Hotel. Waiting to pay tribute to their distinguished pupil were his former headmaster, Frank Marsh, and form master, Fred Dixon. Mr H.C. Barrett, chairman of Woking Council, presented Alec with a television set, an oil painting of him in his England colours, and a cheque for £200.

The assembly of guests at the homecoming included three Surrey stalwarts, Andrew Kempton, Andrew Sandham and the Bedsers' first cricket coach, Alan Peach. Sandham echoed the regret of many who had followed the progress of the series from afar. He thought that if the batsmen had responded as well as the bowlers had performed, England would have won the rubber. Sandham was reminded of the tutelage of Peach, his predecessor as the county coach. 'When I watch Alec bowling I can see Alan Peach when he played for Surrey.'

'Alec has brought honour to our town,' enthused the Woking council chairman. Charm, personality and a love of true sportsmanship characterised his manner as a cricketer and a man: 'We offer our thanks to Alec and Eric for the interest shown and the encouragement they so willingly give to the sporting activities of the young people in our district.'

On the other side of the world, one Australian was also ruefully remembering the dominance of Alec Bedser. Arthur Morris had been given an accolade to treasure after he had scored 696 runs in England in 1948. Don Bradman, his captain, then described him as the best left-hander he had seen. Bedser dented this image when he dismissed Morris five times – twice in one match – in the 1950–51 series.

There was gleeful talk of a hoodoo imposed on him by his England rival. Morris did salvage his reputation and pride and end his servitude with a painstaking double-century at Adelaide. The yardstick for supremacy, with bat and ball, can only be determined by figures over a long period. Morris's mastery was checked but not dimmed in his years of combat with Bedser.

Ray Robinson wittily portrayed the ardour of the contests between two close friends. The fame of Alec Bedser was ultimately sealed when he took his place among the waxen rows of the illustrious at Madame Tussaud's. 'Morris, as a spokesman for the batsmen,' said Robinson, 'could have been forgiven if he had suggested that the figure's proper place was down in the basement – the Chamber of Horrors.'

CHAPTER SEVEN

Snares for Australia's Best

I probably faced more balls from Alec than any other batsman against one bowler. So, as the best bowler, he had more chance of getting me out whether I scored runs or didn't.

ARTHUR MORRIS

It was a kind of double bluff to keep opponents on tenterhooks and often surprised the bowler himself. The wonderful leg-cutter, deviating sharply and coaxed by enormous hands, was the weapon of confusion. For a batsman expecting a late in-swinger it was an uncomfortable experience. The change of movement over the last few yards was so imperceptible that few opponents had time to assess the fine geometry required to avoid an lbw decision.

Arthur Morris was one of the baffled Australians; his adventurous spirit was curbed by the posse of pickpockets waiting expectantly in the leg-trap set by Alec Bedser. 'I started to read the press,' says Arthur dryly in reference to the sequence of dismissals in the 1950–51 series against England. 'I got myself into a mental state of shuffling across my wicket instead of playing my normal game. So often I was beaten because of frustration and annoyance. I was always a bloke who hated not to get on with the game.'

Morris remembers that at one stage he took his block a foot outside his leg stump: 'I didn't know how to handle him, so I thought why not allow Alec a full sight of the wickets.' It was more than a little perplexing for the umpire when he asked for this guard.

The Australian's plight was compounded by the throttling fieldsmen. Before the restriction in numbers, this was, he insists, leading to a cricketing stalemate. Legislation after his career decreed that only two men could be placed behind the popping crease on the leg side. 'It was the best rule brought in since the Second World War because in-swing bowling was killing the game. Scoring opportunities were severely reduced. There is nothing harder than playing a medium-pacer directing his attack in or around your leg stump.'

Morris was always modest and philosophical about his batting fortunes. 'It's just life,' he once said. 'You fail and people are critical. You have the luck to succeed and they say nice things about you.'

His duels with Bedser were spread over seven years and four series in a mutually respectful sporting confrontation. He opened the Australian innings 37 times against England when Alec was the opening bowler. Bedser took his wicket 18 times – a world record for Test cricket – yet Morris averaged 57.42 and scored 8 of his 12 centuries over the course of their meetings. The aggregate of hundreds in matches between the two countries is only exceeded by Bradman (19 in 63 innings); Hobbs (12 in 71 innings); Hammond, Greg Chappell and David Gower (9 in, respectively, 58, 65 and 77 innings).

The odds during the rivalry of Bedser and Morris, as both men strictly maintain, were in favour of a significantly high number of dismissals. 'I probably faced more balls from Alec than any other batsman against one bowler in the history of the game,' says Morris. 'So, by the law of averages, he had more chance of getting me out whether I scored runs or didn't.'

The argument does not run counter to his avowal of the problems posed by his persistent aggressor. He explains: 'You rarely got any loose ones from Alec. He was at you all the time. His devastating leg-cutter, which came in from my off stump, was particularly difficult because it didn't really start "taking" until the third or fourth over when the shine was off.'

An air of resignation did for a time permeate Morris's attitude during the series against England in 1950–51. In five innings in the first three Tests he scored only 45 runs; he was dismissed by Bedser on four occasions at Brisbane, Melbourne and Sydney. He was twice caught by Bailey and Hutton and lbw and bowled on the other occasions. There were two ducks in this procession of mishaps; and to compound his trials he was twice defeated cheaply by Bedser while playing for a Combined XI against the MCC at Launceston, Tasmania.

Alec Bedser, for his part, says he had built up his bowling armoury since his first tour of Australia in 1946–47:

> The development of my leg-cutter gave him problems. The leg-cutter to a left-hander saw the ball coming in to him, while the normal in-swinger was a late out-swinger to him. My ability to move the ball either way caused Arthur to stray out of position

on occasions, because he would move over to his off side . . . When the ball cut back he was likely to be leg before, because in order to try to get behind the swinging ball he sometimes moved too far to the off side. Again, if the ball moved off the pitch there was a short leg at an angle of 45 degrees to take the snick. Arthur could not be certain from my action what I intended to bowl, and as I often surprised myself, the batsman was hardly likely to guess correctly.

Ray Robinson said that the Australian performed a Morris dance all his own in his struggles against Bedser. The 'sideways shuffle' prompted one observation by Robinson in an article in the *Sydney Sun* before the fourth Test against England at Adelaide. 'Morris,' he said, ' was on the move as he played the ball, so that apart from exposing his leg stump, Bedser's late out-swinger was finding the bat's edge with the resultant catch at slip.' Illustrating this was a photograph of one dismissal. It showed Morris at the end of his stroke almost a yard wide of the stumps on the off side as the ball flew waist-high to Hutton at slip.

The Australian selectors were rewarded for their perseverance in retaining Morris in their team at Adelaide. Serving as a good omen was the fact that he had hit a century in each innings on the same ground four years earlier. Less encouraging on the morning of the match, which was to salvage his reputation, was the number of his breakfast table – 13 – allotted to him at the Adelaide hotel. A superstitious man might have taken fright at the arrangement. Arthur did hesitate for a moment before taking his seat. A few hours later he strode out, not without qualms, to open the Australian innings.

In the beginning, it was evident that here was a batsman fighting to regain his confidence. One passage of play indicated the measure of his watchfulness against Bedser. He was so far intent on defence that he scored only 7 runs from 51 balls Bedser bowled to him.

For such an attacking player, this was patience of the highest order. He was right to be circumspect; his resistance was sorely needed. Australia, at one stage, 266 for 3, lost their last 7 wickets for 105 runs. Morris was last out, having batted for 7¾ hours. His 206 was his seventh three-figure score in 14 Tests against England. Bedser's figures for the innings, 26–4–74–3 (8-ball overs), were good, but he did not this time take the wicket of Morris.

Arthur Morris, spotted while a Canterbury High School boy, was the protege of Bill O'Reilly. It was O'Reilly who introduced him to first-grade Sydney cricket with the St George Club and swiftly promoted the 15-year-old to open the innings. Morris has always recognised his debt to one of the greatest of Australia's bowlers. 'Name O'Reilly and Bradman,' comments Arthur, 'and then say the rest of us were quite good.'

Morris was just short of his 19th birthday when he opened for New South Wales against Queensland in the 1940–41 season. He scored 148 and 111 in the match. Archie Jackson, of princely memory, is the only batsman to have recorded twin centuries in a match in Australia at a younger age. Jackson was 18 years and 4 months when he made 131 and 122 for New South Wales against South Australia in 1928.

Morris's exceptional talent was revealed when he reached one important milestone. At 19, his record of 850 runs in one first-grade season for the St George Club exceeded Bradman's aggregate of 785 for the same club. For a cricketer, who started at the top, observed Ray Robinson, Morris was never made dizzy by the altitude. A cool head and a modest mind always dictated his outlook.

The triumphant march was halted on Morris's call-up for war service on the north coast of New Guinea. It was a stay of execution for bowlers, and he returned home to receive scant recognition as a Test contender. Morris had an opportunity to re-assert his claims soon after the arrival of the MCC team in 1946. At Sydney he hustled to 68 runs in an hour. It was not enough for his mentor, Bill O'Reilly. 'You shouldn't have thrown your wicket away for under a hundred,' raged O'Reilly. 'In a Test series, centuries do the talking.'

Morris responded to the rebuke in the best possible manner by scoring one of those required hundreds in his next innings, then another century in his first venture against the English bowling. This was followed by 155, 122 and 124 not out in consecutive innings against England at Melbourne and Adelaide. His three centuries in a row emulated the feat of his compatriot Charles Macartney in England 20 years earlier.

The eminence of a fleet-footed batting adventurer was sealed in 1948. Morris was a member of an invincible group – the first team to remain unbeaten on an English tour. Australia won exactly half their 34 matches by an innings. Eleven of their batsmen between them hit 50 centuries in first-class games. Seven of their 17 players completed 1,000 runs on the tour. Morris, in his finest summer, soared in magnificence as a batsman. He headed the Australian averages in the series with 696 runs at an average of 87. The aggregate included three centuries, and his 182 on a spinner's wicket at Leeds was a ferocious example of his powers on the attack.

Ian Johnson bracketed Morris with Gary Sobers as the finest left-hander in his experience: 'Arthur always had so much time to play his shots. He watched the ball more closely than most and invariably played late off the back foot. He caressed the ball rather than struck it, yet it raced on its way with incredible speed, so correct was the timing.'

Arthur Morris did, in Ray Robinson's felicitous inscription, say hello with his hundreds. The output was reduced for a time when Alec Bedser intervened. Their tussles formed as arresting a spectacle as any international sport could command. Yet their association was never sullied by disagreement. Morris and his wife, Judith, travelled to England in 1998 to attend the Bedsers' 80th birthday dinner in London. In his tribute, Arthur drew attention to Alec's pursuit of his wicket during their days of intense rivalry. It was always conducted without dispute. 'Never once did Alec ever say a harsh word to me while I was batting against him.'

In the emotive atmosphere of a Test match, few others could claim and sustain such exemplary relations.

Trevor Bailey, like Alec Bedser, spent countless hours observing another Australian left-hander, Neil Harvey at close quarters. 'I wonder how many runs Neil would have made if he had decided to stop playing strokes that had an element of risk about them,' said Bailey. Across the years my own memory calls to mind a vision of Harvey as a pocket-sized Clark Gable. He was debonair in appearance and the epitome of audacity as a cricketer.

There was a nerveless disdain for bowlers to match the hauteur of Gable on the picture screen. For one writer, the batting of Harvey reminded him of a pianist so carried away with the music that he went too fast to touch all the notes.

Impetuosity did bring about Harvey's downfall on occasions. His boldness was trimmed by Bedser's swinging deliveries in the 1950–51 series. Harvey's defences were breached so often by Bedser that Lindsay Hassett, the Australian captain, replaced him at the top of the order and went in himself as a shield against the new ball.

Bedser took Harvey's wicket five times in the series. By the end of his career he had advanced this tally to 12. No other bowler had gained supremacy over the Australian more than three times in Tests. For one of these dismissals at Brisbane, Alec had to marvel at the astonishing virtuosity of Godfrey Evans. In his great years, Evans had an uncanny ability to move into top gear, often startlingly so, like someone switching on a battery of neon lights.

Les Ames, his predecessor as the Kent wicket-keeper, admired Evans's ebullience, which was in sharp contrast to his own quietly efficient style behind the stumps. As captain in one county game, Ames watched Evans plunge into a dive to attempt an impossible catch. The ball just eluded his fingers as he sprawled in front of first slip. Evans picked himself up and Ames, standing at second slip, mockingly accosted the crestfallen keeper. 'Gawd,' said Les, 'another one put down. I don't know . . .' Ames would often disarmingly mingle jest and truth. 'If you are going to put it down,' he told Godfrey, 'I should let it go to first slip.'

However Evans's sense of the spectacular did enable him to clutch catches beyond the expectations of most wicket-keepers. They were, as in his acrobatics to dismiss Harvey at Brisbane, a source of inspiration. Jack Fingleton wrote: 'Harvey leg-glanced the ball off the middle of the bat. Evans not only caught it on the leg side, but in one action whipped the bails off. All we saw from the pavilion was a blinding flash of movement, but there stood the umpire with his finger raised.'

The daring of Evans was embossed with the stamp of impish glee. It was a label which Harvey firmly attached to his own brand of cricket. Harvey, always referred to by Alec Bedser as 'young 'un', was the second youngest of six boys from the Fitzroy suburb of Melbourne. His brother, Mervyn, preceded him as an Australian Test batsman; two others, Clarrie and Ray, played in the Sheffield Shield; and Harold and Brian were first-grade cricketers at their home club. Their father, Horace, was a notable club cricketer. From their earliest years in a cricketing household, all his boys were in thrall to the game.

At 19, Harvey scored his first Test century – 153 – which was buoyantly completed by a five (all run) against India at Melbourne. The spontaneity of his cricket was most happily revealed in 1948. The venue was Headingley and the occasion was his Test début against England. Australia had lost three wickets – those of Morris, Hassett and Bradman – for 68 runs. What followed was an escapade, bubbling with youthful impudence and dazzling in its fervour. In an hour and a half Harvey and Miller put on 121 runs. Harvey struck 17 boundaries and hit 112 from 183 balls.

Don Bradman, watching from the pavilion, was seen many times to

NARES FOR AUSTRALIA'S BEST

hold his head in disbelief. He did not expect the onslaught to last so long. His concern was that Neil was trying his luck in on-driving against Laker's off-spin. Afterwards, Harvey had the temerity to tell his captain: 'They were half-volleys, weren't they!' He had laid down the gauntlet and heartily embraced the style of a great Lancastrian. 'Half-volleys,' Johnny Tyldesley used to say – 'you don't get 'em. You have to go and make 'em.'

It does, as one writer said, require a star of exquisite brightness to shine in the constellation overwhelmed by Don Bradman. Bradman was the ultimate record-breaker, but only two other Australians, Allan Border and Greg Chappell, have scored more runs and centuries than Neil Harvey.

At the age of 26 Harvey had scored 12 centuries in 30 Tests. Bradman was two years older and hit 15 centuries in his first 30 Tests. The roll-call of Harvey's opponents during this period included Alec Bedser, Doug Wright, Ramadhin and Valentine, Jim Laker, Frank Tyson, Brian Statham and Hugh Tayfield.

The accent was on attack, but Harvey also had a defensive steel to rival Len Hutton on days of adversity. He stood steadfast and unbeaten while others groped in bewilderment against Tyson and Statham at Sydney in December 1954. There were gripping 60s and 70s that leave many a straight hundred in the shade. No other batsman could have surpassed him in tenacity against Laker and Lock in their pomp. Against Yorkshire at Bradford, on a wicket notorious for its upsets, he banished the gloom of fellow Australians. The tourists, chasing a target of 60, lost 6 wickets for 31 runs. His unbeaten 18 was a tiny gem of resourcefulness. The winning six-hit was a sign that he held no truck with caution.

Harvey held his team-mates spellbound on such crisis occasions. Yet it is said that he awarded the palm to another Australian as his superior. At the height of his mastery, one admirer issued the complimentary verdict: 'You must be tops as a Test batsman now, Neil.' Harvey vigorously shook his head and pointed smilingly in the direction of another batsman – Arthur Morris.

Events were to link Alec Bedser with the greatest batsman of all who came within his sphere of command. In fact, the pleasures of his distinctions against Don Bradman might never have happened, for Bradman was precariously unwell and had resumed his career after a wartime illness severe enough for him to be invalided out of the Army.

The impression is strong that if he had failed in the first Test against England at Brisbane in 1946, he would have retired from the game.

The controversially disallowed catch was a welcome reprieve for Bradman and his admirers; it also served as a spur for cricket in the post-war period. Don went on to score a century at Brisbane and then took stock of his situation. It was reported that Bradman could have come to England in 1948 in other capacities than that of captain. There was, among others, an invitation from a national newspaper in London to write about the Australian tour.

Jack Fingleton related a conversation with a Fleet Street editor. He was told that the offer, later to be doubled, was far in advance of the normal 'special' payment. 'Looking furtively up and down the street, he drew me up a lane out of earshot and whispered the sum. It staggered me.'

Bradman was then in his 40th year and his subsequent decision to travel to England as a cricketer was a gamble in any estimation. It meant that he was the fourth-oldest Australian to make the journey as captain. 'Bradman's deeds of youth,' wrote Fingleton, 'were such that he could not hope to surpass them. He could gain no more, but, indeed, stood to lose much.' On this, his fourth tour of England, Bradman knew that he was placing his reputation at risk.

In his heyday, Bradman was always under pressure to regale his audiences with virtuoso batting encores in the manner of a great actor performing each night without loss of skill and fervour. 'The sight of this small figure,' wrote Ray Robinson, 'striding deliberately to the crease brought something like the roar that goes up when the last preliminary boxing bout ends and the champion climbs into the ring.'

The key to Bradman's command was the intensity of his concentration. 'Every ball for me is the first ball, whether my score is 0 or 200,' he once said. 'And I never visualise the possibility of getting out.'

Bradman did not betray his standards in England in 1948. He was the master counseller of a young brigade. He excelled once again in leading what is acknowledged to be one of the finest Australian elevens. Alec Bedser also defines the enormous burden shouldered by Bradman: 'He bore a responsibility as a national figurehead which perhaps a handful in the whole of sporting history have had to endure. He brought crowds streaming through the turnstiles wherever he played, and his influence on the game cannot be over-estimated. To pit one's skill and wits against him was the biggest challenge any bowler could face.'

Norman Yardley was Bradman's opposing captain in 1948. He knew that he could expect relentless captaincy and this, as an astute and knowledgeable Yorkshireman, Yardley hoped to match. Against Bradman the batsman, he had to contemplate an even more onerous task.

Yardley described what became known as the 'Bedser–Hutton' plan in the following words:

> Alec was to bowl a certain sort of ball that Don was less positive against than he was against the others; his weakness to make an opening single by tickling the ball round behind to the leg was to be exploited. With this in view, we employed three short legs, of whom Len was one, who were to wait just on the spot for the catch we hoped would come from the late-swinging ball.
>
> The theory had first been attempted, under Wally Hammond's direction and advice, in Australia in the previous rubber. It was not then formulated in such detail. Now we had seen it tried, we were able to modify it a bit, and it worked extremely well. The great man's apprehensive feeling until he was fairly well off the mark was about the single weak joint in his shining armour.

An evening discussion on the fateful leg-trap followed a day of attrition in the first Test at Nottingham. Yardley's arresting aim was to staunch an avalanche of runs. Bradman was curbed to the extent that he took an hour and 40 minutes to reach his half-century. By the end of a tedious day of safety-first cricket, Bradman was 130 not out. It was his 18th century against England and one of his slowest.

Bradman himself conceded that, on his last English tour, the advancing years had had the effect of limiting his range of strokes. He was, as one writer said, not establishing the position and timing of his shots against in-swingers as he had done before the war: 'When he contacts the in-dipper from Bedser the bat is pushed farther forward from his legs and out of the inner circle of mastery.'

The Australian captain did, however, strongly maintain that he would not have been caught in Bedser's leg-trap if he had not been 'trying to score runs off the ball.' Like Arthur Morris, he deplored the modern habit of bowling medium pace in-swingers to a modified leg field. In his book *Farewell to Cricket* he referred to being *accidentally* caught at leg slip at Nottingham:

> I need not have played at the ball, but I tried to drive the ball through the field. The ball travelled very fast and hit Hutton on the chest, after which he closed his hands over it. Had the ball

gone a few inches either side, it would never have been caught, as he would not have had time to pick up its flight.

Of his subsequent dismissals by Bedser, Bradman stoutly resisted the notion that he had succumbed to the tactic:

> I refused to be chained down into inactivity by an obvious plan, and paid the penalty with my eyes open, to the delight of some partisan spectators who thought they saw in this old-fashioned device some new theory which would save England.

Bradman, caught acrobatically by Edrich at slip off Bedser, fell 11 runs short of a century in his last Test innings at Lord's. The Bedser–Hutton combination, having operated successfully three times, had now run its course. For the rest of the series the swinging gate was firmly closed against them. But there had been a glimmer of hope in Norman Yardley's ploy. As a postscript, it is interesting to recall Bradman's reaction. He arranged a special net at which he asked his bowlers to concentrate on in-swingers and reproduce as closely as possible the style of Bedser.

Alec Bedser had begun his momentous sequence of successive dismissals of Bradman at Sydney in the 1946–47 series. In England in 1948, the tally increased to six, taking into account his success for Surrey at The Oval. It might even have been seven since, with his first ball in the second innings at Adelaide, he was within a centimetre of bowling out Bradman.

Elation would have turned to astonishment had he managed to dismiss his revered opponent for a pair. Alec says he was delighted to have won one battle; to have achieved more would have been too greedy. 'My compensation,' he declares, 'was that Don possibly had some respect for my bowling.'

Not the least remarkable feature of the ensuing conquests was that Alec had not yet reached his peak as a bowler. At Brisbane in 1946 he had toiled heroically in the sub-tropical sun against Bradman, Barnes and company. One barracker raised his voice in sympathy: 'You'll need your brother before you're through with them.'

Two years later, in England, Bedser was faced by a batsman whose exceptional powers might have been on the wane, but who was still a major force. Bradman's appetite for runs had not markedly declined. He did score 508 runs and averaged 72.57 in the series.

Bedser, an infant in cricketing terms, was able to create an element of uncertainty not apparent in Bradman's pre-war days. It followed the development of a plan which Alec was eager to put into operation. 'As far as I am aware, no one had tried what I did to Don before the war. If the ball swung in, he would hit it through mid-wicket. However, if it swung more than he anticipated, you could fashion a catch on the leg side – in effect, a leg-side "slip" catch.'

Alec explains that Bradman was forewarned after his downfall at Adelaide: 'Don knew after I had bowled him there that he had to play many more balls that were swinging into him than he would have done.' The plot was thus devised to prey on Bradman's mind. Alec freely confesses that he could not accurately determine the movement of his deliveries. 'But if, as with Don, you're not sure whether the ball is going to swing in or go the other way, you've got to play at it. Nine times out of ten the ball swings in, but the odd one goes in the opposite direction. I knew I could do it and the important thing is that Don also knew I could do it.'

The trap in England in 1948 was sprung in consultation with Norman Yardley. 'With two forward short legs and Hutton at backward short leg, it was imperative to bowl a full-length ball either on or just outside the off stump if it was to have any chance of success,' observes Bedser. He rejects reports, current at the time, that his target was the leg stump:

> The angle of my delivery, directed at the off stump, made pad play, as a second line of defence, far too dangerous. I knew that if I could be accurate with my direction and length, Bradman would be forced to offer a stroke and, what was most important, be induced to play forward. Forced into a half-cock position, even Bradman would have no control over the direction of the ball if it swung late into him. Hopefully, any snick would go to backward short leg which, in fact, it did on three successive occasions.

All of Bedser's triumphs have, of course, to be placed in the context of Bradman's dominance, even at this late stage in a distinguished career. Countering the ducks at Adelaide (1946–47) and Nottingham (1948) were scores in England of 146 against Surrey; 138 at Nottingham; 89 at Lord's; and 173 not out at Leeds.

Alec has referred to Bradman's amazingly quick footwork and eye and masterful back-play:

> Bowlers were left no possible margin for error, for anything short was murderously cut or pulled. Once he was set he

manipulated the field like a master puppeteer. His placements amounted to an exact science and were a constant source of concern for me, particularly before I had learnt where to set my field.

There were pre-war accusations of indiscreet batsmanship by Bradman. Some observers thought this was a product of his experiences against Larwood and Voce in the 'bodyline' series of 1932–33. These and other allegations of fallibility on bad wickets were rejected by Bedser in later years, as they were by Hedley Verity, whose own duels with Bradman have passed into cricket lore. Verity once referred to his rival's two innings of 59 and 42 in 1938 against Yorkshire at Sheffield: 'It was a pig of a pitch and he played me in the middle of the bat right through.'

Alec Bedser and Don Bradman were opposed for the last time at the Scarborough Festival in 1948. On the second morning of the match, Alec's first ball to Bradman was glanced waist-high through the backward short leg position – unattended, as Don knew, and he was not inclined to err in that direction again. 'The great Australian went on blithely to his farewell hundred in England,' wrote Ray Robinson. 'He was 153 when he tried to blaze the ball into the backyard of a terrace of houses, but ballooned a catch over point.'

There was a certain rectitude in the partnership which brought Bradman's innings to a close in the snug little ground beside the sea. Alec Bedser was the bowler and the recipient of the catch was his Test ally, Len Hutton.

The statistics revealingly measure the fortunes of Bedser and Bradman. In a glum period for England, Alec's achievements cannot be over-emphasised. In the ten Tests in which they were opposed, the Australian scored 1,188 runs. On the six occasions in which Alec dismissed Bradman, the latter averaged 54.66. Bradman averaged 107.50 when other bowlers captured his wicket.

From his first triumph at Adelaide in 1947, in the subsequent 15 innings of their rivalry, Bedser took Bradman's wicket eight times. His success ratio – 0.35 per innings – is the best in first-class cricket and only exceeded in Test cricket by Bill Bowes. Bedser's feat in dismissing Bradman five times in consecutive Test innings is an unprecedented achievement. His record, among English bowlers, is only exceeded by Hedley Verity, who defeated Bradman ten times, eight of them in sixteen Test meetings, and twice in each innings in two matches.

Don Bradman was unjustly held on a Test average of 99.94, after his second-ball downfall at the hands of Eric Hollies in his final Test against England at The Oval. Four more runs and he would have left the admiring throng with the valedictory average of 100.

In retrospect, the decimal points separating him from this target are just as compelling. They cloak the most ruthless run-scorer of all time with just a whisper of frailty. He was perhaps strengthened in esteem, with his emotions for once uncoiled before the public gaze. 'You don't see too well with tears in your eyes,' said Bradman.

CHAPTER EIGHT

Pride of a Family

*At the start my team was a little afraid to win the championship. I
had to give them a few kicks up the backside. But once they'd won it,
they didn't want to lose it.*

STUART SURRIDGE

The fortunes of Surrey took a dramatic upward turn when Stuart
Surridge began his tenure as captain in 1952. Surridge, at 34, was not a
unanimous choice, but he stunned the county committee with his first
statement of intent. His declaration that Surrey would win the
championship for the next five years was greeted with disbelief.

Surridge's bold formula for success was keen and positive cricket.
Restraint did not govern his game plan; in the words of Alec Bedser, he
never departed from his philosophy of attack at all times, whether
batting, bowling or fielding. One of the secrets of Surrey's eminence in
the 1950s was the understanding built up during the apprentice years of
those who commanded the Oval stage. Surridge was one of the graduates
from the Young Players' nursery.

'We had grown up together,' says Alec. 'When Stuart was made
captain, it was like one of the family moving up. The great thing about
Stewie,' adds Alec, 'was that he only thought of Surrey. He was not
concerned about his own personal performance, or those of other
individuals in the team. He wasn't afraid to make decisions. "Right or
wrong, that is what we are going to do," he would say, and we supported
him.'

Raman Subba Row, the Croydon-born amateur and a later England
representative, recalls the glow of delight at being invited by Surridge to
join the Surrey ranks in 1953. Subba Row had scored 937 runs to head the
Cambridge University averages before his summons to The Oval. Against
Surrey at Fenner's in May, he had earned commendation with his
resistance against the county's front line attack. Alec Bedser took 4

wickets for 14 runs in the first innings. Cambridge were bowled out for 68. It was largely due to Subba Row, in the second innings, that the subsequent defeat was delayed. He stayed for 4¼ hours while scoring 64 before his dismissal by the Bedsers – caught Alec, bowled Eric.

Subba Row subscribes to the prevailing view of Surridge as a 'great leader of men' and immensely skilful in welding the mix of personalities in the team: 'No one was under any illusion as to what the score was when Stuart was in charge.' Surridge's discipline was often harsh and unnerving and he did not mince words with amateurs and professionals alike.

Peter May, the Cambridge batting prodigy, was not excluded from the often withering rebukes. 'He didn't understand Stewie at first,' remembers Alf Gover. 'The skipper used to chase him like blazes.' Peter never forgot one valuable principle which was to become his own cricket credo: 'Remember, Peter, it's no use being second,' urged Surridge. 'You must always be first.'

Subba Row also points out that whatever the disagreements – and these could be explosive at times as in the best of families – Surridge never allowed resentment to simmer in the dressing-room. The verbal sallies crackled like gunfire on occasions before the tempers cooled. Then, with the slate wiped clean, all was well. 'We can start afresh now,' said Surridge.

Alec and Eric Bedser both emphasise the collective spread of endeavour at The Oval. 'We used to tell Stewie what we thought and he would respond with his own ideas. He did have a good side to help him. But Stewie was decisive in a way that would not have occurred to other captains.' Each member of the Surrey team knew their allotted roles. Minimum time was spent on field placings: Surridge would say 'as for me' at the start of his own bowling spells.

Ripples of praise mingled with envy on the county circuit. Even in Yorkshire, where the rivalry was most fierce, the admiration was not stifled. One compliment might have been considered a heresy in the broad acres, coming as it did from a man nurtured by wise and exalted champions of another era.

On the voyage out to Australia in 1954 the England captain, Len Hutton, was in pensive mood. Another Yorkshireman, Bob Appleyard, joined him on deck after dinner. The serenity of the evening was abruptly disturbed by a remark which struck Appleyard like a bolt of thunder: 'Len was musing a little; he was never a man for conversation that was meaningless. Suddenly, amid the silence, he came out with a remark that was almost sacrilege to me, brought up on stories of my heroes of the past.' It was the ultimate tribute from his captain, who had fashioned closer ties with these campaigners – 'I do believe,' said Hutton, 'that the present Surrey side would have beaten the Yorkshire team of the 1930s.'

The revelatory message was rueful in all conscience. It was, in a way, a lament at the passing of the great years of Hutton's cricket education. It expressed dismay that such magical moments seemed lost beyond recall. Sutcliffe, Holmes, Verity, Bowes and Leyland were the heralds of Yorkshire's supremacy. The baton was now transferred to the emerging young men at The Oval.

Hutton was acknowledging their brand of resolution which favourably compared with the inspirational figures of his youth. He also perceived that Surrey's newly found dominance, which was to stretch over seven championship years in the 1950s, was directly attributable to having five quality bowlers in harness at one time.

Alec Bedser, powerful and enduring, was now allied with the slim and wiry Peter Loader. Loader gave an extra dimension to the Surrey attack. He was the epitome of versatility as a bowler. Jim Laker said his colleague could make the 'new ball talk . . . he had the uncanny knack of bowling an out-swinger from both close to the stumps and also from the very edge of the return crease and he could do the same with the in-swinger. No quick bowler of his era,' said Laker, 'could better his change of pace. He could successively bowl a slow off-spinner and the most vicious of bouncers.'

Loader was fortunate to have the highly dedicated Bedser as a partner. 'God's rule – line and length', as one contemporary neatly put it, was faithfully observed by his senior. 'Alec's accuracy and pressure meant that I was the beneficiary of wickets at the other end,' says Loader.

Lock and Laker, with their contrasting spins and disparate personalities, paraded another kind of demoralising aggression. Laker, dour and self-effacing, devised calculating ploys, while Lock, the volatile enthusiast, bestrode the field like a melodramatic thespian.

Eric Bedser, with his looping off-spin, had batting gifts to complement his bowling; and his all-round strengths increased in significance over an illustrious decade. The supporting company, eager understudies all, included fast-medium bowlers Dennis Cox and Jack Parker; and Stuart Surridge, who took valuable wickets with the new ball, especially during the early years of his captaincy.

There are many people who will testify that Tony Lock was the most influential figure in Surrey's great years. His indomitable spirit disarmed even those who labelled him a chucker (a left-arm bowler with a 'very

ABOVE: Sir Alec (right) and Eric Bedser.
'They exude an integrity which is the hallmark of great citizens, and they are examples
for young people of all ages to follow'
– Sir Donald Bradman.

INSET: Motherly care: Florence Bedser
with her infant sons.

BELOW: The Basingstoke Canal amid the pine
woods. (Ian Wakeford)

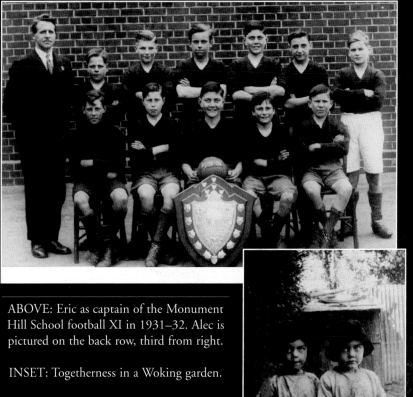

ABOVE: Eric as captain of the Monument Hill School football XI in 1931–32. Alec is pictured on the back row, third from right.

INSET: Togetherness in a Woking garden.

BELOW: All Saints Church, Woodham, where the Bedsers were members of the church choir cricket team. (Ian Wakeford)

TOP LEFT: Florence and Arthur Bedser slice the celebration cake at their diamond wedding in January 1976.

TOP RIGHT: The house the Bedsers built at Woking with their bricklayer father. It has been their home for nearly 50 years.

ABOVE LEFT: Brothers in arms: Alec and Eric during their service in RAF Intelligence in the Second World War.

ABOVE RIGHT: Alan Peach, the former Surrey all-rounder and the twins' first cricketing mentor. (William A. Powell)

TOP: The Surrey team of 1947. Back row: Andrew Sandham (coach), Arthur McIntyre, Tony Lock, Eddie Watts, Eric Bedser, Jack Parker, Alec Bedser, Geoff Whittaker, Laurie Fishlock, Sandy Tait (masseur), Bert Strudwick (scorer). Front row: Alf Gover, Bob Gregory, Errol Holmes (captain), Tom Barling, Stan Squires.

ABOVE: The Surrey team of 1952, the first of the celebrated seven championship years. Back row: Andrew Sandham (coach), Bernie Constable, Dave Fletcher, Jim Laker, Eric Bedser, Tony Lock, Geoff Whittaker, Sandy Tait (masseur), Bert Strudwick (scorer). Front row: Arthur McIntyre, Laurie Fishlock, Stuart Surridge (captain), Jack Parker, Alec Bedser.

TOP: Wally Hammond leads England out to field in the first post-war Test, against India in 1946. Alec, on his début, took 11 wickets in the match.

ABOVE LEFT: A cartoon by Harold Gittins hails the man of the hour.

ABOVE RIGHT: Stuart Surridge and Peter May parade the championship pennant in 1952. (Surrey CCC)

TOP LEFT: Ball control in pre-season training at the Chelsea ground at Stamford Bridge. (Surrey CCC)

TOP RIGHT: Eric in punishing mood as a batsman. (Surrey CCC)

ABOVE: Watchful in the slips, Alec and Eric are paired with Jim Parker against Kent. Tony Pawson is the batsman and Alf Gover the bowler.

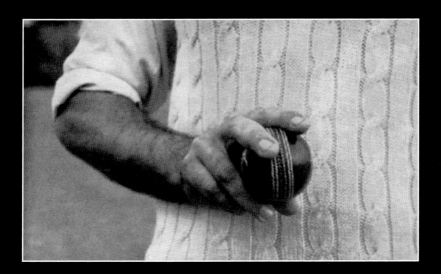

Demonstrating Alec's bowling grips for the in-swinger (top) and the
leg-cutter (above), the latter bowled on a dry wicket taking spin.
It should be noted that the second finger does most of the work.
The ball is held more tightly for swing bowling.

ABOVE: Keeping up with the Bedsers! Arthur McIntyre, proving as always to be an influential ally behind the stumps. Ken Barrington looks on at first slip.
(Surrey CCC)

RIGHT: McIntyre holding the Sportsman's Trophy, awarded to him in 1955 when he scored 920 runs and was involved in 81 dismissals.

powerful throw', to quote Godfrey Evans). Neville Cardus recalled Lock holding 'quite sinful catches, catches which were not there until his rapid, hungry eyesight created them'.

Lock's heroics were in keeping with the compliment paid to him by the Yorkshire player Bob Platt: 'Lockie would be the man you would want alongside you in the trenches.' Fred Trueman describes his old adversary as a man with 'a heart as big as a London double-decker bus [who] didn't give or ask for anything. Lockie was a brilliant fielder, possibly the best of all off his own bowling.'

Fred Trueman, like others in Yorkshire and elsewhere, had no doubts about the illegality of Lock's bowling action. For his team-mate, Johnny Wardle, another slow left-arm bowler and consummate practitioner, it was an affront of offensive proportions. Wardle waged a furious campaign against his Surrey opponent. He considered that he was unfairly disadvantaged in his challenge for England honours. Lock, in his throwing phase as a bowler, also incurred censure for dragging at the crease. Trueman remembers that Lock had a toe plate on his boot which exaggerated the stride: 'We were once playing Surrey on a turner at The Oval. I was batting against Lockie. I saw one ball hit the pitch and tried to get out of the way. It just got quicker and quicker. The ball just feathered my chin, hit Arthur Mac and still went for four byes at the Vauxhall End.'

※ ※ ※

Trevor Bailey has paid high tribute to the partnership of Alec Bedser and Arthur McIntyre. It is a pairing which Bailey believes would have revelled in one-day cricket today: 'It would have been very difficult for batsmen trying to slog against them. They would have paid the price.' He also maintains that Alec's accuracy as a bowler was in large part due to McIntyre (and Godfrey Evans at Test level) standing up to him. 'That was his bonus. Mac and Godfrey both took him superbly. He owed an enormous debt to them.'

McIntyre recalls the challenge presented by Alec's insistence that he stood up as a wicket-keeper: 'There was always a chance of a stumping and we worked out that the percentage of missed chances was low enough to justify the arrangement.'

Alec himself says: 'I preferred Mac to stand up because I pitched the ball up better. If he stood back, you felt subsconciously that it was necessary to bowl shorter to reach him.' Reinforcing the winning concept in Surrey's championship years was one of McIntyre's principles of wicket-keeping: 'It is so important to attack the batter and stop him from wandering round the crease, as quite a lot do.'

The assessment of Alec is that Mac superbly passed the crucial test of any wicket-keeper in his ability to stand up to fast-medium bowling. He recalls his association with McIntyre, 'a magnificent keeper, who did everything so easily and never made a fuss. Mac had the most difficult job in English county cricket, standing up to four bowlers. He often wore a chest pad, but he was rarely hit because his hands were so good and sure.'

Variety was the spice of McIntyre's alert vigil behind the stumps. Encircled by Surrey's brilliant close fielding cordon, he rejoiced in the excitement. 'I was fortunate in that I kept to a world-class attack. There was always something happening to maintain your interest and keep you on your toes.' He cites the seemingly contradictory assets of relaxation and concentration as paramount for a wicket-keeper: 'There is nothing worse than keeping wicket all tensed up. If you are relaxed it means you are on top of your job.'

Roy Tattersall, the Lancashire and England off-spinner of those years, contends that McIntyre was as good as, if not better than, the more spectacular Godfrey Evans. 'I was always very happy with Arthur Mac keeping to me,' observes Tattersall.

Further evidence in support of the match-winning combination of Bedser and McIntyre is provided by Arthur Milton, the former Gloucestershire and England batsman. In one of his early games against Surrey at The Oval, Milton was taken unawares by Bedser's deceptive pace off the wicket. 'It was just short of a length and I was good on the back foot,' he recalls. 'The ball had gone by the time I'd played my shot and rocketed into Mac's gloves.

'In some shock, I looked aghast as the ball was nonchalantly tossed back to the bowler. I turned to McIntyre and said, weakly, "Christ, that nipped off a bit, Mac."

'"Oh," replied Mac, with a grin, "I thought you were kidding."'

'You're bound to have good catchers,' say the Bedsers, 'if you've got the bowlers providing the catches.' It is their way of insisting that fielding standards automatically rise because a chance is expected off every ball. Alec, in *Twin Ambitions*, expanded on this theme:

> The sense of anticipation is so sharpened that concentration becomes second nature. Conversely, a team without an attack to create many chances tends to relax and go through the motions of

concentration. I have often thought this to be the difference between Surrey's approach and that of other teams.

In Surrey's fourth championship year in 1955, the close catching was at its most voracious. In all, 381 catches were taken and three players – Surridge, Lock and Micky Stewart – shared 150 between them. Stewart was later to claim the Surrey record of 604 catches; his tally of 77 in 1957, including seven in one match at Northampton, is the second highest by a non-wicket-keeper, only one short of the record established by Wally Hammond in 1928.

The miracles exacted by razor-sharp reflexes gave Surrey legendary status in the field. Fearlessness was the key accompanied by an almost suicidal disregard for safety. Micky Stewart, in his position in 'bomb alley', often said of his captain, 'Stewie will get us all killed one day.' Then he would reflect that Surridge was just as courageous in the helmetless cordon. He set the example and never asked others to do what he could not do himself. Surridge was placed in the rare category of being worth his place on fielding alone.

∽ ∽ ∽

As you grow older, says Bob Appleyard, the former Yorkshire and England bowler, the memories of battles long ago become fonder. 'Often you admire those players who beat you, however much you disliked it at the time.' The duels between Surrey and Yorkshire superseded the traditional rivalry of Roses matches in the 1950s. They were addressed with a fervour and intensity not exceeded by other encounters in the Test arena.

Two world-class teams were in opposition, separated by the narrowest of threads. The essential difference was that Surrey had a pool of loyal and experienced reserves in their second team which enabled them to maintain their supremacy. One Yorkshire player also echoed the view of many within his own team: 'If we had had Stuart as captain during those five years, we would surely have done as well.'

Watching the combatants, almost literally on tiptoe, were massed crowds, totalling as many as 60,000, in matches at The Oval, Headingley and Bramall Lane, Sheffield. Yorkshire, proud of their heritage, found submission hard to bear, even though they were four times runners-up and third in the championship on two occasions.

The extent of the twin dominance in the championship is revealed by the fact that in one season the two counties, between them, supplied 13 players to England. In 1955, the Surrey representatives were Alec Bedser, May, Barrington, Lock, Laker, Loader and McIntyre. Yorkshire's six were: Wardle, Appleyard, Trueman, Lowson, Close and Watson.

Between 1952 and 1956, the years of Stuart Surridge's reign at The Oval, Surrey were victorious in 86 matches, with winning margins in the championship ranging from 16 to 32 points. Lock, Laker, Alec and Eric Bedser, Loader and Surridge between them took 2,163 wickets, all but two of them with averages of under 20.

Surrey maintained their championship dominance for two more seasons under the leadership of Peter May. In 1959, a new order was established in Yorkshire, with a keen disciplinarian in Ronnie Burnet at the helm. The statistics do, though, confirm an unquestioned authority at The Oval. During their seven championship years, Surrey played 196 games, winning 121 and losing 28. The extent of the achievements can be ascertained from the fact that only three of their victories were obtained as a result of declarations in the last innings of their opponents.

❧ ❧ ❧

'Man for man,' said one writer in 1954, 'the Yorkshire eleven was the equal if not superior to Surrey, but the better-moulded team won the championship.' Surrey, in this season, appeared unlikely title contenders. At the end of July they were eighth in the table, trailing by 46 points (96 to 142).

The sequel was an amazing transformation. In their last ten matches, Surrey won nine outright, including five in two days, and claimed 112 out of a possible 120 points. Yorkshire, in their remaining 12 games, beginning on 10 July, could only muster 52 out of a possible 144 points. They had to be content with second place, 22 points behind the leaders.

The sequence of five victories over Yorkshire in the 1950s included the first double for 36 years. Yorkshire squandered an opportunity in Jim Laker's benefit match at The Oval in June 1956. The match was dominated by the bowling of Lock and Appleyard, who each took nine wickets. It was completed in two days. At the last, Yorkshire, set a modest target of 124 runs, tumbled from 60 for 2 to 100 all out.

The defeat was replicated in another fluctuating battle at Bramall Lane. Yorkshire gained a first innings lead of 61, a commanding advantage in a low-scoring game. Peter May (top scorer in the match with 68) and Ken Barrington added 94 for the third wicket in Surrey's second innings; but Yorkshire's position seemed unassailable when they began the last day, needing only 67 runs, with 8 wickets in hand.

Peter Loader had made the opening breakthrough on the previous evening. On a fresh and breezy morning, he bowled in tandem with Alec Bedser. For over an hour they bowled to the Yorkshire pair of Ken Taylor and Willie Watson. The net was stretched tight, with no fieldsman deeper than cover point. 'Yorkshire,' wrote Jim Kilburn in the *Yorkshire Post*, 'devised a crisis with incredible simplicity. They descended to one of the most miserable, unrealistic displays of batting they can ever have presented. It had neither strength nor sense; it invited disaster and humiliation.'

Tony Lock had been held in reserve and he was not called upon until Yorkshire had struggled to 50 for 4. Lock swiftly bowled Close to give Surrey a faint prospect of victory. In the end, Lock and Loader were almost contemptuous in their mastery. Lock furiously swept aside the Yorkshire tail. His final figures were 5 for 11 in 11 overs on a wicket which gave scant encouragement to spin. Surrey, against all expectations, were the victors by 14 runs.

Surrey could hardly believe their luck. Alec Bedser remembered the fusillade of cushions, pitched on the ground by the disgruntled Yorkshire partisans. The adjacent factories had fashioned their own protest at the impending defeat. Plumes of smoke belched forth from the chimneys as a signal of distress to reinforce the old legend. Micky Stewart recalled, 'After we'd taken three or four wickets, the smoke was so dense I thought they'd set the stadium on fire.'

***

Stuart Surridge, during Surrey's glorious years, once said: 'At the start my team was a little afraid to win the championship. I had to give them a few kicks up the backside. But once they'd won it, they didn't want to lose it.' His sense of adventure and the exciting gambles caused consternation among county members as well as opponents. More often than not matches were completed before the end of the second day. 'We would pack our clubs and drive over to Wimbledon Park for a round of golf,' recalls Dave Fletcher. 'Our members got rather peeved because we were winning so quickly.'

The irresistible surge began in 1952 when Surrey won the championship outright for the first time since 1914. They did not concede any points until mid-June, when Glamorgan led them on the first innings at Llanelli; and the first of only three defeats in the season was inflicted by Lancashire as late as 18 July.

One of Surridge's first notable decisions was to promote Eric Bedser to open the innings with Dave Fletcher. He was rewarded with sterling performances and the new combination became one of the most reliable pairings in the country. Fletcher, rehabilitated after illness, scored 1,674 runs and was second in the county averages. Heading the list was Peter May, then in his last season at Cambridge. May scored over 800 runs in only 14 matches. Eric Bedser also topped 1,500 runs as well as taking 56 wickets. Surridge, one of *Wisden*'s Five Cricketers of the Year, set a new Surrey record in taking 58 catches. Three bowlers – Alec Bedser, Laker and Lock – took 304 wickets between them.

One of the highlights of a historic season was the innings victory over Nottinghamshire at The Oval in August. Alec Bedser claimed 8 wickets for 18 runs, the last 6 for 9 runs in 9 overs. His match figures of 13 for 46 took him to the milestone of 1,000 wickets in first-class cricket. Attacking cricket was the norm then, as it was in succeeding seasons. Many games were achieved against the odds, a sample of which was the triumph over Sussex at The Oval.

John Langridge and Jim Parks both scored centuries in the Sussex first innings total of 365 for 9 declared on the first day. Surrey responded in rapid style: Fletcher and Bedser provided the counter with an opening stand worth 162 runs; and a lead of 67 runs was established before another declaration.

On the last morning, the visitors seemed relatively safe at 101 for three. Then Lock and Eric Bedser summoned urgent spin and Sussex lost their last 7 wickets for 35 runs. Lock, with 10 wickets in the match, took 4 wickets for 8 runs in his final conclusive spell. Surrey needed only 19 overs to score 71 without loss and the match ended with two and a half hours to spare.

A terrific onslaught in the last hour swept Surrey to victory off the second ball of the final over against Kent at The Oval. Surrey had established a first innings lead of 133; but Kent, at the second time of asking, were in no mood to surrender.

Godfrey Evans hit a breezy 92 before being stumped by McIntyre off Alec Bedser. Sid O'Linn, who was to tour England in the South African ranks in 1960, next proved the stumbling block. His unbeaten 111 was an act of defiance. One Surrey stalwart, Tom Clark, said it was the only occasion that he ever saw Alec Bedser bowling round the wicket in his attempt to dislodge O'Linn.

A surprise declaration by the Kent captain, Bill Murray-Wood, released a flood of runs. Surrey were set a target of 188 to win in 92 minutes. *Wisden* reported: 'Surrey pursued aggression to the end without regard to the risk of defeat.' At the call of the last hour 128 were needed, then 50 with 17 minutes left. The eighth wicket fell eight minutes from time and before Surridge struck the winning hit off Dovey, high over extra cover, both he and Clark had survived chances in the deep.

There was another breathtaking exploit against Lancashire in Jack Ikin's benefit match at Old Trafford in 1953. It was preceded by an instance of mistaken identity involving the Bedsers. 'It was coming towards the end of the first day and, just for a lark, Surridge sent Alec in to bat instead of Eric,' recalls Arthur McIntyre. During Lancashire's innings Alec had worn his MCC sweater and Eric his Surrey sweater. When Surrey batted there was an exchange of sweaters between the twins.

Eric's number routinely spun on to the scoreboard at the direction of Bert Strudwick, the Surrey scorer. From the last ball of the final over Alec gave a return catch to Roy Tattersall. Tattersall remembers the confusion and the later exchange of views in the Lancashire dressing-room. 'All the press was taken in by the trick. From 22 yards I certainly thought it was Eric, who normally opened the innings. Cyril Washbrook, with his experience of playing with Alec for England, was the only one of us to detect the change.' Bert Strudwick, busily totting up his figures, was also hoodwinked by the subterfuge. He was furious when told about the revised batting order.

This was a day belonging to Tony Lock. He was as tireless as ever despite the late arrival in Manchester. The Surrey team had had a long coach journey from Taunton and had not reached their hotel until 3.30 a.m. Lock, rubbing the sleep out of his eyes, bowled 45 overs in taking 5 wickets for 89 runs. These labours still left him unfulfilled; his continuing zest also brought him seven catches in the match.

Lancashire offered a stern challenge to Surrey in 1953. At Old Trafford they seemed destined to garner points to close the gap on their rivals. Surrey, at one stage, had lost 5 wickets for 49 runs. The position was retrieved by Peter May, with a typically pugnacious 75. It was then consolidated by Arthur McIntyre, batting at No. 9 because of a broken thumb, and fearlessly answering the call with a magnificent 76.

Their fortunes restored, with a narrow first-innings lead, Surrey once again strutted like champions. By the end of an invigorating day Lancashire were a broken force. Eight of their wickets had gone down, five of them grasped by the attentive hands of Lock at short leg. Alec Bedser and Surridge each took 5 wickets and the victory task of 103 runs was completed in 25 overs before lunch on the third day.

Doug Insole, as one of Surrey's opposing captains, says Surridge was unwaveringly confident in his own judgement: 'Stewie was a great character and some of his declarations were a little bizarre. He wanted to win matches in one day if possible. But he did have the standby of a second innings if matters went awry.'

One example of Surridge's whirlwind captaincy belongs to a Saturday in May 1953 when Surrey beat Warwickshire by an innings in one day. It had happened only once before, in a first-class match at The Oval in 1857. There was a standing ovation by members to reward the team on emulating the feat. Warwickshire were dismissed for 45 and 52. Alec Bedser took 12 wickets, including 8 for 18 in the first innings, and Laker performed the hat-trick.

Warwickshire started their second innings at 5 p.m. As Jack Bannister relates, Alan Townsend mistakenly thought he was safe to run a bath. 'He was in and out, run out before the bath was full.' Next man in was the left-hander, Ray Hitchcock. As he appeared, so the anecdote proceeds, the expectations of another dismissal were such that the Surrey players shook hands with Laker. He was on the hat-trick. It was duly completed when Alec Bedser took the catch to dismiss Hitchcock.

Alec had followed his first innings haul with another three wickets. There was the almost certain prospect of a fourth with Eric Hollies, the Warwickshire leg-spinner, coming in at No. 11. Hollies at that time had taken more first-class wickets than he had scored runs. The execution was not long delayed. Surrey had taken the extra half hour and were looking to bring the game to a swift conclusion.

Bannister recalls the 'wicked, fast-medium leg-cutters' with which Bedser had wreaked havoc in Warwickshire's first innings. 'They were unplayable as the ball spun from leg to off, and divots flew past the batsman's left shoulder.' Hollies was presented with the tasty morsel of a slow-medium long-hop outside the leg stump. He swung hard for runs, but only succeeded in rustically hoisting the ball and was brilliantly caught in the deep field.

Surrey had once again triumphed through the brilliance of their fielding. This was demonstrated by the fact that not one of the visiting batsmen was bowled. Warwickshire, in their second innings, were all out in 70 minutes, 5 minutes fewer than in their first innings.

Warwickshire gained a measure of revenge, winning by 140 runs, in the return match at Edgbaston. On a rapidly deteriorating wicket, Peter Loader took eight wickets, seven clean bowled, before Pritchard and Grove also profited from the conditions to bowl out Surrey for 99. Raman Subba Row recalls the spectacle of fragments of crockery, which had emerged from the soil, sprinkling the pitch. Stuart Surridge collected a cup handle as a souvenir of the match to bring back home for inspection.

Alec Bedser was rewarded with benefit proceeds of £12,866 – by some distance a Surrey record – in the match against Yorkshire, starting on his 35th birthday, in July 1953. Overshadowing all else was the bowling of Laker, who took ten wickets in the match. He took 6 for 38 as Yorkshire were bowled out for 137 in their first innings. May and Clark shared a partnership of 86 to put their side in the lead. The position was strengthened by a ninth-wicket stand of 79 between Alec, second-top scorer with 45, and Laker. Len Hutton, with a masterly 76, out of 172, denied Surrey victory in two days.

Raman Subba Row, held back in the order, was associated with Jim Laker in a thrilling finish against Sussex at Hove in 1954. On a perfect wicket a total of 1,279 runs were scored in the match. Sussex reached 369, with George Cox hugely exultant on 167, on the first day. Tom Clark hit an unbeaten century as Surrey exceeded this with 400 on the second day. Good tactical use of slow bowling then tempted Sussex into a declaration. Surrey were set a target of 239 and lost two quick wickets. In an attempt to catch up with the clock, the entire batting order was altered.

'Stewie said, "We'll have the right-handers in first,"' recalls Subba Row. 'I think he saw me as a slowcoach who would have held up the run-rate.' By the time he was at last permitted to bat at No. 11, Laker had staunchly recorded a half-century, but 19 runs were still required. Subba Row was quick enough to scamper two runs in the last over and Surrey hustled to victory in a tumult of excitement. The outrageous assault told a familiar tale. No one was allowed to sit on the splice with a win in the offing. Victory was achieved in two and a half hours. In a day of helter-skelter cricket, 510 runs were scored in 123 overs.

Jim Laker was again on song with bat and ball in another tense encounter against Northamptonshire at Kettering. Twenty-four wickets fell on a drying track on the first day. Laker and Lock shared the last nine wickets as Northants were bowled out for 125. Surrey also struggled against Tribe and Broderick and finished four runs in arrears. A heavy thunderstorm during the night quietened the wicket to provide a temporary respite for the batsmen. Alec Bedser dutifully obeyed the virtues of economy – he conceded only 8 runs in 13 overs – to keep Surrey in the game until the wicket began to help the spinners again.

Surrey, in the end, required 138 – the highest total of the game – to win and Laker had Loader, his last wicket partner, to eke out the remaining seven runs. Six maiden overs were bowled in miserly succession before the runs, one by one, gave Surrey the narrowest of victories.

Another dramatic switch in fortunes occurred in the same season at Worcester. Nearly two hours were lost through bad light on the first day. On the second morning Surrey tumbled to 116 for 5 in response to Worcestershire's 184. It preceded a remarkable sequence of events. Arthur McIntyre and Alec Bedser were in batting harness in a recovery which gave Surrey a first innings lead of 95.

There was a sensational start to Worcestershire's second innings, Peter Loader took four wickets in his first four overs, in between bowling three wides and four no-balls. Having taken eight wickets in the first innings, he supervised the wreckage again. He claimed a match analysis of 14 wickets for 111 runs. Worcester were bowled out for 99 and Surrey claimed the extra half-hour. By 7.17 p.m. they had won by ten wickets to earn another day's rest in the rain. It fell so heavily in Worcester during the next three days that it ruled out any play there.

❧ ❧ ❧

The fluctuating elements of an English summer presented batting hazards on the uncovered wickets of this time. One of the most delightful sounds for Surrey's vintage cricketers was the gentle patter of overnight rain. Weather forecasting, aided by regular checks with the meteorological office, was an important pursuit for cricketers. It enabled them to gather in their fruits with the same precision as farmers looking to the skies before harvesting their crops.

The possession of a barometer might have been said to be as necessary as winning the toss. For Bill Bowes, in Yorkshire, it was a piece of vital equipment. He avidly consulted his own barometer – a wedding present from one of his mentors, Emmott Robinson, who had told him, 'Tha' wants to look at it night and morning. It's nice to know when there's a sticky wicket in t'offing.'

Stuart Surridge was just as aware as Bowes of the need to take precautions in his master plans. One of these occasions was the match against Worcestershire at The Oval in 1954. The visitors, sent in to bat, were overwhelmed by the spin of Laker and Lock. They lost their last seven first innings wickets for five runs and collapsed to 25 all out. Lock took 5 wickets for 2 runs in 5.3 overs and Laker 2 for 5 in 8 overs.

Alec Bedser remembers the occasions when he thought that Surridge had gone dotty. 'Out of the blue he would announce: "I think we'd better get 'em in." The rest of us might shiver with apprehension and think the skipper had flipped at last.'

Disbelief was again the reaction to another seemingly extravagant throw of the dice against Worcestershire. There was near panic in the Surrey dressing-room when Surridge made his declaration at 92 for 3. Those waiting to bat now had furiously to ready themselves to field. Alec forcibly presented the general view. 'Skipper,' he said, 'you've got to remember that somebody else can play this game as well as us.' Surridge was dismissive in his reply: 'Nonsense. We've got enough.'

The weather sage had once again checked and noted a bad weather forecast. The lowering clouds at The Oval hastened his declaration. Batting, he knew, would soon become a lottery not to be contemplated. The match was only just completed before the heavens opened. It lasted a little over five hours and was concluded by 12.30 on the second day. Worcestershire were dismissed for 40 in their second innings. Surrey batted for only 24 overs, but still won by an innings. The aggregate of 157 runs was the lowest for any completed championship match.

As Alec Bedser said, if ever there was an eccentric declaration this had seemed to be it, even allowing for the fact that Surridge was undoubtedly at his happiest when he was leading the charge on the field. The match-winning conjuror was never more wrapped in his aura of infallibility than in this triumph. In this seductive action, he had confounded his own team as well as beating the rainmakers.

CHAPTER NINE

Record at Nottingham

This was the best fast-medium bowling I have ever seen for an entire match. Alec gave a wonderful exhibition of his craft.

TREVOR BAILEY

The pulse of a great bowler quickened in the enveloping gloom at Nottingham in June 1953. Captured eloquently on film is a famous picture of Alec Bedser which portrays his humility at the pinnacle of his fame. There was the happy smile of fulfilment on his return to a pavilion and a shy bow to acknowledge the ovation.

Bedser enjoyed his finest hour as the relentless record-breaker against the hapless Australians. 'Up he came, over after over, his head rocking as he swung his arm with all the power of the strongest pair of shoulders surely ever given to a cricketer,' wrote Jim Swanton in his narrative of a stunning event. He was later to observe that Bedser's Herculean efforts in this and the previous lost series in Australia deserved the seal of the return of the Ashes: 'If he is not so rewarded, Bedser, I feel, whether subsequently knighted or not, may grow old in melancholy sadness.'

There were, before the exploits of 1953, murmurings of doubt about the prowess of Alec Bedser. The charge was even laid against him that he had not fulfilled his early promise. Reliable, rather than penetrative, was the view of less discerning critics. 'We've seen the best of him,' was one misguided judgement. Trevor Bailey was emerging in tandem with Alec as a Test bowler in the early 1950s. He more responsibly contends that his partner was a 'very good stock bowler, better than anyone else we had got' – before the peak years.

After his labours on his first tour of Australia in 1946–47, Bedser was omitted from the England team in the next home series against the South Africans at Manchester and Leeds. Tiredness did undoubtedly assail Alec, even if he never willingly accepted a rest.

The selectors wisely conserved the energy of their prime asset. Bedser also missed two Tests in the drawn series against New Zealand in 1949. He was one of seven bowlers selected in a vain bid to break the stalemate. But Walter Hadlee, the visiting captain, is derisive about reports that Alec in that season was supposedly bowling a yard short of what should be expected of an attacking bowler: 'I know we were all pleased that he was not selected. When he came back for the fourth Test at The Oval Alec's bowling produced 7 wickets in a demanding display of accuracy.'

It bears repetition that Bedser, with meagre assistance, held sway against powerful batting. 'How heartbreaking to bowl with so little support! Can cricket history furnish any parallels?' asked a correspondent in *The Cricketer*. The Australian sides throughout the 1940s could be compared with any of their predecessors in quality, and especially the length of the batting order.

They were followed in 1950 by the West Indians which, with the 'Three Ws' (Worrell, Weekes and Walcott) united as the batting trinity, exuded an awesome command. 'Here was the best possible school for those with the stamina and attributes to survive it,' commented Ian Peebles. 'In it Bedser learned the patience, cunning and faith in eventual justice which combined to make the best use of his immense natural talent.'

One episode against the West Indies typified Alec's resilience. At Trent Bridge he toiled for an entire day on a plumb wicket. At the close West Indies were 479 for 3. Worrell and Weekes, one stylishly fluent, and the other brutal in his power, shared a partnership of 241. On the following morning the innings subsided in an unseemly gallop. The West Indies lost their last 7 wickets for 79 runs in 80 minutes. It was the outcome of a rally masterminded by Bedser in his most threatening mood. Worrell was Alec's first conquest, with the aid of a catch by Yardley; and then, wrote Peebles, 'girding up his ample loins, the giant sailed in to bag four more wickets in double quick time. Here was the real spark.'

Alec bowled 59 overs for his 5 wickets at Nottingham. He exceeded this figure with a marathon stint of 84 overs in the second Test at Lord's. This was the occasion of the West Indies' first Test victory in England. Ramadhin and Valentine shared 18 wickets to win calypso, as well as cricket, acclaim as 'those two little pals of mine . . .'

As a footnote in the margins of an historic event, Alec rated his own bowling performance as one of his best:

On paper it was not all that startling with 3 for 60, but the three were the wickets of Everton Weekes, Frank Worrell and Bob Christiani, a batsman never to be under-rated. I completed 40 overs in a total of 326. I felt I was on my way. I had now developed my leg-cutter and was able to take full advantage of any help from the pitch.

~ ~ ~

The fanfares were still muted before Bedser's second tour of Australia in 1950–51. R.C. Robertson-Glasgow remembered a conversation with a former Australian bowler at Brisbane. Alec had just begun his first over in the Test. 'No good,' exclaimed the veteran. 'Bedser's just hitting the bat.' The illusion, for that is what it was, did not last long. This observer, along with the bemused opponents, was soon disposed to admiration.

Alec's achievement in taking 30 wickets in the series launched him beyond the tardy reckoning of his critics. Brave deeds in a lost cause were followed by another 30 wickets against South Africa in a series, this time crowned by triumph, in 1951.

The renewed excellence of Bedser's bowling in the first Test at Trent Bridge was matched by the remarkable vigil of Dudley Nourse. Nourse, resisting the pain of a broken thumb, batted for nine and a quarter hours in scoring 208. Alec took 6 for 37 in South Africa's second innings. His splendid counter, however, was unavailing. Athol Rowan and Norman Mann wove a web of spin on a rain-affected wicket and South Africa won by 71 runs.

England levelled the series with a 10-wicket victory at Lord's in a match completed just after lunch on the third day. It was dominated by the off-spin of Roy Tattersall. The Lancashire bowler claimed 12 wickets, including 9 out of the 14 which fell on the second day.

For the South Africans in defeat, the spinning skills of Mann were grooved in economy. Cricket would soon mourn the death of a wily opponent at the age of 31. The encroaching illness did not prevent Mann from heading the South African averages, as he had done on his previous tour in 1947. At Lord's, reported *Wisden*, 'He bowled his left-arm slows with such accuracy that from the time he went on at 70 until he was relieved when McCarthy took the second new ball at 202 his analysis was: 24–11–28–1.

Adorning England's triumph by 9 wickets at Old Trafford was Bedser's twelve wickets in the match. His 7 wickets in South Africa's first innings gave him a tally of 150 in 36 Tests. He deployed late swerve and lift on a damp wicket in a match-winning flourish. In 32 deliveries he dismissed the last five South African batsmen for 11 runs. Alec and his Surrey colleague, Jim Laker, shared 16 wickets in the match. They were also paired as batsmen in an eighth-wicket stand of 53, the extent of England's lead on the first innings. Len Hutton, with rain imminent, was left stranded two runs short of his hundredth century in the victory spurt.

Massive scoring in the following Test at Leeds was a delight for the statisticians, poring over their records, but held little appeal for bowlers. In a curtailed match, there was an aggregate of 1,130 runs over four days at what was described as a laboured rate of 'no higher' than 47 runs per hour. Eric Rowan's 236 (out of a total of 538) was the highest individual score by a South African batsman. Peter May, on his Test début, fashioned a composed century alongside another from Hutton, as England also topped 500. For Alec Bedser, his dismissal of Waite brought him the distinction of equalling Maurice Tate's record of 155 wickets in Test cricket.

જ્જ્જ્ જ્જ્જ્ જ્જ્જ્

Terror struck the Indians like the screech of a nightmare at Headingley in June 1952. Above the excited crowd shone the figures on the scoreboard: 0–4. They were so unlikely that one evening-newspaper office rang its correspondent to check if the score had been given the wrong way round.

Fred Trueman, brimming with hostility and infectious spirit, had taken three wickets in the course of fourteen balls. His sensational Test début might have been laden with the spoils of a hat-trick. 'Hazare came in and I did him with a yorker. It missed his off-stump by a whisker,' recalls Trueman.

Alec Bedser, Trueman's partner at Leeds, was at last presented with an eager apprentice to complement his own bowling sorcery. 'Trueman was the shock in the attack while Bedser was the basis of it,' commented Jim Kilburn in the *Yorkshire Post*.

England were the eventual victors by seven wickets, but they had been restricted to a slender first-innings lead of 41 runs. Then, in a dramatic quarter of an hour, the match seemed almost over. Trueman bowled the first over – up the hill from the Rugby Stand end – and his second ball induced an attempted hook by Roy. The deflected glance from his gloves travelled comfortably to Compton at first slip. Bedser bowled the second over – and his fourth delivery (the one ball of the day which behaved unpredictably) struck the shoulder of Gaekwad's bat, Laker taking the catch in the gully.

To the first ball of Trueman's second over, Mantri played back indecisively and was bowled. Manjrekar played on to the next ball. Trueman then followed the classical procedure in quest of the hat-trick. His yorker defeated Hazare but the stumps stayed intact. A startling passage of play had been watched in a rapt silence. Those balls which did not take wickets but failed to meet the middle of the bat each drew forth a concerted appeal from the crowd.

'After that, rationality returned to the game,' wrote Jim Kilburn. 'The remaining Indian batsmen set themselves to forage and forget.' Hazare and Phadkar raised a century partnership to allow dignity and substance to grow from a desert of distress. Kilburn continued: 'Close to the day's end, with cricket threatening to be capsized in heavy seas of litter sweeping across the ground, Hutton called his fast bowler back to action and Trueman bowled Hazare, who played at him with more optimism than discretion.'

A magnificent all-round performance by Vinoo Mankad could not avert another England victory at Lord's. Mankad, released from Lancashire League duties, scored 72 and 184 as well as bowling 73 overs and taking 5 wickets in England's first innings. The events in the following match at Manchester featured another ravenous conquest by Trueman. His bowling, abounding with confidence and ardour, was accounted the fastest for 20 years.

Play was briefly delayed because of overnight rain. England advanced their score from 292 to 347 before the declaration. Four hours and 50 minutes later, the game was over, the Indians defeated by an innings and 207 runs. It provided the only modern instance of a Test team bowled out twice in a day. Their first innings of 58 lasted 80 minutes; their second of 82 was extended by another 70 minutes though little more convincing.

'In nine overs,' wrote Jim Kilburn, 'Trueman tore the frail Indian innings to shreds as a tiger would devastate a cage of canvas. He hurled himself into thrilling action with the allies of a following wind, a lively pitch and indifferent light.' The violent spectacle can be deduced from England's field-placings for Trueman. It included three slips, three in the gully and two more at short leg. Godfrey Evans, behind the wicket, was stationed 20 yards back in order to take the ball without stooping. Tony Lock, at backward short-leg, protested at the evasive action of one of the

Indian batsmen, Umrigar. The retreat towards square-leg covered his line of vision. 'Polly, do you mind going back?' said Lock. 'I can't see the bowler when you stand there.'

Jim Kilburn paid tribute to Trueman's bowling, which owed less to the generosity of the Indian batsmen than had been the case at Leeds. It was, said Kilburn, without technical, tactical or moral reproach. 'All of his victims save one were clean bowled, or caught on the off side, and those who retreated faintheartedly towards square leg were as safe from injury as they were certain of cricketing ignominy.'

Trueman divided his triumph into two parts: his opening spell was of six overs in which he took 4 wickets for 12 runs. He was rested until the afternoon and on his recall he secured four more wickets to record an analysis of 8 for 31 in 8.4 overs. Someone commented afterwards that he must have written the script for himself. 'Ay,' said Fred in one of the first of his celebrated *bons mots*, 'and I made myself principal boy.'

Tom Graveney remembers that Alec Bedser, as the senior bowler, had expressed his concern at the choice of ends in the Indian first innings: 'Fred had a stiff breeze behind him, while Alec was running in against it.' It was Bedser's turn in the second innings. With the wind in his favour, he prospered hugely. India, a disconsolate force, were devoured again. They lost their last 7 wickets for 27 runs. Alec took 5 for 27 and Tony Lock, on his Test début, completed the rout with 4 for 36.

The series against India was plainly a one-sided affair, but England's outcricket bristled with energy and purpose. Brilliant catches were held to support the conquering bowlers. England did, as was said, look a wonderful side; and the impetus of the success was to carry them out of the shadows. More worthy adversaries would test their resolve, but the pattern had been set to arouse high expectations.

Fred Trueman takes especial pride in his early association with Alec Bedser. Engraved on his memory is the wisdom bequeathed to him by a bowler in his prime. Together, in the four Tests against India, they took 49 of the 70 wickets that fell in the series. Trueman's 29 wickets cost him 13.31 runs apiece and Bedser's 20 wickets were only marginally more expensive at 13.95 runs each.

The advent of the buccaneering and virile Trueman was to release a flush of fast bowling riches. This was much to the pleasure of the newly installed Len Hutton, the first professional in modern times to captain England, who saw their presence as a way to redeem the wounds that the Australians had inflicted on English cricket. Hutton – and Denis Compton – had been the principal targets of the assaults of Lindwall and

Miller. For Alec Bedser, Hutton's emphasis on speed grew like an angry sore to become an obsession.

Trueman's starring roles were to be restricted with the emergence of Brian Statham (his later complementary Test partner and happy companion), Frank Tyson, Alan Moss and Peter Loader. There was also the matter of strained relations with Len Hutton on the troubled tour of the West Indies in 1953–54. The two Yorkshiremen were both on trial – one as captain and the other, a raw, inexperienced and quick-tempered newcomer. Trueman was prone, as beginners are, to acts of indiscretion, mostly in the sheer excitement of just being young. He did need firm leadership. However, Hutton reflected afterwards that he had scarcely time to look after himself let alone anyone else.

Hutton was cast in an unenviable role as captain in the Caribbean, a region where emotions can run high among spectators. He was always quiet and withdrawn as a man and uncomfortable when rowdiness was on display. Any form of horseplay was distasteful to him. Therein lay the cause of the clash of personalities with Trueman. The England captain had also to be wary of not blotting his own copybook on his first tour abroad as leader. There is strong evidence of opposition to his appointment within the cricket establishment. As John Arlott observed, any indication of inability to discharge the diplomatic or disciplinary side of his duties could be taken as confirming the inadequacy of a paid player for the post.

The influential presence of Alec Bedser in the West Indies would surely have eased Hutton's vexations. Sir Leonard, in his autobiography, *Fifty Years in Cricket*, maintained that Alec's withdrawal from the tour was a severe blow. The selection of Bedser would, he said, have ensured that Trueman, 'his lively young colt', was not called up too soon:

> I had planned to give Alec as near to a holiday in the West Indies as possible, without too much involvement in the lesser matches played on pitches like a macadam road surface, and reserve him for the Test matches. Bedser's capacity for hard work and his zest for the game might have made him unwilling to accept the arrangement, but his support and down-to-earth common sense would have been invaluable on a troubled tour.

There were conflicting pre-tour assessments of the merits of the

Australians in 1953. E.M. Wellings, writing in the *London Evening News*, prophesised that it would prove to be the weakest for over 40 years. John Arlott, in another commentary in the same paper, stressed Australia's all-round potential. Arlott won this particular argument. By the end of the summer eight Australians shared wickets ranging from Lindwall's 85 to the 45 of Miller, and the only defeat suffered by Lindsay Hassett's team was in the final Test at The Oval.

A more recent judgement by Trevor Bailey is that Australia deserved to win at Lord's and Leeds. Australia could not call upon adequate spin resources. Bruce Dooland, who narrowly shaded Roy Tattersall and Alec Bedser in the English bowling averages that year, was playing in county cricket, as was another Australian spinner, George Tribe.

A renewed association between Fred Trueman and Alec Bedser against Australia in the Coronation Year of 1953 would have helped to lessen the heartbeats in a fluctuating series. Lord Justice Birkett had given his usual felicitous welcome to the Australians at the Cricket Writers' Club dinner at which Trueman was presented with the Club's trophy for the best young cricketer of 1952. It was a deserved choice, as his later renown would confirm in full measure.

Len Hutton reflected on a blossoming partnership between Bedser and Trueman. He considered it an ideal combination. Certainly, it would have spared the exertions of the Surrey man in a memorable summer. The demands of National Service delayed their reunion until the tumultuous finale at The Oval.

❧ ❧ ❧

The spotlight has wavered uncertainly upon Bedser's epic endeavours against Australia. In this peak year, Alec achieved a series aggregate of 39 wickets, at an average of 17.48 runs each, to beat the previous record held by Maurice Tate. They included match figures of 14 wickets for 99 runs in the first Test at Nottingham. It was the best return by an English bowler since 1934 and has only been surpassed against Australia by Rhodes, Verity and Laker.

Crawford White, writing in the *News Chronicle*, enthused about Alec's feat: 'I suspect that both Rhodes and Verity had a deal of help from a treacherous wicket. Bedser achieved his figures on a Trent Bridge wicket as good as most batsmen here have seen in the past.'

Alec himself, with his pride undiminished by the passing years, believes that he has received less than his true deserts for his part in regaining the Ashes. He bowled 265 overs in the series and his nearest contender was Johnny Wardle, who completed 155.3 overs in taking 13 wickets. England went into three Tests (at Nottingham, Manchester and Leeds) with only four bowlers. 'Len was frightened of not getting enough runs,' recalls Alec. 'If I had broken down, he would have been lost. There was no one else.'

Trevor Bailey, as Bedser's opening partner, was a key witness in the stirring events at Nottingham. The audience also included another great bowler, S.F. Barnes – then aged 80, he watched Bedser overtake his English Test record of 189 wickets.

Purple patches in cricket are rare enough not to excite idle praise. 'Alec gave a wonderful exhibition of his craft,' says Bailey. 'It was the best fast-medium bowling I have ever seen for an entire match.' He places Bedser's performance in the same category, if in a different style, to the controlled fast bowling displayed by the 22-year-old Michael Holding against England at The Oval in 1976. The West Indian took 14 wickets (9 of his victims clean bowled) in that match in a flurry of youthful enthusiasm. 'For 33 overs in the first innings and another 20 in the second innings, I cannot remember once slackening my pace, or even thinking that I should,' recalled Holding. Trevor Bailey, equally captivated in both instances, observes: 'Great bowling produces great matches.'

The bowling rhythm of Alec Bedser was just as strictly maintained against Australia at Trent Bridge. Alec remembers a good wicket, intermittently freshened by slight drizzle: 'The ball did swing, but you had to bowl to a full length.' Australia, at the end of the first day, were 157 for 3. Bedser bowled 25 overs and conceded only 26 runs for his 3 wickets, those of Hole, Morris and Harvey. By the end of the series, he had greatly eased England's task by dismissing Morris five times and Harvey on six occasions.

Jim Swanton recalled the conditions on the first day: 'The air was damp, the light murky and gusts of drizzle were periodically blown down the field from the north-east.' Swanton declared that he had never seen Bedser bowl better either in Australia or at home. 'By sheer strength he strove to generate some pace off the wicket. He was never off a good length and with the second new ball especially he was the picture of hostility.'

In his recital of the astounding events of the second day, Swanton wrote: 'The mastery of Bedser, and later of Lindwall, was attributable not in any way to the turf, but to the raw and damp atmosphere in which they swung the ball with extraordinary skill.' Bedser, it should be noted, had bowled 37 overs for Surrey in the preceding county match at The Oval. 'This morning at Nottingham,' reported Swanton, 'Bedser seemed not unnaturally a little stiff after yesterday's great effort. After lunch, he swept through the Australian ranks in the manner of a truly magnificent bowler.'

At lunch Australia were 243 for 4. 'Thereafter,' commented *Wisden*, 'the game moved so swiftly that by the end of the day most of the spectators felt exhausted through the sustained excitement.' Lindsay Hassett had moved so certainly to his century that his dismissal by Bedser came as a surprise. It was Alec's leg-cutter, sharply deviating once again to hit Hassett's off stump. The Australian captain wittily described his downfall: 'I tried to play three shots off one ball and almost made contact the third time.' Hassett added that he was proud of the fact that he was a good enough player to touch the ball on the way to the stumps.

Ron Archer, who first toured England in 1953, recalls the dismissal of Hassett. 'I have never seen a better ball than the one which bowled Lindsay. It went down the line of the off stump, swung late to pitch just outside leg, and then cut back to hit the top of the off stump.'

Hassett's innings, lasting six and a half hours, was a remarkable effort of sustained application. 'In view of the afternoon's events, one may well wonder what might have happened had he gone early,' commented Jim Swanton. Bill Bowes, writing in *The Cricketer*, told how Bedser and Bailey, with the new ball, effected a rout which had not been seen since the famous Verity match at Lord's in 1934.

Australia, from 243 for 4, lost their last 6 wickets for 6 runs in 45 minutes. An acrobatic leap, as if jet-propelled, by Godfrey Evans provided the catalyst for the tumble of wickets. Evans spectacularly took the catch to dismiss Benaud off the bowling of Bailey. 'It was a genuine leg-glance,' wrote Swanton. 'Evans, standing back, must have made something like ten feet before he took off and held the ball left-handed as he hit the ground.'

Alec Bedser returned figures of 7 wickets for 55 runs in 38.3 overs. Searching spells with the three new balls of the Australian innings demonstrated his mastery. They were: 1 for 7; 2 for 5; and in the last phase 4 wickets, all clean bowled, for 2 runs.

Trevor Bailey recalled the hasty dispatch of the Australians and the bewilderment of the England players at the seeming hysteria of one of the defeated batsmen. Don Tallon was hard of hearing and known as 'Deafy'. The conditions, said one writer, presented the phenomenon of a grey November day in June. Hassett had instructed Tallon to 'give it a go', intending that his wicket-keeper should appeal against the light. Tallon wrongly interpreted the message. He judged that it was necessary to go on to the attack. 'Deafy came in and started to "smear",' says Bailey. 'We couldn't understand what was happening.'

Australia led by 105 runs on the first innings and then succumbed tormentedly once again to Bedser. Alec stresses that there was no question of him breaking down. The absence of relief bowling meant that he and Bailey had bowled 82 overs between them in Australia's first innings. The omission of Statham had also increased their burden. Bailey, who conceded only 17 runs in 10 overs, was the admirable foil. He exerted pressure at one end, while Bedser kept on taking wickets at the other end.

Alec had also to school himself to withstand the pain of a bruised foot when he bowled again. While batting, he had been struck on the right instep by a yorker from Lindwall. 'I could feel the foot swelling,' he recalls, 'so I decided not to take the boot off in case I couldn't get it back on again. I went out and bowled and gradually the pain and swelling disappeared.'

The heart and middle of the Australian second innings was destroyed by Bedser in half an hour. Hassett was deceived by a wickedly lifting ball. 'It removed the prop and stay of the Australian batting, and it sowed in Australian minds a distrust of the wicket which was reflected in all that subsequently happened,' reported Jim Swanton. The ball which beat Hassett reared from a good length, hit the bat handle and glove, and passed in a gentle arc to Hutton in the leg-trap.

Hutton, sensing the moment was propitious, now tightened the noose. Harvey, Miller and Benaud were dismissed in rapid succession. At this stage Bedser had taken 5 wickets at a cost of 22 runs in 11.1 overs. Tom Graveney remembers that Alec bowled only one bad ball in the match, a long-hop down the legside to Harvey. As the ball left his hand, Bedser groaned at the anticipated concession of four runs. 'Neil went for the hook,' says Graveney. 'It went straight to me, hip-high, at square leg and, thankfully, I caught it.'

Arthur Morris was the only Australian who held the slightest certainty of confidence amid the prevailing turmoil. His batting, said one writer, was in a category far removed from any of his companions. Morris was the sixth man out, bowled by Tattersall. He had scored 60 out of a total of 81. Two superb catches in the deep field, first by Graveney and then Simpson, removed Davidson and Tallon. Bedser finished off the innings by taking the last two wickets to exact a yield of 7 for 44 in 17.2 overs.

Roy Tattersall was Alec's accomplice with a controlling spell of off-spin. His three wickets were coupled with two catches to aid Bedser's final thrust. Both were taken off steepling hits, hanging precariously aloft, by Lindwall and Hill. Tattersall was fielding at mid-on and did not have to move as the balls plummeted down from the leaden skies. Don Bradman, reporting at Nottingham, said they soared so high that they could easily have gathered snow before the descent. Each of the catches, he said, were fine examples of judgement and sure hands.

Australia were bowled out for 123. What followed was a hurtful anti-climax. England required 229 to win and were a tantalising 109 runs short of victory when the match ended. Nearly 40 hours of rain and drizzle from 6 p.m. on Sunday until 10 a.m on Tuesday ruled out play. The weather robbed England of a highly probable victory; but it could not diminish the lustre of one of the century's most outstanding bowling feats. At Nottingham, Bedser was confirmed in his eminence. His bowling marked the turn of the tide for England.

ᵔᵔ ᵔᵔ ᵔᵔ

England collected the Ashes in August, with what on paper seemed the utmost ease, by eight wickets. Len Hutton, tired but happy, stood on The Oval balcony above a rapturous multitude. Thirty years on, in 1983, Jim Swanton cast his mind back to the rejoicings:

> For those of us, who had been watching the struggle over so many years, the truth was hard to believe until the crowds surged in a multi-coloured mass in front of the pavilion.
>
> The country was taken up by the euphoria of the moment to a degree unknown before, since the great boom in the sale of television sets occasioned by the Coronation allowed millions to both see and listen.

The excitement aroused by the thrilling pageant at The Oval led to a swift rearrangement of television schedules. Ronnie Aird, the secretary of the MCC, issued a statement in which he said that because of the 'enormous public interest' the MCC had decided to allow the BBC to transmit the whole of the final day's play. The decision was forced by the aggravations of the previous day when the state of the game had played havoc with other television programmes.

Ron Archer was still a schoolboy when he first watched Alec Bedser bowl at Brisbane in 1946. Seven years later, at The Oval, he gallantly sought to stem the England advance after Laker and Lock had stunned Australia. Four wickets, those of Hole, Harvey, Miller and Morris, had been taken in the course of 16 balls for just two runs. The breathtaking procession was halted by a stirring counter-attack headed by Archer, the 19-year-old from Queensland. Archer hit a six and seven fours in a valiant 49. He and Davidson added 50 in 38 minutes. *The Times* reported that 'Archer held the tattered standard high from the moment he arrived on the scene. He led the answering challenge with brilliant forcing strokeplay.'

Archer today conceals his youthful assault and refers instead to the fact that he was the batsman off whom Alec Bedser took the return catch for his record-breaking wicket. Over the years Archer has been the recipient of many kindnesses in his friendship with the Bedsers. 'I suspect there is a "soft spot" for me because mine was the wicket which beat Maurice Tate's record. I really can't give Alec credit for a great ball on that occasion. It was simply a bad shot and I could produce them very easily!'

∾ ∾ ∾

Alec Bedser should, in retrospect, have bowed out of Test cricket still wreathed in the laurels of 1953. His last tour of Australia, at the age of 36, in the winter of 1954–55, was blighted by a debilitating attack of shingles. He tells of how he contracted the illness on the voyage to Australia and of the failure to diagnose the ailment. He had complained to the MCC masseur, Harold Dalton, about unceasing back pains. Intensive massage was thought to be the palliative to reduce his discomfort. By the time the team arrived in Perth his back was disfigured by an ugly rash.

Alec's travail was not helped by the lack of medical advice which, in later years, would have brought the order to return home. The apparent indifference to his condition might also have stemmed from his stoical contempt for injuries at other times. It does, though, seem incredible that Alec was allowed to bowl 16 overs against an Australian XI at Melbourne and a further 30 overs against New South Wales at Sydney.

He was still far from fit when he bowled for the MCC in the state match against Queensland in late November. At Brisbane he told the selectors, 'I'll battle on and try to play.' He was, even then, unaware of the seriousness of his predicament: 'I'd played in so many matches when

120

I'd stuck it out. I didn't realise the effect that shingles had had on my constitution.'

The Brisbane wicket performed an act of caprice to outwit the Englishmen. 'It was very humid and the ball was swinging all over the place on a green pitch,' recalls Bedser. Seven days later, under the impact of the hot tropical sun, it was transformed in character for the first Test. Len Hutton failed to recognise the change in this early challenge of his leadership. He put Australia in to bat and they gratefully scored over 600. *Wisden*'s correspondent was sympathetic:

> The wicket looked a beauty, but Hutton had inspected the wicket most carefully and he carried out his plan . . . Although on subsequent events he could be condemned, the fact remains that England allowed about 12 possible chances to go astray. If the England fielding had approached any reasonable standard Hutton might well have achieved his objective.

Alec Bedser bowled 37 (eight-ball) overs for 131 runs and one wicket. 'I tried to bowl at 95 in the shade, with my back full of sores,' he says. He deserved a better reward for his fortitude. Morris was dropped off Bedser before he had scored. That lapse by Keith Andrew, who was deputising for Godfrey Evans, occurred in the third over of the match.

It was estimated by Ray Robinson, an Australian observer, that six other chances went begging off Bedser. Morris again escaped on 55 and 89 and Harvey was twice reprieved. Two of Australia's most dangerous batsmen took full advantage of their good fortune: Morris (152) and Harvey (163) between them scored over half of Australia's total. Trevor Bailey, in his view of a disastrous episode, considers that the balance of the England side was wrong: 'We made a complete hash of picking the team, with no spin bowlers in the Test. We went in with four seamers instead of making use of two good spinners – Appleyard and Wardle.'

The selection of Frank Tyson, after only one full season in county cricket, to tour Australia was regarded as a 'shot in the dark' by Jim Swanton. 'But,' he added perceptively, 'it may prove to be a very penetrating shot.' Tyson was the bowler who replaced Bedser at Sydney to help bring about the England revival. 'I was never close to Alec since I think my replacing him in the Sydney Test rankled,' says Tyson. 'He was, after all, the senior bowler and Andrew, Peter Loader, Jim McConnon and I had been told on ship that we would probably be the supernumerary players on the tour.'

Alec Bedser, for his part, takes leave to question the dramatic reversal in Tyson's form unless, as he contends, the wicket was overwhelmingly in the bowler's favour at Sydney. Tyson had conceded 160 runs in 29 overs at Brisbane. It was widely reported that he then heeded the earlier advice of one mentor, Alf Gover, to shorten his run. In the preceding state match Tyson had reverted to the old principle: six shuffling steps followed by ten deliberate raking strides. At Sydney, swept along by half a gale behind him, Tyson was a man of fury. His bullet-like yorkers dipped unnervingly into the Australians' stumps. None of the batsmen, excepting Harvey (forlornly isolated on 92 not out in one of the finest innings of his career), knew how to counter Tyson's speed. 'Few bowlers – fast, medium or slow – have ever dominated a match as Tyson did this one,' commented Bill O'Reilly.

Tyson bowled unchanged, with inspiring intent, through the closing 90 minutes. His six wickets completed a tally of ten wickets in the match. England's victory margin was, though, perilously close, a mere handful of 38 runs. Tyson's success could not have resulted without the unflagging support of his partner, Brian Statham – his contribution, 'holding up the upwind end over after over till it seemed he could give no more', would on other occasions place England in his debt.

Statham proved also the immaculate foil – not to be confused with playing second fiddle – for his allies of more spectacular pace. As one writer neatly put it, Statham was so accurate that on a yielding turf the marks where the ball pitched were grouped like rifle shots around a bull's-eye.

Ron Archer, as an Australian opponent, endorses the impact of Tyson in his alliance with Statham: 'Frank was really someone special that summer.' Tom Graveney expresses his praise with equal fervour: 'Tyson, with his remodelled approach, bowled like the wind. I've never seen anyone quicker.'

Archer remembers a 'very juicy and well-grassed pitch' at Sydney. Arthur Morris, regarded by Archer as the best captain under which he had played, put England in to bat. According to some reports, his decision was made because he expected Bedser to play and feared he would bowl his side out in such conditions. Archer believes it was a 'send-in' wicket irrespective of the opposition bowlers. Trevor Bailey considers that Bedser was very unlucky not to play at Sydney. 'The conditions were tailor-made for swing bowling,' he states. 'I was quite useful, but not nearly as good as Alec. He would have had an absolute field day. If he had been selected at Sydney, I swear that he would have got at least six wickets.'

Len Hutton was never a robust man and he suffered recurring bouts of ill health. A combination of physical and mental fatigue had led to an enforced rest for a month during the summer preceding the Australian tour. That he subsequently felt able to carry out a demanding assignment was a relief to his many admirers. As England's greatest batsman, he tellingly furthered the cause of professional cricket as the most appropriate leader for the series. However, his pioneering quest was not achieved without toll on his stamina.

'Hutton's captaincy grew in authority, though he always seemed to feel himself on trial, restricted by custom and circumstances,' commented Jim Kilburn, the Yorkshire historian and a close friend. 'He was persistently anxious not to tread on corns. He wanted his team to be all of the same frame of mind and then he would guarantee more victories than defeats. Victories were important to Hutton; he did not play in Test matches as a pastime.'

Geoffrey Howard, the MCC manager in Australia, believes that Hutton – who, as a professional, had never captained Yorkshire – was being asked to do a job for which he had no real training. 'He was fortunate in having such a good collection of players under his command.' One Yorkshire observer said Hutton succeeded as a captain not because he was a born leader of men, but because he was a superb tactician who planned everything down to the last detail. There was also the necessary streak of ruthlessness and a competitive urge instilled in him from his earliest days as a cricketer. 'Len did not believe in sparing the opposition once he had got them on the floor,' remembers one contemporary player.

Howard retained his affection for Hutton in a good relationship in Australia. He attempted to discharge all other responsibilities so as to enable the captain to concentrate entirely on the cricket: 'Len was a worrier and I don't think I was. He would not have been a good chap with whom to share your problems.'

When he needed counsel he turned to a 'very remarkable man', George Duckworth, the MCC baggage master and scorer. Duckworth, the former Lancashire and England wicket-keeper, was especially helpful in maintaining discipline within the party. 'Duckie' was also unerringly direct in his dealings with the players, according to Howard: 'He would march straight into the dressing-room at the close of play and unhesitatingly tell the team, if it was necessary, exactly what he thought of them.' Howard remembers his accord with Duckworth and presents a fine tribute: 'Basically, with George, it was his love of the game and his loyalty to it.'

Bob Appleyard remembers a tense low-scoring series in which Hutton exhibited increasing signs of strain. Adding to the burden was the fact that he lacked a consistent and solid opening ally. He had four different partners: Reg Simpson, at Brisbane; Trevor Bailey at Sydney; Bill Edrich at Melbourne and Adelaide; and Tom Graveney in the final Test at Sydney.

Hutton, in fact, had to be persuaded to play in the vital third Test at Melbourne, where England gained a 2–1 lead in the series. He was in a low state and had scored only 75 runs in 4 innings in the preceding Tests. Geoffrey Howard remembers Hutton was so overwrought that he asked for a doctor to be called on the night before the Test at Melbourne. Edrich and Godfrey Evans joined Howard when the examination was carried out on the morning of the match. The doctor announced a clean bill of health and urged Hutton to take a shower, have breakfast and go to the ground.

It was, as later transpired, a psychosomatic illness. 'Len was devastated; he wanted to be told that he was unfit,' recalls Howard. The reason for Hutton's indisposition was that he had decided to leave Alec Bedser out of the team. He was deeply worried about the impending omission of his senior professional. Melbourne was also one of Bedser's favourite bowling venues. He had taken 22 wickets in 3 Tests there.

'Len didn't want to hurt Alec; but he refused to delegate the task to Edrich, who was prepared to convey the sad news,' says Howard. To make matters worse, Hutton did not advise Alec of his decision. Bedser, having already changed for the match, was confounded to discover that his name was not included on the team sheet pinned up on the dressing-room notice-board. 'Len had actually taken Alec out to inspect the wicket,' says Howard. 'With all the other problems pressing on his mind, he still couldn't face communicating his decision to Bedser.'

Trevor Bailey also reflects on the winning hand which led to the omission of Bedser at Melbourne: 'It wasn't an easy decision for Len because he had a great respect for Alec.' Bailey accepts that England would have won at Sydney with Bedser in their ranks; but he is less sure whether he would have prevailed at Melbourne. 'We needed two spinners there and also in the next Test at Adelaide.' It was the saddest possible conclusion to a great Test career. 'Alec never got another opportunity because it was decided to persist with speed and spin.' By such narrow margins choices are made: Bedser's illness was a major factor and, but for it, the whirlwind advance of Frank Tyson might never have happened.

Victory in Australia was, in the event, the close of an era. A new young guard, led by Peter May, was waiting to take over and signal their supremacy. The careers of two great cricketers from the north and south had been inextricably linked. They would separately make their departures. It was the husbandry of their talents which had enabled Alec Bedser and Len Hutton to win acclaim. Each of them, shrewd and circumspect in voice and manner and steadfast in outlook, had laboured long to lead England to prosperity.

Alec Bedser would play only one more Test, against South Africa at Manchester in 1955, while Len Hutton withdrew from the captaincy and shortly afterwards announced his retirement. Their unceasing toils in England's cause had ended, but they would never be forgotten.

CHAPTER TEN

Supreme in their Seasons

If Bedser's labours as a bowler could be collected and piled up around him in some visible shape, he would be seen to be standing beside a mountain.

JOHN WOODCOCK

The threads of coincidence were spun to link two bowlers, accounted equal in status in their distinguished eras. Alec Bedser and Maurice Tate travelled down identical paths. They were both denied apprentice years because of two world wars and did not emerge as Test candidates until their late 20s. An allotment of three tours of Australia was the prize of their worth. They each established records – Tate with 38 wickets in the 1924–25 series, Bedser with 39 in England in 1953.

The final stages of their careers again moved closely in parallel. Tate and Bedser, respectively aged 37 and 36, were both ousted by the demands of express speed on their last tours of Australia. Tate was a late choice in Douglas Jardine's team in 1932–33. He was sidelined by the presence of Larwood, Voce, Allen and Bowes. An attack of shingles excluded Bedser from the reckoning in 1954–55. The debilitating illness enforced his withdrawal from four Tests and his position was then usurped by the pairing of Frank Tyson and Brian Statham.

On each occasion the tactics yielded overwhelming victories, the latter the first in Australia since Jardine's conquest. It is said – and clearly with truth since his pre-war seniors, Bowes and Verity, were witnesses on the 'bodyline' tour – that Len Hutton had not forgotten the legend passed down to him by Jardine. The disappointments which beset Tate and Bedser were shared by their devotees; but the results were such as to alleviate any grievance.

There is inevitably a mystique which looms over a division of merits involving players from different generations. This is nowhere more apparent than in the assessments of Bedser and Tate. Don

126

Bradman, as ever, was present at the kernel of these discussions.

Bradman regarded Alec as the equal of Maurice, who was 33 when he first bowled to the emerging Don in the 1928–29 series. Bradman was 18 years older and, by his monumental standards, a less devastating batsman when he first tussled with Bedser in the 1940s. Alec was then still a learner. His success in breaching the Australian's defences, while still in his formative years, has aroused speculation as to the outcome of their duels if they had stood shoulder to shoulder in maturity.

Writing in 1950, Bradman observed: 'I think all Australian batsmen of the modern generation believe that Bedser is the best medium-pace bowler they have ever met. Had they faced Tate in 1924–25, it is probable they would have found him better still. Anyhow, both were magnificent.' The question that remains is how Tate and Bedser would compare with the third bowler in this imposing trinity. Jack Hobbs (with batting credentials to count) and Bill Bowes both placed S.F. Barnes as unquestionably the finest English bowler in their experience.

Barnes wrought havoc in the leagues and in Minor Counties cricket in his native Staffordshire. Apart from brief excursions with Warwickshire and Lancashire, he rejected the daily round of county cricket as too irksome. But his detours into Test cricket brought him a yield of 189 wickets at an average of 16.43 in 27 matches against Australia and South Africa before the First World War. In the 1911–12 series in Australia, Barnes and Frank Foster, the Warwickshire left-arm fast-medium bowler, shared 66 wickets. Their partnership is still regarded as one of the greatest in England's history.

A succession of Barnes's rivals had cause to endorse the verdict of Sir Pelham Warner. Speaking at a dinner in Barnes's honour at Stoke-on-Trent in 1927, Warner recalled the first time he had batted against the master craftsman in 1903: 'Barnes pitched me one on the leg stump. It came off the wicket like a streak of greased lightning and hit the top of the off wicket.' Warner cited another example of the prowess of Barnes in a Gentlemen v Players match at Lord's: 'He was literally cutting up the pitch with his finger spin and the ball was flashing right across the wicket.'

At the turn of the year in 1912, Barnes took 4 wickets for 3 runs in a spell of 9 overs against Australia at Melbourne. By lunch he had bowled 11 overs, including 9 maidens, and claimed 5 wickets for 6 runs. Victor Trumper was not among Barnes's victims on that occasion. 'I kept him quiet which was as good as bowling many men,' said Barnes. 'You couldn't dictate to Trumper. He played as he liked and not as you liked.' But even Trumper's skills were not always proof against Barnes. Later, during the Australian tour, he did overcome his respected rival.

Charles Macartney, who was batting at the other end, described a ball, delivered at fast-medium, that swerved in the air from leg stump to off and then broke back to hit the leg stump. Macartney said it was the sort of ball a player might see when he was tight.

On the coir matting wickets of South Africa in 1913–14, Barnes was unplayable and performed record feats. He claimed 49 wickets at an average of 10.93 runs each. They included 17 for 159, only bettered by Jim Laker, in the first Test at Johannesburg; and another 14 wickets in the fourth Test at Durban.

Barnes was aged 55 when he opened the bowling for Wales, one of his many affiliations, against the touring West Indians at Llandudno in 1928. Wales were the victors by eight wickets and Barnes took 12 in the match. Trevor Bailey recalls a conversation with the renowned Barbadian opening batsman George Challenor, who scored over 1,500 runs on the 1928 tour, but was among the routed opponents that day. His testimony, persuasively in favour of a man more than 25 years his senior, was that Barnes was the greatest bowler the world had ever seen.

Douglas Jardine was another fascinated onlooker when he captained Barnes in a press match in 1938. The veteran, then aged 65, took 7 wickets for 35 runs. Jardine commented: 'Barnes was now slow-medium, but his action was still packed with spring and rhythm and he moved the ball a little one way and a little the other way.' From his position in the slips, Jardine could not detect any difference in the finger movements which produced the variations. 'We could imagine what a terror he must have been making the ball do its work at fast-medium.'

Alec Bedser would later bowl his leg-breaks in a similar style to the incomparable Barnes. His delivery was then termed a leg-cutter, because it was maintained that genuine spin was imparted only by slow bowlers. 'Those subscribing to that belief,' reflected one writer, 'should have faced Barnes, Macaulay, McDonald and others. Only the very fast could afford not to use spin on pitches shorn of every trace of greenery.'

The issue of spin, as delivered in the fast-medium style, is also addressed by Peter Richardson, the former Worcestershire, Kent and England batsman. He remembers a noise like the buzz of a wasp which snapped Bedser's opponents to urgent attention. One instance of this devilry occurred in a match against Worcestershire at The Oval. 'This was a spinner's wicket,' recalls Richardson. 'In normal circumstances Alec would not have bowled at all. It was his brilliance bowling his leg-cutters which made him as difficult to play as Lock and Laker.'

Reg Hayter referred to a remarkable resemblance in the bowling of Alec Bedser and Maurice Tate: 'Both these burly men could have been used as text-book models for their particular style of bowling.' Hayter described the 'moderate but lively approach, the gradual acceleration finishing with an explosive burst of energy'. There was, he said, the perfect sideways action, high arm and unchecked follow-through. Every feature of the best in bowling was present.

The Tate gates at the sea end at Hove happily commemorate one of Sussex's favourite sporting sons. They are perfectly positioned, for it is from them that the mists curl seductively in from the shores beyond to hasten the spring in the stride of bowlers. Tate, in one of his typically confidential asides, would often turn to his captain, Arthur Gilligan, and say: 'See that green patch, skipper? That means the tide's coming in.'

The metamorphosis of Tate as a bowler occurred after ten years with only modest success as an off-spinner. The reversion to the fast-medium style transformed him almost overnight into England's leading bowler. In ten months between his Test début in June 1924 and March 1925, Tate took 65 wickets in two series against South Africa and Australia.

His newly found hostility was released in tandem for Sussex and England with Arthur Gilligan, who was then regarded as the fastest amateur bowler in the country. In all matches in 1923, Gilligan and Tate shared 382 wickets. It is extremely doubtful whether any other pair of fast bowlers from the same county can claim such a record in one season. It did seem that the partnership was destined to prosper and become one of the deadliest in cricket history. At Birmingham, in 1924, Gilligan and Tate bowled out South Africa for 30 (11 of them extras) in 48 minutes. The innings lasted for only 75 balls. It was the lowest total ever made in a Test match in England. In 6 overs Tate took 4 wickets for 12 runs. Gilligan's performance in the same innings was the most memorable of his career. He returned figures of 6 wickets for 7 runs in 6.3 overs.

The Springboks were beaten by an innings and Gilligan took 5 more wickets for a match record of 11 for 90. The rest of the England attack – Frank Woolley, Percy Fender, Cecil Parkin and Roy Kilner – were reduced to the roles of onlookers. They did not take a wicket as the Sussex pair shared 19 (and the 20th was a run-out).

In the thrilling weeks before a sickening blow on the heart effectively ended Arthur's career as a fast bowler, Tate and Gilligan blazed an all-conquering trail. In his own reminiscences, Gilligan described how he was incapacitated as a bowler during the match between the Gentlemen and Players at The Oval: 'It was in the first innings and I had made 34, when a good length ball from Dick Pearson got up sharply from the pitch and struck me right on the heart. I went down like a stone and was out for a couple of minutes. I continued my innings, but hit the next ball straight into the hands of Jack Hobbs at cover.'

Gilligan scored 112 before lunch in the Gentlemen's second innings on the following day. 'I helped Michael Falcon to add 134 for the last wicket. I was a stupid fellow. That was probably the worst thing I ever did.' Tate, who was in the Players' team in that fateful game, later paid tribute to Gilligan's courage, but concluded that Arthur should have withdrawn from the match after the injury. 'If he had not made that historic century, he could have had an even greater career than he did.'

Contemporaries between the wars remembered the infectious spirit of Maurice Tate – the final swing of the arm, said one, could be likened to the 'merry plunge of a porpoise as it goes over the top'. Bill Bowes recalled how Tate, in his follow-through, would graze his left knuckles on the ground.

John Langridge, as an alert eye-witness at first slip, was fervent in his praise. 'We could rely on Maurice to take five or more wickets, sometimes before lunch,' he said. 'There was no one better of his type. A superb delivery close to the stumps, no wavering off line, foot in the blockhole and a devastating swing. The ball pitching on leg would hit the off stump as the batsman shaped to play to the on.'

John Arlott was another admirer, writing:

> Bowling into the wind on a heavy seaside morning, Tate would make the ball dart and move in the air as if bewitched. The ball would whip into Tich Cornford's gloves with a villainous smack and the little man would hollow his belly and was lifted to, or off, his toes, as the ball carried his heavy-gloved hands back into him.

Pelham Warner had watched, with keen interest, the burgeoning promise of Alec Bedser in wartime cricket at Lord's. He had forecast then that Bedser's qualities would match those of Tate. In a letter to Alec in the 1950s, he offered his congratulations and said that Bedser was superior to the Sussex man. It was, even if regarded as a courtesy to a modern exponent, a fine tribute from a veteran observer. Elsewhere, the opinion was expressed that these two great bowlers did not have much in common, except in their pace and the course of their careers.

E.M. Wellings thought Tate was an instinctive bowler: 'He has confessed that, whereas he was aware of how he swung the new ball, his away movement off the pitch with the older ball just seemed to happen. If he did not know what was going to happen, the batsman had no chance of being forewarned.'

For another writer, Raymond Robertson-Glasgow, it was Tate who beckoned as the 'more natural genius', while Bedser maintained the 'greater invention and variety.' Ian Peebles tellingly alluded to the respect afforded to Bedser by his major batting rivals:

> They will inform you that although you might manoeuvre Bedser on to the defensive you could not get him down. At any moment he might produce the ball that dipped in flight and came the other way on pitching, a combination against which no human bat is certain proof.

Peebles said that one of the most remarkable aspects of this delivery was that, in certain conditions, Alec could produce it seemingly at will. 'Like Barnes, he gained his effect through conscious manipulation by somewhat the same, but not completely similar, methods to the old master.'

The contrast in styles of Bedser and Tate was also stressed by Peebles. Tate did have the facility, an art not to be underestimated, of pitching on middle and leg and dispatching the off stump with fine fury. This was achieved by the purely natural use of the seam. Peebles added:

> Because of this, although I never saw anyone quite like Tate on a green wicket, Bedser was an infinitely more flexible and adaptable performer.
>
> On a wicket which, through dust or moisture, gave the ball any grip Alec was, in his heyday, the most economical and destructive bowler in the world. His height and action gave the batsman the complication of steep lift, in addition to sharp turn from the leg, allied to unerring accuracy.

Bedser's physical advantages were also outlined by his Surrey captain, Peter May. 'Alec is able to wrap a vast hand round the ball, reducing it seemingly to golf ball dimensions,' he noted. 'Then, with fingers almost as big as bananas – outsize yet sensitive fingers – he flicks across the seam, "cutting" the ball so that when it grips the turf it will veer sharply.' May also recalled another subterfuge which was quite as deadly as the leg-cutter. 'Alec had the ability to go through the motions of sending down this type of ball but making it go straight on.' The unwary batsman expected the cutter and was foxed into playing down the wrong line. The ball would then nip between bat and pad and bowl him.

Doug Insole, the former Essex captain and a prolific scorer in county cricket, was once regaled with Bedser's repertoire of bowling tricks. In one particularly venomous over, Insole played and missed at five balls and edged the sixth through the slips for four. He was probably fortunate to manage the snick, but it brought forth an acid response from Alec: 'I always said you were the luckiest batsman in first-class cricket – and now I've bloody well proved it.'

Insole, like other contemporaries, places Bedser's leg-cutter in the same tormenting category as the googly in that it creates an indecision on the way to play it. His penchant for on-side strokes was an irritant to Alec. It did, though, enable him to enjoy, however briefly, interludes of prosperity against his Surrey rival. 'I remember once hitting him through mid-wicket,' says Insole. Eric Bedser, standing at mid-off, was just as angry as his brother at the audacious gesture. Eric called out disapprovingly, 'He's hitting you through there again.' Alec paraded a glare of disdain. There was a great heave of his formidable shoulders. 'If he does it again,' he replied, 'he's out.'

Bedser was always meanly on guard against the concession of runs. The temper of his cricket did not relax even among the festival frivolities at Scarborough. He would certainly have shared the indignation of one Yorkshire bowler, Johnny Wardle, who strongly objected to his average being torn to shreds on September days. He contended that, if fun was to be had, it should be at the expense of batters bowling – and not him.

Doug Insole remembered one occasion when he captained an MCC team, with Alec Bedser in his ranks, against Yorkshire at Scarborough. Ted Lester, a local townsman, had registered a duck in the first innings. 'Give the lad one to get off the mark,' said Insole to Bedser at the start of Yorkshire's second innings. Alec grumbled but acceded to the request. He sent down a ball just short of a length. Lester, a fierce hitter, smote it mightily, just failing to clear the ropes for six at the Trafalgar Square end. Alec looked disbelievingly at his captain. 'Is that your idea of giving this bugger one off the mark?' he enquired.

The episode, however trivial, reflected Alec's rugged common sense which saw little value in betraying his instincts as a bowler. Pretence was anathema to him. Ian Peebles recalled a somewhat off-beat, but extraordinarily apt, wit — usually benevolent, but not without edge should the occasion warrant it.

Effusive demonstrations were ridiculed by Bedser. He was never a man to engage in rhapsodical flights. The response to one spectacular catch by Godfrey Evans off his bowling at Leeds in 1952 was entirely in character. Vjay Hazare was the victim, athletically taken off the bottom edge of the bat. Evans had reason to be jubilant that his agility had enabled him to accept an extremely difficult chance on such a slow-paced wicket. Alec was a little uncharitable, perhaps, in suppressing the enthusiasm: on the wicket provided, he said, it was impossible for him to get the ball high enough to hit the top edge.

❧ ❧ ❧

Alec Bedser was true to his goal as a bowler; but it is salutary to remember that but for those taxing endeavours he could well have entered the lists as an all-rounder. Batting was perforce a secondary exercise, but he was stoutly resistant in this mode. He displayed courage against pace and drove freely with power off the back foot. However the division of responsibilities at The Oval meant that Eric gained greater renown as a batsman. As Jim Swanton observed, the elder twin was 'a rather more flexible version of that of his distinguished brother which has often served England so well'.

A.A. Thomson neatly renderd his appreciation in a pleasing paradox: 'As Eric was somewhat the better bat and Alec a more than somewhat better bowler, it used to make a straightforward little joke to assert that, if Alec bowled well for England, that was Alec, but if Alec batted splendidly for England, as he did at Leeds in 1948, handsome off-drives and all, then obviously it must be Eric.' Thomson added: 'But you had to keep a straight face telling that one. No doubt the twins delighted in innocent deceptions, but never one as innocent as that.'

Alec was not misleading anyone against the Australians in 1948. His opponents remembered his driving and thought he was one of England's best batsmen. At Trent Bridge, in alliance with Jim Laker, who was top scorer with 63 in the England first innings, Alec helped his Surrey partner to more than double the score.

Even more commendable was his resistance at Manchester. While Denis Compton, bearing stitches in a head wound, personified heroism with an undefeated 145, Bedser was a solid and imperturbable comrade. They shared an eighth-wicket stand of 121 in two and a half hours. 'On

133

a day so marrow chilling that the bowlers had to divest themselves of two sweaters apiece,' reported Denzil Batchelor, 'Bedser began the morning's play by facing Lindwall and Johnston armed with the new ball. He confronted those engines of war with disciplined resolution.'

The partnership was concluded by a foolish run-out, when Bedser had made 37 and the England total had risen to 337. 'There seemed no end to this bravely blossoming alliance,' commented Batchelor. 'It suddenly committed suicide in a wantonly nonchalant manner. A half-hit to the covers by Compton was fumbled and a run, at first abandoned, was at last attempted. Loxton's throw was neatly gathered and the wicket broken with Bedser still pressing to gain the crease.'

Alec was characteristically downbeat, or just plainly mischievous, when asked to convey the secret of playing the feared Lindwall at his best. He responded by saying that he did not waste time moving his feet. Bedser and Lindwall vied with each other as batsmen at Leeds. For Alec, there was the distinction of a nightwatchman exceeding expectations and fulfilling the wildest hopes.

Lindwall also played a key role, scoring 77 at a crucial juncture. His defiance, broadly expressed in a flurry of hitting, enabled Australia to restrict England's lead to 38 runs on the first innings. Australia were handsome if unexpected victors at Headingley. But, as Lindwall said, his innings helped to turn the game: 'We would have had no chance if I'd got out. It made all the difference.'

Raymond Robertson-Glasgow described the protracted batting vigil of Alec Bedser as the day's truly romantic story. Having been sent in as nightwatchman on the Thursday evening, Bedser carried out a day shift as well. 'But we must not squeeze the truth just to enjoy the paradox,' stressed Robertson-Glasgow, 'for Bedser is so nearly an all-rounder when permitted.'

Alec shared a third-wicket stand of 155 with Bill Edrich and was not dismissed until 3.10 on Friday afternoon. His innings of 79 included eight fours and two sixes. One observer, watching the mounting frustration of the Australians, reported that 'the batsmen stayed in comfort and dignity, offering no suggestion that this was an alliance between numbers 3 and 10'.

At lunch, the total was 360. In the afternoon the pair moved on serenely until Edrich, hooking Morris for 4, hoisted his 100 and 400 for England. This was the climax of the stand – but not quite its end, for not until the score had reached 423 did Bedser slightly mistime his drive, offering Johnson a hard return catch. Jack Fingleton wrote:

with the Duke of Norfolk, his managerial ass
1962–63 tour of Australia.

E: Checking form as the Duke's special guests

New and old friends: Trevor Bailey, as a Dulwich schoolboy, (*left*) flanked by the twins at Chichester in 1941. (Trevor Bailey)

A happy reunion (*below*) with Bailey (left) and another former England colleague, Godfrey Evans, at the Cricketers Club of London in April 1998. (Chris Hogg)

On camera with Denis Compton,
Len Hutton taking the photograph.
(Surrey CCC)

On camera again, with a
young friend at home.

Hutton as England captain en route for Australia in 1954. Behind
him are (left to right) Colin Cowdrey, team masseur
Harold Dalton and Alec Bedser. (Alan Hill)

TOP AND ABOVE: Meetings with Her Majesty: Alec, introduced by Surrey captain Stuart Surridge, is presented to the Queen during the match against South Africa in 1955 (*top*); and pictured at the investiture of his knighthood at Buckingham Palace in 1997 (*above*).

Bedser came in to keep watch overnight, but so brilliantly and
confidently was he batting at one time that he seemed certain to
become a centurion. I have never seen a man so embarrassed as
Bedser was when he returned to the pavilion. He was positively
blushing at being acclaimed a hero.

David Sheppard, one of the young guard on the tour of Australia in
1950–51, provides an amusing postscript to Bedser's batting command at
Headingley. With the impudence of youth, Sheppard cheekily asked his
senior, 'Why don't you practise your batting, Alec? You could make a
great many runs if you really tried.' Bedser replied: 'Oh, I have to do all
the bowling. I can't do all the batting as well!'

South Africa, the setting for Bedser's second post-war tour in 1948–49,
provided another summons for his batting nerve. Alec was paired with
Cliff Gladwin, the Derbyshire bowler, in the victory by two wickets in
the first Test at Durban. It was sealed by a leg-bye in which, as one writer
reported, the two batsmen ran 'as if their shirts were on fire'.

England were set a target of 128 to win in two and a quarter hours.
They lost 6 wickets for 70 before Compton and Jenkins came together to
add 44 and check the menacing speed of the 19-year-old Cuan McCarthy.
McCarthy, on his Test début, took six wickets and excitingly strove to
arrest the pursuit of runs. He looked likely to propel South Africa to
victory. In the closing stages, a tense battle was waged. The encircling
neon lamps shone brightly in the shops surrounding the ground. Inside,
the cricketers, soaked by rain, moved like shadows in the gloom. At the
last, all emotion was drained and the only thought was that this was a
game no one should lose.

Eight runs were required and the hands of the pavilion clock stood at
one minute to six when Tuckett began the final over. The first ball hit
Bedser's pad and the batsmen ran one. Gladwin, striking it on the rise,
pulled the next one for four. It went whistling over the head of Eric
Rowan, the mid-wicket fieldsman, to smack against the pickets in front
of the pavilion.

'There was all Derbyshire and pitheads and the village green in this
glorious cow shot,' enthused Jim Swanton. Rowan misjudged the dipping
flight of the ball. He stepped eagerly forward when he should have gone
back and the ball soared a couple of feet out of reach. A leg-bye off the
third ball yielded another run but the score advanced by only one off the
next four balls.

Alec Bedser declares that bad captaincy delivered the match to

England. 'Wade, the South African wicket-keeper, stood back, and he was the nearest fielder. There were runs to be had before they woke up and realised what was happening.' The crucial boundary – struck by Gladwin – occurred, says Alec, because the erring Rowan was 12 to 15 yards in when he should have been stationed on the boundary. Cool heads would have scuttled England's cause, but thoughts can become scrambled in moments of crisis. The magnet of cricket, the hair's breadth between success and failure, is revealed at such times.

'Whatever happens, we are going to run,' Bedser told his partner before Tuckett ran in to send down the last ball. It rebounded from Gladwin's leg to drop into the blockhole. 'I'd made up my mind to put my body in the way of the ball,' said Gladwin in his version of the scampered winning leg-bye. 'It struck me on the thigh and away we galloped.'

'COMETH THE HOUR, COMETH THE MEN', was the headline which greeted the famous victory at Durban. Yet the umpires were wrong to allow the run to count. It demonstrated the illogicality of the leg-bye as a batting aid. Strictly according to the rules, the match should have ended in a tie. Law 30 read: 'If the striker wilfully deflects the ball with any part of his person, no runs are scored and the batsmen may not change ends.'

Fred Root, the Derbyshire star of other days, said that if he had been operating as an umpire he would have declared the run void. In the high excitement at Durban, the umpires did contravene; but they obeyed the spirit of the game.

❧ ❧ ❧

John Woodcock referred to Alec Bedser as 'loyal, kind and incorruptible'. He portrayed the tale of a cricketing giant in the following words: 'If his labours as a bowler could be collected and piled up around him in some visible shape, he would be seen to be standing beside a mountain.'

The gargantuan labours yielded 1,924 wickets, including 236 at under 25 runs each in 51 Tests. Put even more succinctly, he played in 485 matches and bowled 106,192 deliveries. Alec especially cherishes his haul of 104 wickets, an average of almost 5 wickets per match, in 21 Tests against Australia. 'The talk today is all about strike bowlers. What about me? My idea of a strike bowler is someone who gets batsmen out.'

Bedser was only the second bowler since before the First World War to pass the century milestone against Australia. Those who achieved this target before 1914 were Yorkshire's Bobby Peel (102 in 20 Tests at the best average of 16.81) and S.F. Barnes, with 106 in 20 Tests. Wilfred Rhodes took a sabbatical from bowling during his reign as England's opening batsman. He took 97 wickets in 34 Tests before the war and then swung his bowling arm again to register a tally of 109 in 41 Tests. Another 25 years would elapse after Bedser's achievement before Derek Underwood added his name to this elite of bowling centurions against Australia.

'Alec was unique. Goodness knows what would have happened to English cricket if he hadn't been there at the time,' reflects Bob Appleyard. The testimony of a stern Yorkshire rival to an enduring warrior is given substance by astonishing figures. In Bedser's peak years from 1950 to 1953 he bowled 6,293 balls at approximately 2 runs an over, and took 121 wickets (average: 18.16) in 21 Tests. In his record season of 1953, Alec took 6 wickets against Australia at Leeds to overtake Clarrie Grimmett's world record of 216 wickets.

Alec Bedser, as can be seen, offered irrefutable evidence that 'the best practice for bowling is bowling'. What is more, he rarely broke down, which argues powers of resilience at variance with the moderns, who are constantly subject to injuries despite – or because of – the intensity of today's fitness regimes.

Bob Appleyard also stresses the need for consistent spells of bowling as an aid to fitness. All Bedser's overs were bowled from an unvarying run-up of ten paces and in a manner to preserve maximum efficiency. It was estimated that they lasted two and a half minutes each. Alec, says Appleyard, 'was so grooved in his action, which was rhythmical and economical and lessened the strain, that he was able to continue for long periods'.

The comparison with today's bowlers is strengthened by other sets of figures. Alec bowled 1,332 overs for his 162 wickets in 1953. Before the first Test at Nottingham in June, he bowled 400 overs in taking 62 wickets. Other times, other manners; but even making a charitable case for current England bowlers – resting, not always wisely, between international duties – there is a sharp discrepancy in the amount of work required of them.

Trevor Bailey, in a recent assessment, placed Derek Shackleton and Tom Cartwright, both very accurate, if at a slower pace, as comparable to Bedser. Fazal Mahmood, who learned his trade on the matting wickets of the sub-continent, is given the rating as the best exponent of the leg-cutter after Bedser. In the wet season of 1954, Fazal was the triumphant bowler who sprang the surprise, admittedly against suicidal batting, in Pakistan's first Test victory at The Oval.

In the fast-medium style, Bailey also advanced the credentials of Ian Botham – in Test but not county matches – and Terry Alderman. On two tours of England, recalls Bailey, the Australian successfully proved the value of bowling straight. Alderman possessed a splendidly concealed delivery that came straight on, and lbw dismissals to him were frequent (19 out of 42 Test wickets in 1981). Bailey adds, 'Alderman showed that it is possible to take a large number of wickets in Test cricket without being genuinely quick.'

Doug Insole does cite the benefits of uncovered wickets – sadly denied to the moderns – which accrued to Bedser, although his record overseas was proof that he was not disadvantaged in other conditions. Alec, like Maurice Tate, depended hugely on the close-up support of his wicket-keepers, Arthur McIntyre and Godfrey Evans. The hands of Herbert Strudwick, Tate's England ally, bore savage evidence of his work over many summers. Strudwick, as the later Surrey scorer, paraded fingers shaped at odd angles – as one writer said, like the 'distress signals of a semaphore'.

In his early days with Surrey, before his rule was assured, Strudwick continued to play despite breaking the middle finger of his right hand. He rigged a metal plate between the first and third fingers to isolate the middle one. He must have been in constant agony, for the protection would not have prevented jarring. Strudwick did not permit any challenge from his rivals. He kept his place while the break was healing.

Doug Insole, developing the wicket-keeping theme, emphasises that Godfrey Evans was in the same situation with Kent as Arthur McIntyre was with Surrey. It was commonplace then for wicket-keepers to stand up to fast-medium bowling until it was decreed that certainty of catches was paramount. Standing back, as was said, would be like a warder exercising remote control. Doug Wright was considerably quicker than most bowlers of his type. His often eccentric leg-spin was propelled at brisk medium-pace and required the utmost vigilance from Evans.

McIntyre, in his turn, was equally resourceful keeping to Alec Bedser. In this instance, Alec's accuracy was the key element. 'They say that the hardest job in cricket is keeping to an off-spinner on a turning wicket,' comments Peter Richardson. 'Well, imagine what it was like keeping to Alec at his pace in the same circumstances.'

Over the years, Arthur Morris maintained that if there were any easy runs to be gained from Bedser, it was advisable to gather them early in his spell. By the third over Alec was in the groove, dropping the ball just short of a driveable length, but far enough up to make the back stroke a matter of quick decision and quicker action. Attention soon had to be paid to the ever-present threat of the leg-cutter. David Sheppard remembers how it would stop and lift as well as turn, so that the ball became almost unplayable: 'It became one of the stock sayings of many cricketers of our era, when we saw a wet wicket, or a rough village wicket – "Alec would bowl well on this."'

In the beginning, Bedser's major weapon was his stock in-swinger. As he moved into his peak years he became, in effect, two different bowlers. There was the accuracy and control and the ability to swing the ball late into the batsman. The leg-cutter, by contrast, was a direct result of the experiment of holding the ball across the seam to stop it swinging. This magnificent ball did, says Trevor Bailey, give Bedser the ascendancy over Maurice Tate. Only Sydney Barnes was his superior in propitious conditions. 'The reason why it was so devastating stemmed from the size and strength of Alec's fingers,' explains Bailey. 'The tips of my fingers, quite apart from being more delicate, only just reached the first knuckle of his, which meant that he could spin his leg-cutter with the knowledge that on a wet or dusty pitch it would virtually always turn sharply.'

Defeatism was not a state of mind which ever affected Peter Richardson and Trevor Bailey in their batting ventures. Yet both remember their pride in earning precious runs against a great bowler. Staying at the wicket for two to three hours against Alec Bedser constituted an achievement beyond the norm. Bailey still winces at the memory of his tussles: 'The most significant feature was that Alec was responsible for bruising the inside of my right hand. He just kept on hitting the bat. Alec jarred my hand more than any other bowler I faced.'

CHAPTER ELEVEN

An Inseparable Brotherhood

The joy that Eric has got from Alec's success is so blatant. This is one of the nicest things about them as brothers.

PETER RICHARDSON

Two bright-eyed children, sunny in their innocence, gaze inquiringly at the camera, as if someone has disturbed a private playtime. It is a charming study of two companions and already the signs are that a rare and precious partnership will evolve between the sturdy twins, Alec and Eric Bedser. It has, as they now say in old age, given them contentment and an in-built insurance against loneliness. The brothers are secure in their togetherness: 'We don't enjoy things so much unless we're sharing them.'

The mysteries of identical twinship have exercised expert minds throughout the ages. This remarkable phenomenon is explored in literary and dramatic legends. Tales of mistaken identity were a favourite topic of Greek playwrights over 2,000 years ago. The engrossing riddle also appealed to Shakespeare, who was reputedly the father of a boy–girl twin pair. His play *Comedy of Errors* involves a mix-up of two sets of identical twins, one pair of noble birth and the other their servants. He also deployed a variation on the theme in twinning a brother–sister combination in *Twelfth Night*.

One writer opined: 'It is exhilarating to be with another individual who is uniquely able to understand you, who seems to anticipate your thoughts before you form them.' Another maintained that such an alliance should not be lightly discarded. 'In a world where there is increasing personal isolation, it may be good to know that there is always someone with whom one is closely linked in thoughts, experiences and mutual concern.'

It is almost narcissistic, observed one commentator, to be able to stand aside and look at your almost-self, and to talk to someone who is inside the same physical package. One small boy, it is related, would exclaim to his twin, 'Stand over there a minute – I want to see what I look like!'

'Our absolute and complete affinity is hard to explain,' says Alec, of his relationship with Eric. 'But it is true and very real to us – so much so that as long as we can remember we have never been happy apart.' The lessons of serene co-existence were discovered in their infancy. The strength of the union was not ignored by their mother. She was quick to reject the entreaties of neighbours and friends at Woking that Alec and Eric should be separated and allowed to go their different ways.

Florence Bedser was aware of the potential harm – and the mental anguish afflicting other twins – that could ensue from this action. 'Mother said, "If they want to be together, that is how it must be. We must let nature take its course,"' remember the Bedsers. She also took what, the brothers say, was the easiest and most economical course of dressing her boys alike during their childhood. She gave her considered verdict: 'Why should they not enjoy their twinship?'

It did, however, tend to accentuate the confusion of identification when, in later years, Alec and Eric painstakingly continued the habit. Their measurements were also identical, so it became the routine for one or other of them to visit the tailor and then order two sets of clothes. One contemporary, Billy Griffith, echoed the prevailing bewilderment when he said, 'I never cease to wonder at the ease with which Alec and Eric assume each other's identity or when – if they are separated overnight – the twins appear clad in exactly the same clothes.'

There were times when they were divided by vast distances, but still managed to extract the same attire from their respective wardrobes. Bob Appleyard eavesdropped on one episode. Peter May, in company with Alec and Appleyard, issued the challenge one morning in Australia. Eric was on a trip, visiting friends about 200 miles away up country. 'We'll ask Eric what he is wearing,' remarked the knowing Peter to his companions. A quick telephone call confirmed that both Bedsers were dressed in the same outfits.

Trevor Bailey cites another example of the unerring double-act. 'When I travelled back with Alec after a Test match in Leeds, Eric was there to meet us in London. He was dressed without variation, even to the extent of a similar pair of cufflinks.'

Ron Archer, a former Australian cricket rival and friend, follows the general trend in being better able to recognise the Bedsers when they are together: 'It is difficult if you haven't seen them for some time, perhaps as long as a year in my case.' On his business trips to England, Archer would often arrange to meet Alec and Eric at the East India Club in London. Then he would be confronted with the familiar dilemma. 'One of them would greet you at the door. He would say, "My brother" – never Alec or Eric – "is parking the car."' Archer adds, 'They do enjoy putting you to the test.'

One of the earliest instances of mistaken identity occurred during a match at Woking. As 15-year-olds, Alec and Eric were relatively unknown. Eric was accused of trying to bat twice when Alec walked to the crease. The umpire said, 'You've already been in.' Eric had to emerge from the pavilion to 'show himself' and convince the official that he was one of a pair. Afterwards, an alert local journalist complemented his income by sending the story to the national papers. 'We were so scared by the subsequent notoriety,' recalls Alec, 'that we stayed at home until the publicity had died down.' It probably served as a lesson, since from then on they always firmly resisted the temptation to trick anybody, especially during a first-class match.

The Bedsers, as was said of other identical twins, have gone through their lives, keeping time like two precise watches. They share expenditure and nothing is questioned. Birthday cards or presents are never exchanged. It would be pointless cluttering up their home with the same gifts. Their apparent clairvoyance has been manifested on many occasions. It does enable them to carry out practical tasks jointly. One can start a letter and the other can finish it without their correspondent being aware of the distinction.

Conversations, too, can proceed in tandem. It was not uncommon on promenades around The Oval for interrupted talks with Surrey members and other friends to be continued by either Alec or Eric at another point on the ground. It mattered not a jot since the interlocutor would be unaware, in any case, that he was speaking to a different twin.

The Bedsers are infallibly linked by a kind of telepathy. They do, however, dismiss any hint of collusion in setting up puzzling situations. 'You must have some fun being so alike, but sometimes it must be embarrassing' – thus went a question once addressed to Eric. 'Oh no,' he replied, 'it's the other people who get embarrassed.' Eric insists: 'When people mistook us, it was not through our instigation. They just got muddled.'

Few people other than those with whom they were daily linked in their cricketing years at The Oval could identify the Bedsers with certainty. Peter May, their Surrey captain, recalled that he had lived in their company for several months before being able to voice with confidence,

'That's Alec' or 'That's Eric'. Even then, it was quite possible to trip into error, especially if they happened to be apart.

J.J. Warr, the Cambridge and Middlesex bowler, has testified to the accord of the Bedsers and the parallel thinking which exists between them. He recalled bowling to Eric at Lord's in the days of uncovered wickets. 'It had rained and the bounce was unpredictable.' One short-pitched delivery from Warr reared past Eric's bat and struck him on the cap 'roughly in the middle of the Prince of Wales feathers.' Warr, in some concern, dashed down the pitch to apologise to his Surrey rival. Eric was unharmed and simply said, 'I should have hit the bloody thing.'

Alec, meanwhile, had appeared on the visitors' balcony to check that his brother had emerged unscathed. Warr was curious to know how Alec had reacted to the incident. He made enquiries at lunch. 'I thought he might have said something derogatory about the bowler.' He could not have been further from the truth. Word for word, in complete unison with his twin 150 yards away, Alec had remarked: 'He should have hit the bloody thing.'

Trevor Bailey presents another example of the Bedsers' affinity. The match was between Surrey and Yorkshire at The Oval. Tony Lock had just taken a spectacular catch of the brand which forged his renown as a close fieldsman. Alec turned to the not-out batsman, Norman Yardley, and confided: 'He's a good catcher in the gully, he is.' From third man, up strolled Eric to dispense his wisdom. 'He used exactly the identical words with precisely the same inflection,' adds Bailey.

Peter Loader, a former Surrey and England colleague, maintains that the regularity of incidents demolishes any suspicion that they are fixed. At the close of each championship it was the custom to organise outings to a West End show for Surrey players and their wives and girlfriends. One year, in a dressing-room discussion, Alec nominated a musical which drastically departed from those in the hit category and then in vogue. Eric was out of the room when the idea was mooted. When he returned, he was asked for his choice and unhesitatingly concurred with Alec's preference.

Visiting England on another occasion, Loader, who is now resident in Perth, arranged tickets at The Oval for fellow members at his local golf club in Australia. His guests had not previously met the Bedsers. They were thrilled to join in talks with Alec in the Long Room. Beers were ordered and Alec was then called away. The Perth visitors were still jingling the change in their pockets when Eric arrived to meet the assembly. 'Aren't you going to buy me a drink?' he asked. Bewilderment reigned until Loader explained that they were now in the company of a different twin.

Alec's humour, said A.A. Thomson, was so dry it made you thirsty. Thomson remembered the Bedsers giving a running commentary on a film of their travels. 'They talked in alternate dollops of dialogue and the effect was wonderful – like a couple of Greek choruses. The discourse, spoken with straight faces, was better than the film, and the film was good.'

Bizarre and freakish are the tales of connecting weight losses occurring while Alec and Eric were occupied in separate activities. The brothers have always maintained the same weight within a pound or two over their normal 15 stone. Doug Insole provides an instance of the physical toll, affecting both brothers. It occurred on a sultry day, during a match between the Gentlemen and Players at Lord's.

Eric was due to meet his brother at the ground before they jointly travelled on to the next Surrey game. 'Alec had bowled a considerable number of overs that afternoon,' recalls Insole. He confidently predicted that Eric would be several pounds heavier than Alec at this juncture. Alec was adamant that this would prove to be a false prophecy. So, on Eric's arrival at Lord's, the weight comparison came under inspection. Each of the brothers, in turn, sat on the old-fashioned weighing machine inside the doors of the tennis court. 'They were absolutely identical in weight,' says Insole. 'It was quite amazing.'

The course of mistaken identity has led to many anecdotes, none better than when they are actually true, as in the one about a bemused Sydney barber. Alex Bannister said he would have loved to witness the blank astonishment when Alec appeared in the salon, ten minutes after Eric had had his hair cut. Alec, having been assured by his brother of the efficiency of the barber, entered the shop to a stunned silence.

At length the barber said, 'Jesus, mate, I've just cut your bloody hair. It doesn't take long for it to grow.'

'No,' said Alec, not yielding his identity. 'It's your hair oil – pretty strong stuff. I'll lay off it this time.'

Even Alec and Eric, accustomed as they are to the unusual tempo of their lives, were taken aback by one remarkable coincidence. It was stranger than fiction. Packages of 15 one-pound premium bonds were awarded to them when Surrey won the championship for the sixth year in succession in 1957. They had lain in a drawer at their home for 35 years. One day, in the same post, two buff envelopes dropped through their letter box. At first, they thought, with some irritation, that it was just another income tax demand. Each in turn opened his envelope. Both contained a winning cheque for £50. 'It was unbelievable,' comments Alec, 'because our bond numbers were miles apart.' A statistician was asked to calculate the odds against such an occurrence. 'They are virtually incalculable,' said the adviser. 'But let's start at 20 billion to one.'

The twinship of the Bedsers in their cricketing heyday did carry the hazards of adulation. Many admirers – and parents of other identical twins – registered their appreciation by christening their sons with the names of Alec and Eric. On only one occasion, because the mother and father were distant relations, did the Bedsers assent to the use of their names. They also agreed to become godparents to the new arrivals. This occurred during the MCC tour of South Africa in 1948–49.

Alex Bannister accompanied the Bedsers on the drive from Port Elizabeth to East London. They stopped for tea at Kingswilliamtown. An entry in a local paper caught their eyes. It announced the birth of twins to Mr and Mrs Sid Bedser in Kei Road. The christening was arranged for the following Sunday, which was the signal for intense press interest. 'A small army of journalists and photographers descended on a remote community,' recalled Bannister. 'Fittingly, Alec was handed to Alec and Eric to Eric, although so many changes took place during the service that probably only Mum could make a positive identification by the end.'

'The babies were so tiny that we could have held them in the palms of our hands,' remembers Alec. The christening ceremony in the small, corrugated church ended with the organist informing Alec that he had supported Kent all his life and that his happiest memories were of the times when they beat Surrey.

There was a sad sequel to an intriguing story when the South African Alec was killed in a car accident. The Bedsers had last met the boys, by then two strapping young men, when they called on them in London. They were well able to sympathise with the grief which must have assailed the younger Alec's brother.

Peter Richardson, as a cricket contemporary and close friend, does not subscribe to the slightly mocking tone of others, lacking discernment, on the ways and manners of the Bedsers. For him their association has an uncommon grace and harmony: 'The joy that Eric has got from Alec's success is so blatant. This is one of the nicest things about the brothers.'

Differences in features have increased as they moved into the veteran stage. It is now considered that Alec, after thousands of overs of hard bowling, bears the leaner and more rugged countenance. One observer referred to Alec's chin, jutting like a boxer's and expressing a determination which conceded no favours in his cricketing days. On the matter of chins, Eric sports a tell-tale scar. Arthur McIntyre remembers that he was the culprit as a bowler in the Surrey nets. Eric top-edged a ball into his face. He retains the marking of the wound on his chin to this day.

A study in personalities places Eric as the intellectually shrewder twin. He was regarded as the 'figures man' when the brothers embarked on their highly successful business partnership following retirement from first-class cricket. The senior Bedser – 'thoughtful and sympathetic' – possessed a temperament which, Doug Insole believes, enabled Eric to transcend any limitations as a cricketer and make the most of his abilities.

Even more important, it is his quiet influence which was a major factor in Alec's days of triumph. Peter Loader has also noted that Alec generally adopts a deferential posture towards his brother. 'Eric is the boss and quite likely to correct Alec if he deems it necessary.' Bob Appleyard also takes the view that Eric is the leader. 'It is an arrangement which just happens, and they both accept it.'

There is a strain of self-effacement in the younger Bedser, which is markedly apparent in conversations with him. This is not to say that Alec cannot be forceful in argument. His status and experience in the higher echelons of cricket does mean that he takes a leading role in matters of public relations. Both, it almost goes without saying, are honest, straightforward and without malice in all their dealings. Above all, it is the quality of kindness which peeps out from beneath their gruff exteriors.

Alec and Eric do not flaunt their gestures of kindliness – these are carried out with a discretion which makes them all the more worthy. Ron Archer remembers one December visit to London in the 1970s. There was a little business to transact during his stay in England and his company had paid the air fares. But it was his annual leave and he had to meet all other expenses personally.

Archer, accompanied by his wife, Margaret, booked a room in the swankiest of hotels overlooking Hyde Park. The accommodation was luxurious and adjacent to the lure of the premier West End stores. After two nights he telephoned the Bedsers to advise them of his arrival. They were appalled to learn about the hotel costs – £100 per night – and immediately organised alternative accommodation at only £25 at the Charing Cross Hotel.

Margaret Archer was highly displeased when told about the proposed change of venue. The Bedsers then persuasively countered with an argument to overcome her objections. 'They suggested that I should buy her a pair of Italian shoes each day and said I would still be well in pocket,' remembers Archer. All was forgiven when Alec and Eric made another decisive thrust. Ron and Margaret were informed that further discounted accommodation had been booked for them in Devon, a part of England hitherto unknown to them. 'It was just magnificent,' recalls Archer, 'the weather was perfect and we saw more in three days than we would have done in three weeks in the height of the summer.' The Archers have never forgotten those acts of generosity by the Bedsers.

❧ ❧ ❧

Golf – success in which is assured, according to five-times Open champion Jimmy Braid, if you 'keep your head down and hit the wee ball in the ass' – is a game which has received almost as much attention from the Bedsers as cricket. Alf Gover was among those senior professionals at The Oval for whom Alec and Eric caddied as youngsters, and he has described the twins as 'naturals' at golf. They first practised, as boys, with one rusty club, pitching up to a solitary hole dug out of the heather on Horsell Common. Among their golfing idols was another Open champion, Henry Cotton.

It was only after the Second World War that the Bedsers acquired full sets of clubs to pursue the game in earnest. Alec and Eric are still swinging with precision after 50 years as members of the West Hill Club at Woking. Eric was into his 60s when he recorded a hole-in-one on his home course to win the Johnny Walker international award for the feat.

The Bedsers started with a handicap of 16 and reduced it to 5. The greens are a little more elusive now, compelling a bigger handicap. At 14, though, it demonstrates that the veterans are still no mean challengers on their weekly forays at Woking. One contemporary has referred to their extraordinary fitness as octogenarians. In recent times, he was told that Alec and Eric had played 36 holes on two consecutive days 'and pulled their own trolleys'.

'They play golf far too seriously for me,' says Trevor Bailey. 'There is usually a session on the driving range before they start a round.

❧ ❧ ❧

Unlike many retired celebrity cricketers today who cross the floor into the media, the Bedsers had to draw upon their own resources. The decision to go into business was taken in the mid-1950s when they were still actively engaged and earning as cricketers. From the proceeds of Alec's Surrey benefit, later supplemented by Eric's benefit, they allocated £500 each to establish a typewriter and office equipment company in a small shop at Woking.

Jack Fagan, a golfing friend, with extensive experience in the trade, was their first business associate. 'If we were blessed with sensible parents,' recalls Alec, 'we were also very lucky to link up with Jack.' Fagan supplied the expertise and his wife, Florrie, worked in the shop and attended to the book-keeping. The Bedsers, with the aid of influential contacts in cricket, were the sales team.

'We worked for five years for nothing,' says Alec, 'and never took a penny out of the business while we were still playing cricket.' From 1955 to 1960 they divided their time between cricket and the fledgling business. The hectic round began at seven in the morning and continued until ten when they travelled to The Oval for cricket duties. At the close of play, showered and changed, they put on their business hats again to work in the evening.

By the time of their retirement from cricket, the Bedsers had built up the business sufficiently to grant themselves a salary. A small business at Staines was their next acquisition and it was followed by a transfer to new premises and the takeover of another well-established concern in St Bride Street close to Ludgate Circus in the City of London. The turnover was instantly doubled, increasing to £700,000 by 1962, when the Bedsers went into partnership with the stationer Ronald Straker.

The Straker–Bedser empire extended to 25 shops in London and the Home Counties, with 180 employees on the payroll. It did, as Alec and Eric now admit, severely diminish their control. 'We became minority shareholders in a family business. It was the worst thing you can do, but we didn't know that at the time.' By 1971, when Straker–Bedser was taken over by the office equipment chain Ryman, the turnover had reached £1.75 million. The inexorable march of events led to another swift change of ownership when Montagu Burton, the clothiers, purchased the business from Ryman.

'Despite the changed pattern of our business activities,' remembers Alec, 'no obstacle was ever put in the way of my duties as a Test selector or of any other cricket interests. Eric was always willing to cover for me. Although Ryman and Burtons never demurred when I was away from the office, I never took holidays as such.'

The eventual dissolution of their partnership and surrender of their shareholding was an amicable procedure. The tentacles of amalgamation, together with financial liabilities which they could ill afford, were conclusive factors. 'We were just happy to withdraw without financial loss,' say the Bedsers.

In the hour of need they turned to David Evans, a sports enthusiast and chairman of Breengreen (Holdings) plc, which was an office-cleaning and refuse-disposal company. Evans was a schoolboy soccer international and Aston Villa professional and accomplished enough as a player to score 60 centuries in club cricket. He proved to be a worthy friend, having told Alec and Eric some time earlier that positions as consultants would be available to them, if their association with Burtons failed to prove fruitful. A telephone call to Evans confirmed that his promise held good.

Loyalty of such unwavering kind has never been forgotten by the Bedsers.

⁕ ⁕ ⁕

Ian Peebles referred to the robust and intelligent attitude which Alec and Eric brought to their flourishing business. 'Here, indeed, was a happy fulfilment of the parable of talent.' Quietly and without fuss, the brothers won equal esteem for their charity works in London. It earned each of them the distinctions of the Freedom of the City. It was said, not implausibly, that they would have made a most impressive joint Lord Mayor.

We now salute 'Sir Alec', the knighthood having been conferred in 1997 for his services to cricket. It is an award which he cherishes as the first and only English bowler to receive the honour.

At his side is brother Eric, unfailingly supportive as the consort through an industrious lifetime. 'I owe so much to my Other Half,' says Alec. 'And if it is deemed that I served the game, then cricket is also in his debt.'

CHAPTER TWELVE

Travels with His Grace

His efficiency and devotion to the whole business was quite remarkable. The MCC can never be better served than they were by him.

DUKE OF NORFOLK

The union of the aristocrat and the professional, brought together on the tour of Australia in 1962–63, was forged by equal measures of humility. The report verdict of the Duke of Norfolk, a surprise choice as manager, proclaimed the diligence of Alec Bedser. The congratulations which later emanated from Lord's served to reinforce what was by any account an onerous beginning to his career as an administrator.

Bedser was the first professional to be appointed as assistant manager on an Australian tour. If he was then cast in the role of probationer, his business acumen shone forth. The authority he brought to the task was subsequently confirmed in his record term of 12 seasons as chairman of the Test selectors.

Doug Insole, who preceded Bedser as chairman, has reflected on the attributes which earned commendation. 'Alec was obviously going to be a competent manager because he had all the strands pulled together. He was a good administrator, as he had shown in his own business. All his dealings around the cricket scene were very efficient. He had the background of being a great player and the immense respect of people he had played with and against in England and overseas.'

The consultations were earnest and prolonged at Lord's during the summer of 1962. All the MCC committee members were in agreement that firm diplomacy was the prime requirement of any candidate as manager on the forthcoming tour of Australia. They had, as their objective, the need to mend bridges following the throwing controversy which had blighted the previous tour under the captaincy of Peter May in 1958–59.

England, it could be said, were hoist by their own petard in Australia. Having gone out as firm favourites to win the series, they were beaten 4–0. At home, as well as abroad, throughout the 1950s, a *laissez-faire* attitude persisted towards bowlers with suspect actions. It was not offset by protestations that the livelihoods of professionals were at stake. Tony Lock was one of those who escaped punishment: hailed as a master of vicious spin, he was, however, widely portrayed as a thrower on the English county circuit. The lingering revulsion at illegal bowling was not lessened by the qualifying verdict of Alan Davidson, one of England's opponents. He maintained that upwards of 20 bowlers – including some respected names – stood guilty of transgressions.

The cries of outrage did not not begin until serious injury threatened, with the arrival of throwers of unbridled speed. Confronting Peter May and his team in Australia were dubious challenges. Throwing was a disfiguring feature in every state. Ian Meckiff, the Victorian left-arm bowler, became the chief target of criticism among the tourists; he was subsequently banned from first-class cricket.

Gordon Rorke, a giant of a man at 6ft 5in., was another member of the fearsome Australian bowling battalion. Tom Graveney recalled an 'absolutely terrifying' experience: 'We just stood there like rabbits against him.' For another England batsman, Arthur Milton, the biggest problem was judging the line, length and pace of the deliveries. The eccentric nature of the bowling, fluctuating so wildly, could not be countered with any certainty.

The managerial considerations in 1962 at first centred on Billy Griffith. A wise and strong administrator, he was due to succeed Ronnie Aird as the MCC Secretary late in that year. Griffith had won the advocacy of Doug Insole as the best prospect as tour manager. But the judgement, in the corridors at Lord's, was that Griffith had a more pressing commitment in his new tenure at home. The decision on the managerial appointment was deferred at one meeting attended by the Duke of Norfolk. He was disinclined to favour Griffith in the circumstances. Afterwards, over drinks, Insole took issue with what he considered to be a misguided opinion. He told the Duke, 'I'm sorry that you don't agree with me about Billy. I think he is your man and should be released for the tour, which is very important from the point of view of Anglo-Australian relations.'

Insole also broached the matter of the captaincy of Ted Dexter and the dangers of personality clashes with a man who could be austere and forbidding. Dexter had led the MCC in India and Pakistan the previous winter. He had his critics as a captain, but no one could deny his adventurous spirit. Yet he had to withstand other claims in a fierce contest for the leadership in Australia. His long-term possibilities as captain were perceived to be in contrast to his major rival, David Sheppard, who was then embarked on a career in the ministry. The friendship between Dexter and the Norfolk family was to prove, in the event, a substantial factor.

It was affirmed when the Duke emphatically declared that he did not envisage any problems with Dexter. 'I can manage him,' said the Duke. 'But you're not going as manager,' replied Insole. The exchange concluded with the counter of the Duke: 'No one has asked me.' The momentum for his appointment now gathered pace; the MCC president-designate, Lord Nugent was informed: 'You may now have a candidate as manager.'

Lord Nugent, thus encouraged, officially invited the Duke to manage the tour. The question which was never resolved is whether he had entertained the job as a long-cherished ambition, or if it was the result of a sudden inspiration. It would seem, as Alec Bedser relates, to have fallen into the latter category. In the evening following the meeting at Lord's, there was a discussion with the Duchess at Arundel Castle. 'Why don't you go?' she said. 'You haven't very much to do over the next few months.'

Ted Dexter has recently intimated that but for his own appointment as captain – and the ease of their relationship – the Duke might not have gone to Australia. The unexpected presence of Bernard Norfolk was, in his view, an inspired selection: 'It was the best piece of public relations that anyone had ever dreamt about. He was a marvellous friend to all of us on that tour.' The ambassadorial qualities of the Duke are also acknowledged by Doug Insole: 'He was an upmarket figure and his appointment as manager gave our tour quite a cachet.'

❧ ❧ ❧

In the beginning, the MCC tourists must have been mystified to have such an august statesman thrust upon them. But any alarm over elitism was quickly dispelled, for the Duke was seen to be as 'shy and impressionable as a boy' in the company of the celebrity cricketers. One of them, David Allen, the Gloucestershire off-spinner, remembers the dry wit and friendliness of the Duke: 'He was a rallying influence, liked by all the players. He was very generous and opened so many doors for us.'

'The Duke was a gentleman and without snobbish pretensions,' says Alec Bedser. 'There was never any social barrier between him and the players, who at first had not known what to expect. The Duke travelled in the same compartments and shared the same dinner tables like any other manager.'

The protocol of respectful address did, though, have to be pursued. 'Your Grace' was soon discarded as too extended for regular usage. The players opted for the easier expression of 'Sir' – only lightened to 'Bernard', as Ted Dexter says, when they were together in the swimming pool.

The prevailing harmony cannot disguise the indisputable fact that over the six months of his assignment, involving up to 16 hours a day, Alec Bedser had to maintain an exhausting timetable. In fact, despite the assumption, back home in England, that the Duke would oversee the financial arrangements of the tour, Alec quickly learned that he would have to shoulder this responsibility.

Each day he rose early to deal with the accounts, arrange hotel bookings and deal with the demands of the players. At the close of play he had to check gate receipts, which were then shared between the Australian and English authorities. The necessary attention given by Alec to all the details of the tour even led to misinformed criticism that he should have devoted more time to the actual cricket – his original brief – and less to other chores.

Crawford White, as a senior cricket correspondent and friend, remembers how Alec, with Eric as his aide, nursed the Duke through his management tour. 'Every step of the way, Alec quietly showed the Duke the ropes and kept the show on the road. It was a classic performance of diplomacy, with the Duke, a good sport, happily taking the plaudits from the adoring Aussie elite – from the racing fraternity as well as cricket's top brass.'

There was confirmation of Bedser's stewardship after the tour. The presentation by Alec of an immaculate set of accounts astonished the staff at Lord's. They had grown accustomed to rewriting documents offered by co-managers or treasurers who had had only this job to occupy them.

'No wonder you were overworked,' said Lavinia, the Duchess of Norfolk, in a letter many years later. 'I could have told you before you left that Bernard had never been known to fill in a stub of a chequebook. Each time he went to London I had to give him money for his rail ticket.' The Earl Marshal of England, exalted for his organisation of the great state occasions, was out of his depth in book-keeping concerns.

His fallibility in financial matters was emphasised soon after the MCC party arrived in Perth. At Alec's invitation, the Duke took charge of a group of 12 players for a two-day fixture at Kalgoorlie, a gold-mining town 375 miles from the West Australian capital. Alec stayed behind to supervise net sessions in Perth. The Duke was given a chequebook and asked to perform the nominal task of paying the hotel bill in Kalgoorlie and to specify the date and amount on the stub. On his return, the chequebook contained just a single scrawled entry: 'Kalgoorlie'. Alec had to contact the hotel to obtain confirmation of the bill and gain a receipt. 'I realised that the Duke had probably not been used to such mundane things, so I thought it prudent not to entrust him with a chequebook again,' he recalls.

At Kalgoorlie, the Duke and his party were accommodated in a faded country hotel. The amenities could charitably be described as rudimentary. The Duke was not fazed by these surroundings. Jim Swanton remembered the communal washroom at Kalgoorlie: 'There were several handbasins but only one mirror, so that only one of us could shave at a time.' The Australian patrons, unaccustomed to such intimate proximity to the Earl Marshal, let alone in his pyjamas, made polite noises. 'After you, Your Grace,' they chorused in unison. Their companion bowed gravely in dissent. 'Not at all,' he replied. 'It's your turn.'

◦~◦ ◦~◦ ◦~◦

Ted Dexter scarcely deserved the luxury of instructive net sessions with the newly retired Alec Bedser in Australia. In all his days with Sussex and England, he was aggressively inclined as a batsman. He was at his most audacious, wielding his bat like a cleaver, against the veteran Bedser on one occasion at Hove: 'Alec was bowling with the new ball up the hill. I set myself to go for the first one he swung in. Bang! – I hit it over square leg and straight into the houses behind the scoreboard.' He relates how Alec shrugged his shoulders and said, 'I came into the game getting stick. It looks as if I'm going to end the same way, so perhaps it's time I finished.'

Alec did not forget that unseemly assault at Hove. Dexter remembers his net tussles with the old craftsman in Australia. In the hours of valuable practice, he was able to examine the qualities which had elevated Bedser to his illustrious state: 'Here was the benchmark for any bowler.' Alec, with formidable precision, might have been bowling in a Test

154

match. His challenge was undiminished in this tutorial for the England captain. 'Alec was as reliable as ever, swinging and seaming the ball.'

In later years, Alec would often remind Dexter of how he had won these practice battles – 'And I was coming up to 50, remember!' Dexter adds, 'Alec likes the last word when it comes to who can bowl and who cannot.'

The guidance of Alec Bedser is also cherished by David Allen, the emerging England off-spinner in the 1962–63 series. 'Alec, as he showed behind the scenes, was a hard worker,' he says. 'If you gave 100 per cent as a cricketer, you got his backing and he then enjoyed your company.' Allen's career just overlapped with that of Bedser. He was a member of the Gloucestershire team which faced Surrey in the last of their seven championship seasons in 1958. The match was at Bristol and Allen shone as a batsman, scoring 47 out of a total of 149. He was ultimately one of Bedser's seven wickets in the innings.

Allen recalls: 'As a young man playing against this great bowler, then on the verge of retirement, I went to hit a delivery on the leg side and struck it straight back at Alec, who took the catch.' This produced an implicit reprimand from Bedser. His response to the dismissal was tantamount to an instruction to his opponent to show better concentration. 'Bloody typical,' said the veteran, in a caustic aside loud enough to be heard by the departing batsman. 'He gets nearly 50 and is still caught off the edge.'

Bedser, away from his Surrey battle station, was a mentor rather than a critic as assistant manager in Australia. Allen, who was expected to be a front-line bowler on the tour, had disappointingly failed to make an impression. Halfway through the series, he took the difficult decision to adjust his bowling approach. The aim was to increase his run-up by two yards in order to achieve a smoother rhythm: 'I wanted to gain more adaptability and become more versatile on all pitches.'

Allen was not playing in the match at Adelaide. Bedser was advised of his intention to modify his action. 'Why not give it a try?' said Alec. They both changed and went into the nets. The work-out, lasting nearly an hour, proceeded under Alec's earnest inspection. Finally, he said: 'I think that's good enough.' Allen remembers that Bedser quietly observed without insisting on a particular method. 'He was just so reassuring and his care and understanding gave me confidence.'

Allen believes the practice session was the turning-point for him as an England cricketer. It resulted in his selection for the final Test at Sydney. His five wickets in the match included those of Norman O'Neill in both innings, and the prized scalp of Neil Harvey, who was playing in his last Test match.

A more recent testimony to Bedser's influence was provided by former Australian captain Bobby Simpson, who first toured England in 1961 and, starting in 1964, captained Australia in 39 Tests. At the age of 41 he came out of retirement to lead Australia in 1977–78 following the defection of most of the national side to Kerry Packer's World Series Cricket organisation.

David Allen recalls how Simpson, in this crisis, drove home the principles of orthodox and positive cricket among the the young recruits under his command. 'He dragged Australia up by insisting on the virtues of playing straight, line and length bowling and alert running between the wickets.' Simpson dwelt on his own learning curve in a conversation with Allen during the World Cup in England in 1999. He remembered a great man who had become his model as a young cricketer. That counsellor, in his early days, had been Alec Bedser.

Players with worries could always count on the concern of the Duke of Norfolk – an insomniac, as Ted Dexter recalls. Ken Barrington was one of those prone to anxiety in Australia in 1962–63. He was, at times, affected by sleeplessness. The MCC manager was aware of Barrington's problem. 'Ring me at any time if you're not sleeping. I've always got a supply of pills,' he said.

At two o'clock one morning there was a shrill ring on the telephone in the Duke's room. It was one of his own better nights and he was aroused from a deep slumber. Barrington, on the other hand, was struggling vainly to get some rest. His own quarters were a considerable distance away. The Duke, having ascertained the number of Barrington's room, dropped the required pill into his dressing-gown pocket and marched purposefully along the carpeted corridors. He was just about to knock on the player's door when he heard the sound of loud snoring.

Calm had descended on the troubled Barrington. His call had disturbed the Duke but it had also eased his own mind. The master of the malapropism now slept not like a log but 'like a lark'. If he sang just as happily at breakfast next morning, he soon tumbled into dismay when he realised his offence – but His Grace, if he was not exactly amused, did not consider it necessary to rebuke a man who had sought solace in the early hours.

In his tour report, the Duke referred to Alec Bedser's extensive network of friendships, built up over many years, with cricket officials in the various Australian states. The success of the tour, he said, was largely due to these invaluable contacts: 'No one could ever take on a tour such as that of Australia and New Zealand without an assistant manager, but no one, in the future, will be as lucky as I was unless they have Alec Bedser. He has been a real friend in every sense of the word.'

There was a practical acknowledgement of Alec's services following the tour. Horse racing was one sporting activity in which the Duke, as an eminence of the turf, achieved an instant rapport with the Australian public. It was a pleasing diversion for Alec as he accompanied the Duke to major meetings. On one of these occasions, the prestigious Melbourne Cup, he ventured the remark that he and Eric had never been to Ascot or Epsom.

In the April, after the tour, the brothers were invited to stay at Arundel Castle. The Duke had not forgotten Alec's casual inquiry. 'By the way,' he said, 'you want to go to Ascot, don't you? I'll send you the tickets.' As the months went by, it seemed that the Duke would neglect to fulfil his promise.

He was, however, true to his word. Late, but not too late, the invitation was confirmed. A week before the Ascot meeting, the Bedsers received tickets for the Royal Enclosure, parking and meals. The generous gesture was renewed over the next few years. Alec and Eric, as the Duke's regular guests, were able to doff their top hats to their benefactor on this special racing occasion.

CHAPTER THIRTEEN

Selector with a Sense of Duty

Alec was totally reliable, with all the right ideas about the way cricket should be conducted.

DOUG INSOLE

Alec Bedser, in his exacting new role as a Test selector at the start of the 1960s, was closely associated with a swiftly changing order. His record reign coincided with the abolition of the distinction between the 'gentlemen' and the 'players' in 1962–63 and the subsequent abandonment of one of the oldest fixtures in the cricket calendar.

Usurping the old amateur supremacy was a surge of player power, which carried perils and impending conflict. Bedser, involved as he was in this time of dissent, had to call heavily on his reserves of tenacity and patience in the years ahead. His renown as a cricketer – and, perhaps more importantly, his integrity and status as a former professional – earned him acceptance as a trustee of the game. He never allowed popular clamour to cloud his judgement.

The scale of his endeavours as the longest-serving selector have never been matched. He was a member of the Test panel from 1962 to 1985 (23 seasons excluding the 1970 series against the Rest of the World). The sequence included 12 seasons as chairman when his teams won 10, drew 3 and lost only 5 out of 18 series.

Alec possessed a civility which won over those who might have posed a threat to a less resolute man. If his censure – and caustic appraisal of players – did at times confound, the smallest dribble of praise from him was worth more than any rave review. He had played cricket in a modest age when he and his contemporaries were content to let their deeds speak for themselves. Alec would clearly have relished the admonition of one MCC president, who briskly punctured the conceit of one particular player thus: 'If he was half as good as he thought he was, he would be twice as good as he is.'

'Alec's judgement was always respected,' says Doug Insole. 'He was totally reliable, with all the right ideas about the way cricket should be conducted.'

There was, inevitably, a disdain which greeted over-inflated reputations. Alec's severity as critic still reflects his impatience with less than the best. But it also conceals a deep regret at the decline in standards in a game which he has played and observed for over 60 years.

Insole, then chairman of the selectors, conveys the tenor of Bedser's disposition in one story. Soon after Alec's elevation to the selection panel, he presided at a Test match dinner. Alec was introduced to the assembled players. 'If he says you're fairly useful,' Insole wittily explained, 'you can be reasonably sure that he means you are among the best in the world.'

There were to be interesting times, involving complex personalities and situations to engage the England selectors. Ranged alongside Bedser prior to and during his reign as chairman, which began in 1969, was an expert contingent of former professionals. His colleagues – and regional representatives – included Sir Leonard Hutton, Willie Watson in Yorkshire; Cyril Washbrook (Lancashire); Ken Barrington (Surrey); John Murray (Middlesex); and Don Kenyon and the esteemed former umpire Charlie Elliott in the Midlands.

Alec spent upwards of 100 days each season watching and inspecting the progress of players. Selecting was a fascinating task, even if the financial rewards were negligible and restricted to travelling expenses. His appearance at games would often bring about a big leap in the endeavours. The likely men would say, 'We'd better try a bit harder – the chairman's here today.'

Sometimes, when championship dates clashed, Eric Bedser would take time off to view other candidates. Attention was always paid to the knowledge of serving umpires on the county circuit. They were invaluable advisers on those players who might otherwise have escaped the net. But, as Alec explains, 'You could write down eight names straight away in good periods. And really there are only around 20 players who would come into the Test category.'

Alec emphatically cites 'class' as the quality he always looked for in selecting England cricketers. The cavalcade of talents occupying his attention, and that of other selectors, over two decades included Tom Graveney, a player who was renewed in purpose when he moved from Gloucestershire to the splendid batting pastures at Worcestershire's New Road headquarters. Graveney had earlier failed to fulfil his potential as a Test cricketer. 'Tom was tending to get out with frivolous shots in circumstances which didn't require them,' remembers Doug Insole.

Graveney's recall to the England colours at the age of 39 in 1966 heralded a happy renaissance. He discovered, as a veteran, the measure of greater resolution to enhance his stylish stroke-play. Insole contrasts the progress of Graveney with Ken Barrington. The Surrey player eliminated the gambles of extravagance, which had dominated his approach as a young cricketer, to achieve reliability as a sheet-anchor batsman.

Among the surprise selections of those years was Philip Sharpe in 1963. He was probably the only player to win England honours, almost exclusively because of his prowess as a slip fieldsman. Sharpe's 71 catches in 1962 gave him a Yorkshire record and only Wally Hammond, Micky Stewart and Peter Walker have taken more catches in a season. His form as a batsman in 1963 did not justify selection; but, in the event, he topped the averages against the West Indies.

Don Wilson, the slow left-arm bowler and Yorkshire colleague, remembered how Sharpe used to take catches with his 'small, very small hands' a long way behind his body – indicating superb anticipation and reactions in delaying a catch until it was a certainty. 'Phil instinctively knew which way the ball would go as it left the bat,' says Wilson. 'He stood wider to me, covering first and second slips, and his agility gave us a spare man in the field.'

David Steele, looked upon as a county journeyman, was one player who came into the lists as a 'hunch' selection. Prematurely grey and bespectacled, he appeared to have been drawn from the ranks of *Dad's Army*. It was a deceptive impression. At Lord's in 1975 – having first taken a wrong turning into the basement – he emerged to astonish the waiting Australians. 'Who's this guy coming out? Groucho Marx?' exclaimed Jeff Thomson.

Embattled as he was against searing pace, Steele was the exemplar of honest defence. His resolve matched his surname. It was easy to identify with this David against the Goliaths. In his first three Tests he scored 365 runs, including four fifties. He headed the England batting averages and became the folk hero of the summer. Bedser remembers the intrepid Steele as a 'gutsy player' and 'good off the back foot'. The selection was made at the instigation of Tony Greig, who had noted the ability of the Northamptonshire recruit against quick bowlers.

The successful introduction of Steele occurred in the aftermath of a torrid series in Australia. Alec Bedser, who was present in the first of his tours there as manager, remembers the magnificence of Lillee and

Thomson. Their unnerving aggression on 'lively, fast wickets' was liberally sprinkled with bouncers. Harold Larwood, watching them in company with Bill Bowes, thought they exceeded their ration. 'They bowled more in some overs than I did in an entire match,' he said.

Jim Swanton said the speed of Thomson, first unfurled at Brisbane, was a revelation. He remembered the broadcast tribute of Lindsay Hassett, the former Australian captain, in a survey of the series. Hassett thought one over bowled by Thomson at the Wooloongabba was the best he had seen from a fast bowler. The England batsmen were facing a bowler whose speed, at 99.7 mph, is still unsurpassed more than 25 years later. 'The purists,' wrote Swanton, 'talked of Thomson's action as slinging, and maybe the left shoulder did fall away a shade early in the delivery stride. Yet there was no lack of rhythm, and the muzzle velocity he generated from a relatively short run was amazing. As he ran to the crease, I could see more than a hint of Keith Miller.'

Alec Bedser said that Thomson, in his peak summer, had a disconcerting tendency to make the ball rise steeply from little short of a good length at top speed. 'He was faster than anyone I've ever seen. He could be erratic, but he bowled a hell of a lot of good 'uns.'

England, their batsmen cowed in spirit, were beaten 4–1. It is a signal testimony to the mastery of Lillee and Thomson that, when England won by an innings at Melbourne, both had been sidelined by injuries. Alec adds, 'The best batsmen of any age would have been sorely troubled by these superb bowlers.'

Many people have testified to Bedser's personal consideration and kindness. Colin Cowdrey stressed his avuncular care for players. Because of injuries on the 1974–75 tour, he was sent out to strengthen the beleaguered English ranks. At the age of 42, and only four days after his arrival, he was called upon to stand up to the might of Lillee and Thomson. 'He so wanted me to do well,' said Cowdrey of the chairman. 'And he was terribly anxious that I didn't get hurt.'

David Gower was another to be given reassurance by Bedser. He was dropped from four Tests against the West Indies in 1980. Alec was alertly responsive to Gower's disappointment. There was a consolatory letter to fortify him and make clear that there was a place available when he had recovered form and confidence.

❧ ❧ ❧

Alec Bedser was plunged into the first of his crises as a selector in the mid-1970s. It was a prolonged saga in which Geoffrey Boycott fully tested his powers of diplomacy. 'Geoffrey was a fine player and England needed him,' says Doug Insole. 'Alec was instrumental in bringing him back into the Test fold.'

Alec remembers – and is still perplexed – by Boycott's 'self-imposed' exile from Test cricket, which lasted for three years from 1974 to 1977. 'You are not conscripted to play for England. It is your decision' – that was the substance of one of the many conversations Bedser had with the Yorkshireman. 'I tried as much as I could to accommodate Geoffrey,' says Alec. 'I didn't want the press to allege that I was not doing my utmost to get the best players to represent England.'

The saga began without warning at Old Trafford during a less than taxing series against India in 1974. Eknath Solkar, a moderate trundler, was the catalyst for Boycott's decision. Solkar, in one of those quirks of cricket fate, dismissed Boycott four times in six innings for England, the MCC and Yorkshire. 'Geoffrey was so distressed by his performance that he asked if he could see me at Manchester,' recalls Bedser. Their talk lasted for more than an hour, at the end of which Boycott – then the Yorkshire captain – said his energies should be conserved to aid his county. Alec, however much he wanted to retain Boycott, was not prepared to plead with him to stay. Finally, he said: 'Do I understand you correctly? You don't want to play for England.'

In the following two seasons, Alec telephoned Boycott to ascertain whether he wished to be reconsidered as an England candidate. Each time the answer was in the negative. The suspicion had grown that Boycott was offended because he had not been offered the England captaincy and that he felt the post had gone to other less qualified players.

Boycott, it transpired in a letter to Bedser, had even contemplated retiring from the game at the start of the 1974 season. He was then aged 34. One observer at the time said, 'This fellow is worrying himself into premature retirement.' Two years later there was more reassuring news, at least on the batting front, from Yorkshire. Boycott's form – and presumably his heart for cricket – had produced a bumper crop of runs. He scored 1,915 runs at an average of 73.65. 'It made me think that his old thirst for runs might bring about a thaw in his attitude,' said Alec.

The assumption proved correct, as was shown by a tentative enquiry from a Yorkshire journalist. The caller, acting as a go-between, wanted to know if Alec would meet Boycott. The appointment was later confirmed and, in an episode cloaked with secrecy, a halfway rendezvous was arranged at a motorway service station at Watford Gap. Boycott rejected a meeting in the station coffee lounge and insisted that their conversation should be held in the anonymity of Bedser's car.

It was a long and animated talk in which Boycott repeatedly contended that the selectors and the Lord's hierarchy had set their minds against him. Perceived inadequacies in social background were given as the reason for his isolation. Alec quickly reminded his companion that he and his fellow selectors – Sir Len Hutton, Don Kenyon and Charlie Elliott – had endured similar hardships and were all products of a tough upbringing. Referring to Boycott's ambition to captain England, Alec said: 'The first thing, Geoff, is that you've got to play. Are you available, or not?'

Boycott was thereupon given 24 hours in which to reach a decision. Another telephone call followed and the impasse seemed as large as ever. Clearly, the situation now called for a sterner attitude. 'When I put this phone down,' said Alec, 'I'm going to tell the newspapers exactly what has happened.' Boycott relented and said, 'I'm available.' He was restored to the England team at Trent Bridge and was able to bask in the glory of his 100th first-class century – adoringly greeted by his Yorkshire followers – in the following Test at Headingley.

Alec is not a man to complicate issues, although he must have raged in private throughout his patient public declarations during the affair. He has, though, a capacity for friendship, even in the most unpromising circumstances. He remains steadfast in his view of Boycott as technically the best of England's batsmen during the period in which he played: 'I have a good relationship with Geoff. I think he appreciated my forthright stance and that my only concern was England's cause.'

Boycott himself has said how much he respected Alec for the patience and consideration he was shown during a time of personal turmoil. 'Alec has said since and quite fondly (I think) that he considered me a fine player, if "a bit potty" as a person. He cannot have found our relationship easy over the years when he was England chairman. I was bedevilled by personal problems which clearly would not have made much sense to him.'

❧ ❧ ❧

The exciting command of Tony Greig set the pulses racing and won the admiration of many cricket followers, not least that of the chairman of the selectors. Alec Bedser was responsible for installing Greig as England captain; and it was at his request that a suspension ban was lifted.

Greig had suffered this imposition following the 1973–74 tour of the

West Indies. His offence was exuberantly, and perhaps unwittingly, to run out Alvin Kallicharan in the first Test at Port of Spain. The batsman had begun to return to the pavilion, believing that play had ended for the day. Hasty apologies had to be made to Kallicharan – and the Trinidad authorities – and the appeal withdrawn to defuse a potentially explosive incident.

The action did, though, typify the impulsive nature of a cricketer of character. Greig was recruited by Mike Buss, one of several Sussex players who had coached the future England captain at Queenstown in South Africa's Cape Province. At Hove, with scarcely a break in his stride, Greig was an invigorating presence. The fair-haired giant provided a wake-up call to the committee and the members slumbering in their deckchairs.

As with the England squad, Greig built up an immense reservoir of goodwill and refreshing camaraderie in Sussex. In my book, *The Family Fortune*, I expressed my sadness that such a combative and inspirational cricketer should have chosen to pitch himself and others into a sordid squabble. Alec Bedser similarly, before the engulfing trauma of the Packer affair, had welcomed the spirit and determination of a dynamic personality: 'The tougher the situation the stronger was his response and, added to his considerable ability and flair for the big occasion, a talent for leadership emerged.'

Alec regarded the growing influence of Greig as deserving as his former Surrey captain, Stuart Surridge. Each of them travelled down the same decisive path – never imperilled by doubt, both of them madcap adventurers in pursuit of victory. Greig, in his curtailed reign of 18 months, was ranked along with Mike Brearley and Ray Illingworth (tactically outstanding, in Bedser's opinion) as the best of England's captains since the Second World War.

Greig's defection to Kerry Packer – and his role as an agent in recruiting other England players – polarised opinion in cricket circles. It was doubtless, from his personal standpoint, a crusade for a better deal, and the controversy did have the effect of increasing financial rewards in the game. But it also foretold, as Bedser declares, that money not so much talks in modern sport as yells at the top of its voice.

Jack Bannister, in an article in *Wisden* in 1986, reflected on the immensity of the change in fortunes. Test match payments had increased roughly four-fold in the biggest financial revolution in the history of the game within a decade. The introduction of the minimum wage in 1979 had more or less tripled the salaries of county players. By 1985, the top six players in the country earned £40,000 from actually playing cricket, without taking account of sponsorships and advertising contracts.

More immediate matters occupied Bedser in his discussions with Tony Greig. He had, as he thought, established a climate of trust. There was a fearful sense of betrayal when he learned that Greig, while still England captain, had been involved in negotiations with Packer representatives during the Centenary Test in Melbourne in 1977. 'Tony had done as good a job as captain as anyone,' says Alec. 'What I found disgraceful was that he kept this intrigue to himself.'

In April 1977 Alec travelled to Hove for preliminary talks with Greig on the composition of the MCC team to play against the Australians at Lord's. It proved to be a pointless exercise and one, moreover, charged with duplicity. In the evening, Greig publicly divulged that he was now contracted to World Series Cricket.

Alec, having vigorously supported Tony's claims to the England captaincy, was now ruefully forced onto the back foot. 'You should have advised me of your intentions,' he told Greig. 'I would have respected your confidence. Our trust,' he added, 'should have been a two-way thing.'

⁂

Alec Bedser was doggedly straightforward in all his relations, including those with the competitive media. He was, like others, dismissive of the trivia and froth of the tabloid press. Their wilder excesses were the price he had to pay for being in the sporting spotlight. Entertainment for their readers took precedence over cricket issues of value. Ted Dexter, as one of Bedser's successors as chairman, takes a philosophical view on the waves of criticism which assail those in such a high profile post. 'Life is reasonably tolerable when you're winning,' he says.

Alec says: 'I was always available for comment and used to tell the press the truth.' One experienced member of the press corps remembers how the Bedsers were very methodical in a military sense. He once rang the chairman and Eric answered the call. 'He's out at a meeting. Back late. But do ring him in the morning. At half past six!'

The caller probably belonged to the privileged elite which received background information for their back-page topics. Alec always knew that he could rely on discretion in such hands. His guidance also had another purpose. Others, less informed and callow in judgement, would be ticked off by their seniors in the press box if their stories owed more to the imagination than the actual facts.

The style of plain speaking which distinguished Alec as a selector was well demonstrated towards the end of his term as chairman. Ian Botham, sacked as captain in 1981, tried to salvage his pride by resigning from the post. Alec has said that, but for the unavailability of Mike Brearley, Botham would not have been saddled with the leadership in the West Indies in the previous winter. Botham had, though, earned commendation amid the problems on his first series as captain. There was the saddening blow of the death of Ken Barrington, the much revered tour manager, and the militancy of the Guyana government when Robin Jackman replaced Bob Willis (who had to return home with injury almost by return flight). It was, by any standards, a formidable baptism. As a proud man, he was angry about the following events.

Botham's personal crisis began when he was twice dismissed for a duck in the second Test against Australia at Lord's. A great player trudged back to a glum and silently disapproving pavilion. 'We knew what Ian's failures meant to him,' says Bedser. The England selectors had been sure that Botham had the ability to grant all their wishes as captain. 'But we saw a dream fading and our plans falling apart,' adds Bedser.

Botham had been given two matches as captain against Australia. His reverses were underlined by telling statistics. In 12 matches in charge of England, between June 1980 and July 1981, he had scored 276 runs at an average of 13.86 and his 35 wickets had cost 32 runs apiece. The cares of captaincy were threatening to ruin his cricket. 'We decided, reluctantly, during the match at Lord's, that we had to ditch Ian,' says Bedser.

Jim Laker, in the *Daily Express*, wrote that there had always been the worrying thought that the additional burden of the captaincy would affect Botham's performances. 'We needed him at his brilliant best to beat Australia,' he said. Botham himself had anticipated the selectors' decision. Alec remembers that the ousted captain asked if he could publicly announce that he had resigned. Their meeting was held in the attendant's cubby-hole outside the England dressing-room. 'By all means, if that's the way you want it,' replied Alec. 'You say it that way.'

Alec did qualify this by reminding Botham that the media would not be duped by such a subterfuge at the ensuing conference. He would not offer a lie, even of the whitest hue. 'If I'm asked a direct question, I'm going to give them a true answer.' Evasion was not his style and, in any event, remaining silent would easily be construed as a tacit admission.

In addition, it would present the selectors as weak in their treatment of Botham after his lapses as captain. 'A far more important point,' he later wrote, 'was the selectors standing four-square behind him and keeping him in the team when it would not have created a sensation if he had been left out of the next Test.'

Alec remains unstinting in his praise of Botham as a cricketer: 'From the beginning he revealed his talents. He was very strong and didn't break down. Ian was a genuine all-rounder, the last we've had – and he had the priceless gift of making things happen in a Test match.'

Botham's demotion, staggering as it was to him, unleashed a furious response. At his side was the recalled Mike Brearley, whose captaincy rekindled the flames of a cricket passion. Botham was revived in spirit under Brearley's understanding leadership. There was an awesome vengeance in the magnificent 149 – his seventh Test century – with which he retrieved an apparently lost cause at Headingley. It was complemented by a bowling performance which is sometimes forgotten in recollections of an amazing Test. Bob Willis, on the last morning, bowled 15.1 overs and took 8 wickets for 43 runs. Australia were dismissed for 111. England were the victors by 18 runs after odds of 500–1 had been offered against them at the close of the third day.

Redemption for Botham continued throughout the rest of an enthralling summer. His batting, endowed with a lustful fervour, so caught the imagination that he was said to rival the Edwardian aggressor Gilbert Jessop. The hundred at Leeds was followed by another, as England retained the Ashes at Manchester. Botham hit six sixes – a record in Anglo-Australian Tests – and reached his century in 86 balls. Alderman and Lillee, armed with the second new ball, were struck for 66 runs in 8 overs after tea.

Between times, there were marvels with the ball, too. At Edgbaston, as *Wisden* reported, 'the crowd, dotted with green and gold, were beside themselves with agony and ecstasy, as only 12 days after Headingley, history repeated itself.' Australia, with 6 wickets left, required only 46 runs to win. They did not legislate for another miracle wrought by Botham. In 28 balls he took 5 wickets for one run. 'One after another, five Australian batsmen walked into the point of his lance,' enthused *Wisden*. England – and their young hero – had defied the odds again to win by 29 runs.

A spectacular revival was, in the end, a direct consequence of an unpalatable decision. For Alec Bedser, in his last season as chairman, the momentous exploits of 1981 were the most pleasing of farewells. It was an irresistible conquest with which to bring down the curtain. 'All who know him and admire his sense of duty and enjoy his bluff humour will have been delighted that he ended on a winning note,' observed John Woodcock, the editor of *Wisden*.

The happiness of the occasion ensnared another cricket correspondent: 'That was a marvellous performance by Ian Botham,' enthused Christopher Martin-Jenkins.

'Yes,' said Alec. 'Well, he's a good cricketer.'

CHAPTER FOURTEEN

Defending Cricket's Certainties

*We have stifled the County Championship, the means of producing
good Test players.*

Sir Alec Bedser

Each generation has its own impulses and formula for success, but the principles of cricket remain unchanged. The censure of the veterans, including Alec and Eric Bedser, could perhaps be less forcibly expressed, but it harbours a distress at the betrayal of the timeless values. Cricket, as a box-office attraction, now rings incessantly to the tunes of the pyjama game. It is a medley which carries the raucous appeal of a pop concert and the diehard traditionalists fear it will engulf the County Championship.

Reconciling these opposing forces is a challenge which today's rulers will neglect at their peril. Grave misgivings in a vexed debate are voiced by Alec Bedser. 'Remember that selectors don't make cricketers' was the warning he issued during his record term as chairman. 'The system produces them – for better or worse.'

A plea to recognise the quickening tempo of modern life was made by Sir Donald Bradman in an article in *Wisden* as long ago as 1939. Fifty years later, in another report commissioned by the almanack, he reflected on the renewed acceleration which had transformed cricket: 'Despite my deep feeling for the traditional game, and my conviction that the vast majority of players and the public regard Test cricket as the supreme contest, we must accept that we live in a new era.'

Sir Donald, while confessing his love for both forms of the game, said nothing could match the cut and thrust of a Test match where the advantage see-saws and the result is unpredictable to the last ball. The tied match between Australia and the West Indies at Brisbane in December 1960 fell overwhelmingly into this category. It was endowed with superb batting and fielding, spin and speed, and victory dictated by adhering to the principles upon which the game was founded. 'I cannot imagine any sporting event being more exciting,' observed Bradman.

A fascinating tussle did, commented Bradman, starkly illustrate the Achilles' heel of a limited-overs match, namely the premium placed on defensive bowling: 'One can get bored to death watching countless singles being taken when even the world's fastest bowler may be operating with no slips and five men on the boundary.'

On the credit side of the ledger, Sir Donald said one-day cricket had eliminated the 'unutterable bore who thinks that occupancy of the crease and his own personal aggrandisement are all that matters'. Another advance had been the requirement for fieldsmen of great speed and agility. 'The standard of fielding at all levels of cricket has undoubtedly lifted. Running between the wickets, too, has taken on a new dimension. Runs must be taken to maintain an essential run-rate.'

Bradman's assessment is endorsed by Ted Dexter, the ringmaster – and a pioneer in one-day strategies – who piloted Sussex to their triumphs in the early years of the Gillette Cup competition in the 1960s. 'Cricket then had to be played differently,' he says. 'In bowling and fielding the stress levels are now hugely increased.' The intensity of the modern game prompts his conclusion that rest periods, insisted upon by the current England management, are an essential guard against injuries. In any 12-month period, he believes, players must have a complete stand-down, both physically and mentally, for six weeks. There should be no cricketing activity without the express permission of the board.

Dexter provides, as an example of his claim, the newly found spirit of Andrew Caddick, who 'has put injuries behind him and bowled more overs for England than ever before'. Caddick, in a recent interview, said, 'I've proved to myself what keeps you fit is bowling.' Dexter adds, in a tone of wry amusement, 'It might have been Alec Bedser talking.'

❧ ❧ ❧

Wilf Wooller, a vigorous and articulate spokesman, was never inclined to drift into nostalgia. The former Glamorgan captain, speaking on his 80th birthday, optimistically believed that the vast amounts of money yielded by Test cricket would make administrators less beholden to the one-day game:

> I have always liked 'cakes-and-ale' cricket, but the longer game carries the elements of a fine symphony orchestra. This is the great music but it doesn't bring in the millions. We have to

recognise this and try to achieve the proper amalgam of the two forms of cricket.

The crux of the matter is the increasingly unpalatable truth that the traditional game's cerebral nature, of fluctuating fortunes, affords contemplation for only a small and dedicated core of county followers. Others – the vast majority – are attracted in their thousands to the immediacy of the one-day game. Their busy lives demand that cricket is reduced to instant gratification.

So we arrive at the paradox of county cricket, the essential proving ground, played to near empty stadia while the one-day game conspires to defeat orthodox cricket. The problem is exacerbated, in the view of Alec Bedser, by the tendency to decry the championship: 'The structure which produced Test cricketers has been stifled. Why did we want to abandon a three-day competition on uncovered pitches which gave us some of our greatest performers?'

David Allen, the former Gloucestershire and England off-spinner, remembers the spirit which governed his approach as a young cricketer. In the West Country, Allen came under the rigorous professional leadership of Jack Crapp and George Emmett. 'Our method was keen and positive cricket,' he recalls. 'You attacked as a bowler when conditions were in your favour. As a batsman, you had to make sure you got runs on flat wickets. You didn't look to play safe; you imposed yourself on the opposition.'

The fourth day of the championship, as has become increasingly apparent, is largely an irrelevance. It merely serves as an extension which reinforces go-slow attitudes. Bedser urges an increase in the number of balls delivered each day: 'If the old rate of 120 overs in a full day could be reached there would be no need for a fourth day.'

The abysmal over-rates which appertain today simply fuel disaffection among supporters. As long ago as the early 1950s, at the close of his career, Les Ames remembered the exhortations: 'Come on, come on, we've got to slow the buggers down.' Modern cricket tactics, as Ames also said, would have debarred Don Bradman from ever again scoring 300 in a day.

Geoffrey Howard, the former Surrey secretary, recalled one conversation with Colin Cowdrey after a tour of the West Indies. 'There were,' said Cowdrey, 'only three balls, on average, an over, which were in reach of making a shot.'

Alec Bedser refers, without fear of contradiction, to one inescapable fact: the longer the match, the greater are the skills required. 'I have consistently maintained that there must be a sensible balance between one-day competitions and the traditional fixtures.'

Alec, in his roles as a selector and as a member of the Surrey committee, has been embroiled in a catch-22 situation: 'On the one hand there is the struggle to remain viable and retain local interest by succeeding in one of the limited-overs competitions. Equally there is the need to have a truly representative Test side. There is the danger of one prospering at the expense of the other.'

He concedes that covered pitches are a necessity for the one-day game. But he is not alone in advocating a return to three-day championship matches played on uncovered wickets: 'You had to be a good back-foot player in those conditions. All our great Test players came into that category.'

The state of wickets in general is also a factor with regard to reduced playing standards in England, at both county and Test level. Bedser dwells on the regional differences in soil content and covering of squares which excludes rain and air, so that wickets lose their natural character. Because of covering, so it is alleged, less emphasis has been placed on the preparation of pitches. One observer has said, 'Much less rolling takes place and the groundsman's main concern seems to be with the growing of grass.'

Johnny Wardle, the former Yorkshire and England bowler, committed himself to a study of groundsmanship. His work, unpaid, at cricket and golf clubs in South Yorkshire, were lasting memorials to his talents in this field. Shortly before his death, at the age of 62, in 1985, he inveighed against the introduction of heavy loam in the search for quicker cricket wickets:

> It is very difficult soil to work with: water will not penetrate it, neither will the grass roots which are so vital in binding it together. The wicket cracks both vertically and horizontally, resulting in uneven bounce. Batsmen are having to wear helmets and other protective clothing. Never mind what anyone says, all the great players of the past would have needed protection had they played under these conditions.

Wardle maintained that medium-paced bowling had replaced spin because it was harder to play on modern wickets with their uneven bounce:

The old-fashioned slower wickets used to dust a little and help only the spinner and were never dangerous. The ordinary medium-pacer came in for some hammer. One had to be pretty quick, with some swing, or slow with plenty of spin and flight to succeed.

There were trenchant words, too, from Wardle on the covering of wickets:

The captain with four or five fast bowlers has no need to worry about the weather. I wonder what the averages of some batsmen would be like if they had to face Laker, Lock, Appleyard and Underwood on rain-affected wickets. Even such a great a batsman as Vivian Richards would be brought back to earth with a bang.

Having accepted that limited-overs cricket is now an economic necessity, the key question today is how it should be played without eroding the standards required in Test matches. Evidence is mounting of deficient technique among English batsmen: the game is cursed by suicidal stroke-play where once we could rely on discretion and responsibility in the Test arenas. Dangerous habits formed in youth are now being perpetuated at senior level. The consequence is that we have bred a race of 'bits-and-pieces' players.

A sparse legacy has been underlined in recent England selections. In one instance, a No. 3 county batsman was relegated to No. 7 in the order. He was placed in an unenviable role, in the absence of an all-rounder, of squeezing out runs with the tail.

Forty years ago, after his retirement, Alec Bedser deplored the fact that young players expected fame to come too easily. It smacked of a lack of dedication. 'If it does not come early,' he wrote, 'they do not want to put in that extra effort so necessary to bring about success.' He also believed that too many of the less mature players were inclined to treat the game merely as a wage-earning occupation.

Standards of fitness formed the basis of another of his talking-points: 'There are far more injuries nowadays. Players break down more easily if they are not strong, and I am certain that the hard work at the nets in one's youth does build up muscles able to stand the strain of a long days in the field.'

Alec today strictly maintains that he would not allow any youngster until the age of 17 or 18 to play limited-overs cricket (as opposed to the time-governed one-day game, which he and Eric played in their young days). 'It gives boys the wrong idea of what cricket is all about. They are not learning how to get people out.'

Geoffrey Howard is also dismayed by the spirit of the game which, he says, is now slothfully enveloped in containment. 'Cricket has gradually become more defensive, with bowlers of medium pace pitching just short of a length on the middle and leg stumps. Before this happened, the spinners bowled mainly to the off and sought to gain dismissals on that side of the wicket. The fielders on the leg side were there to stop runs or take catches off bad balls.'

Don Wilson, in his days as head coach at Lord's, diligently sought to eliminate the safety-first approach: 'Our game now produces defensive bowlers. Bowl 10 overs and take none for 30 and you're a hero.' Wilson adds, 'There is something wrong when it gets to that stage. Cricket ought to offer more enjoyment than that. You can't delight in bowling if you don't want to get people out.' He cites the example of Fred Trueman in his Yorkshire days. 'He wanted to get everyone out. Marvellous self-confidence. He'd come in after getting none for 85 and say, "No bloody luck at all. Should have had 8 for 20. Buggers played and missed all day." And he believed it.'

Concern is deepened by the overthrow of the slow bowler, especially in the attacking mode. In Yorkshire, Bill Bowes once expressed his astonishment when an aspiring young slow bowler revealed that he had bowled only 100 overs in a season. The boy was a victim, one of many throughout the country, of the one-day system.

Bowes offered his conclusions nearly 20 years ago. He believed that the game had passed the point where a revival of the spinner's craft could easily be contemplated. The counties, he noted, had decided that a fast or medium-fast bowler could do a good job in similar circumstances.

Ray Illingworth, commenting on a frustrating dilemma in the 1980s, said the situation was the worst in his experience. 'Thirty years ago you could get a dozen left-arm bowlers from the Bradford League who could do a fine job for Yorkshire, and perhaps one of them would have turned out to be a great bowler,' he said. 'Today I cannot find one that is good enough for county cricket.' Yet the profits of spin, as Saqlain and Salisbury still demonstrate at The Oval, should not be disregarded. As

TOP: Two pairs of twins: Alec and Eric with the Yardley boys, sons of England captain Norman Yardley, at the Scarborough Festival.

ABOVE: Twinned again as veterans with the Australian pair,
Steve and Mark Waugh.

TOP: The Invincibles: A composite group of the triumphant Australians, led by Don Bradman, and their England opponents in 1948.

ABOVE: Sharing a century. Alec during his stand with Denis Compton against Australia at Manchester in 1948.

OPPOSITE : Record at Nottingham. The scorecard showing Alec's match figures of 14 for 99 against Australia in 1953. A standing ovation (*top*) acknowledged the epic feat.

ENGLAND v AUSTRALIA
Played at Nottingham, June 11th, 12th, 13th, 15th, 16th, 1953.

Match Drawn

Captains – L. Hutton & A. L. Hassett. *Wicket-keepers* – T. G. Evans & D. Tallon. *Umpires* – D. Davies & Harold Elliott. *Toss won by* – Australia. *Close of play scores* – 1st day, Aust. 157-3 (Hassett 67, Miller 19); 2nd day, Eng. 92-6 (Bailey 2, Evans 0); 3rd day, Eng. 41-1 (Hutton 10, Simpson 8); 4th day, no play. *Test debuts* – Davidson and Hill (Aust.). Kenyon, Graveney, May, Wardle and Benaud were making their debut in the series.

AUSTRALIA

G. B. Hole	b Bedser	0	b Bedser	5
A. R. Morris	lbw b Bedser	67	b Tattersall	60
A. L. Hassett	b Bedser	115	c Hutton b Bedser	5
R. N. Harvey	c Compton b Bedser	0	c Graveney b Bedser	2
K. R. Miller	c Bailey b Wardle	55	c Kenyon b Bedser	5
R. Benaud	c Evans b Bailey	3	b Bedser	0
A. K. Davidson	b Bedser	4	c Graveney b Tattersall	6
D. Tallon	b Bedser	0	c Simpson b Tattersall	15
R. R. Lindwall	c Evans b Bailey	0	c Tattersall b Bedser	12
J. C. Hill	b Bedser	0	c Tattersall b Bedser	4
W. A. Johnston	not out	0	not out	4
Extras	(B2, LB2, NB1)	5	(LB5)	5
Total		249		123

ENGLAND

L. Hutton	c Benaud b Davidson	43	not out	60
D. Kenyon	c Hill b Lindwall	8	c Hassett b Hill	16
R. T. Simpson	lbw b Lindwall	0	not out	28
D. C. S. Compton	c Morris b Lindwall	0		
T. W. Graveney	c Benaud b Hill	22		
P. B. H. May	c Tallon b Hill	9		
T. E. Bailey	lbw b Hill	13		
T. G. Evans	c Tallon b Davidson	8		
J. H. Wardle	not out	29		
A. V. Bedser	lbw b Lindwall	2		
R. Tattersall	b Lindwall	2		
Extras	(B5, LB3)	8	(B8, LB4, W2, NB2)	16
Total		144	(1 wkt)	120

BOWLING

	O	M	R	W		O	M	R	W
ENGLAND									
Bedser	38.3	16	55	7	..	17.2	7	44	7
Bailey	44	14	75	2	..	5	1	28	0
Wardle	35	16	55	1	..	12	3	24	0
Tattersall	23	5	59	0	..	5	0	22	3
AUSTRALIA									
Lindwall	20.4	2	57	5	..	16	4	37	0
Johnston	18	7	22	0	..	18	9	14	0
Hill	19	8	35	3	..	12	3	26	1
Davidson	15	7	22	2	..	5	1	7	0
Benaud	—	—	—	—	..	5	0	15	0
Morris	—	—	—	—	..	2	0	5	0

FALL OF WICKETS

	AUS 1st	ENG 1st	AUS 2nd	ENG 2nd
1st	2	17	28	26
2nd	124	17	44	—
3rd	128	17	50	—
4th	237	76	64	—
5th	244	82	68	—
6th	244	92	81	—
7th	246	107	92	—
8th	247	121	106	—
9th	248	136	115	—
10th	249	144	123	—

TOP: Alec takes the return catch at The Oval (*left*), dismissing
Ron Archer to bring his series total to 39 wickets and
surpass the record of Maurice Tate (*right*). (Sussex CCC)

ABOVE *(left and right)*: Twin beneficiaries against Yorkshire:
Alec with Norman Yardley (note the gasholder decorated for
the Coronation, in the background) in 1953;
Eric spins the coin, watched by Ronnie Burnet, in 1958.

members of a dwindling band, they have played a major part in Surrey's recent championship successes.

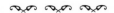

Alec Bedser, amid all the modern innovations, condemns the futility of attempts to replicate in England cricket as it is played in Australia. Climatic differences mock such exercises as day/night matches. 'We are trying to gear our cricket on similar lines to a country which enjoys six months of sunshine. We have only three and a half months, so a lot more work is needed.' Our competitive cricketing cousins in Australia, operating in a much reduced catchment area and without the back-up of a long-established professional structure, have developed a profitable formula. Their policy has been to give a swift call-up for those players who merit recognition.

There are reasons, says Bedser, for Australia's attitude: 'They gave their youngsters a chance because it was a financial necessity with older players, as amateurs, having to leave the game to earn a living. Simple economics helped to push young players forward.' Neil Harvey, one of Australia's greatest batsmen, was playing for his state on merit at the age of 17. His talent was forged in the company of men.

The Australian cricket structure remains relatively unchanged, apart from the establishment of a national academy at Adelaide. The only other difference — compelled by the current programme of year-round international cricket — has been the departure from the amateur custom, to give professional status to an elite squad of some 20 players. In every other respect, the path to fame is pursued at schools and upwards through the various grades. At the independent schools the senior boys, from the age of 15 upwards, are opposed in 'proper matches' of 100 overs each side and played over two weekends.

'Go out to Moore Park in Sydney on a Saturday morning,' says Bedser, 'and you will see as many as ten matches taking place there.' It is a buoyant scene with the zest of the boys, all smartly attired in whites, complemented by the huddles of encouraging parents on the ring of the field. This enthusiasm in a country where cricket still exerts an irresistible appeal explains why Australia enjoys its present world supremacy.

Australia, as England's oldest cricket rival, has always been a magnet for followers in both countries. The symbolic Ashes are defended with a zeal beyond all other trophies. For Alec Bedser, in his heyday, there was the tension of a great occasion and a glow of pride in his conquests over such resolute opponents. The mighty amphitheatre of Melbourne was one of his favourite arenas. It was there, as a newcomer in the 1946–47 series, that he experienced the awesome tumult of a Test match in Australia.

Alec recalls: 'I shall never forget the first Test I played at Melbourne. The crowd of 80,000 was making a terrific din as I walked back to bowl the first ball of the match.' The sudden hush which descended on the multitude was almost eerie as he moved in, with his familiar rolling gait, purposefully towards the crease. 'You could have heard a pin drop at that moment.' It was succeeded, as bat met ball, with a roar like a crash of thunder echoing around the vast stands. Another Test match between England and Australia had begun in a blaze of excitement.

The passing years have not diminished in the memory the thrills of so many epic tussles. Alec Bedser, along with Eric as his devoted companion, are nowhere more venerated for their integrity than in Australia. Two sprightly octogenarians, still among the most instantly recognisable sportsmen (if not separately named), are fêted as men of honour. They now enjoy honorary status in Australia and are welcomed as old and trusted friends on their annual visits to a land of warm and hospitable people. Such are their united voices, it is impossible to guess which of them will begin the many talks of cherished times.

Statistical Appendix

Compiled by Paul Dyson
(acknowledgements to Michael Pearce for supplementary work)

THE BEDSER TWINS

CHRONOLOGY

	A.V. BEDSER	E.A. BEDSER
Born	Reading, Berkshire, 4 July 1918	
First-class début	Surrey v Oxford University, The Oval, 21 June 1939	
County cap	1946	1947
Benefit	1953 – £12,866	1958 – £7,700
Final day of first-class cricket	Surrey v Glamorgan, The Oval, 30 August 1960	MCC v Cambridge University, Lord's, 29 June 1962
President of Surrey	1987	1990

ALEC VICTOR BEDSER

CHRONOLOGY

First day of Test cricket: England v India, Lord's, 22 June 1946

One of *Wisden*'s Five Cricketers of the Year: 1947

Became world record holder of most Test wickets: England v Australia, Headingley, 24 July 1953

Final day of Test cricket: England v South Africa, Old Trafford, 12 July 1955

Test selector: 1962–85 (chairman 1969–81)

Awarded OBE: 1964

Awarded CBE: 1982

Awarded knighthood: 1997

BATTING AND FIELDING

Season by season

	M	I	NO	Runs	HS	Avge	100	50	Ct
1939	2	2	1	12	12★	12.00	–	–	2
1946	26	37	8	494	38	17.03	–	–	10
1946/7	15	22	5	264	51	15.53	–	1	8
1947	30	41	12	727	126	25.07	1	2	32
1948	27	38	6	493	79	15.41	–	2	15
1948/9	14	17	3	271	77★	19.36	–	1	8
1949	26	34	8	468	53	18.00	–	1	30
1950	31	47	5	503	66	11.98	–	3	26
1950/1	13	16	3	164	42	12.62	–	–	10
1951	27	33	10	403	73	17.52	–	1	15
1952	31	32	10	273	87★	12.41	–	1	16
1953	31	34	13	250	45	11.90	–	–	23
1954	30	26	7	262	58	13.79	–	1	10
1954/5	7	11	2	85	30	9.44	–	–	3
1955	34	40	23	165	43★	9.71	–	–	13
1956	27	35	13	163	23	7.41	–	–	15
1956/7	2	3	1	10	10	5.00	–	–	2
1957	34	24	13	130	17★	11.82	–	–	10
1958	17	19	9	112	31★	11.20	–	–	5
1959	30	33	15	259	31	14.39	–	–	19
1959/60	2	4	2	57	42★	28.50	–	–	1
1960	29	28	12	170	25	10.63	–	–	16
Total	485	576	181	5735	126	14.51	1	13	289

For each team

	M	I	NO	Runs	HS	Avge	100	50	Ct
Surrey (County Championship)	311	362	126	3441	126	14.58	1	8	184
Surrey (other matches)	59	67	22	667	87★	14.82	–	1	43
England (Tests)	51	71	15	714	79	12.75	–	1	26
An England XI	5	5	3	8	5	4.00	–	–	4
The Rest	2	3	2	48	23	48.00	–	–	2
MCC	32	37	6	501	77★	16.16	–	2	15
MCC South African XI	1	1	0	8	8	8.00	–	–	–
South	3	3	0	11	6	3.66	–	–	2
Players	12	16	5	237	59	21.55	–	1	9
T.N. Pearce's XI	5	7	1	67	40	11.17	–	–	2
C.G. Howard's XI	2	3	1	10	10	5.00	–	–	2
H.D.G. Leveson-Gower's XI	2	1	0	23	23	23.00	–	–	–
Total	485	576	181	5735	126	14.51	1	13	289

Summary

	M	I	NO	Runs	HS	Avge	100	50	Ct
Surrey	370	429	148	4108	126	14.62	1	9	227
England (Tests)	51	71	15	714	79	12.75	–	1	26
Other teams	64	76	18	913	77★	15.74	–	3	36
Total	485	576	181	5735	126	14.51	1	13	289

Against each opponent (excluding Test matches)

In United Kingdom

	M	I	NO	Runs	HS	Avge	100	50	Ct
Derbyshire	18	24	9	251	35★	16.73	–	–	10
Essex	22	28	6	185	42★	8.40	–	–	18
Glamorgan	17	20	9	248	73	22.55	–	1	6
Gloucestershire	17	22	8	108	25	7.71	–	–	17
Hampshire	19	20	8	202	53★	16.83	–	1	12
Kent	18	19	8	180	31★	16.36	–	–	12
Lancashire	16	21	7	173	41★	12.35	–	–	6
Leicestershire	19	16	6	170	48	17.00	–	–	14
Middlesex	29	42	18	395	34	16.46	–	–	15
Northamptonshire	19	23	13	263	66	26.30	–	2	8
Nottinghamshire	29	23	8	156	31	10.40	–	–	22
Somerset	16	11	3	200	126	25.00	1	–	7
Sussex	18	23	8	254	57	16.93	–	1	11
Warwickshire	15	19	4	208	66	13.86	–	1	11
Worcestershire	19	20	3	204	58	17.00	–	1	12
Yorkshire	24	35	9	291	51	11.19	–	1	7
Cambridge Univ.	9	4	3	18	12★	18.00	–	–	6
Oxford Univ.	10	10	2	145	87★	18.12	–	1	7
MCC	14	17	3	226	35★	16.14	–	–	11
Gentlemen	12	16	5	237	59	21.54	–	1	9
The Rest	7	8	4	9	5	2.25	–	–	3
North	3	3	0	11	6	3.66	–	–	2
Combined Services	2	2	1	14	10	14.00	–	–	–
HD.G. Leveson- Gower's XI	1	1	0	8	8	8.00	–	–	–
England XI	1	1	1	12	12★	–	–	–	1
Australians	4	6	1	86	40	17.20	–	–	2
Indians	5	8	2	51	31★	8.50	–	–	3
New Zealanders	4	4	1	61	45★	20.33	–	–	6
Pakistanis	2	1	0	12	12	12.00	–	–	–
South Africans	7	10	5	37	13★	7.40	–	–	6
West Indians	4	6	2	49	15	12.25	–	–	2

Note: The figures against the counties are all for matches in the County Championship except for one match for Surrey against each of Essex (did not bat, two catches) and Middlesex (23, 13★, 2 catches). He also played in two matches against Yorkshire for MCC (7 and 4).

Overseas (listed by country)

	M	I	NO	Runs	HS	Avge	100	50	Ct
Australian XI	2	2	0	10	7	5.00	–	–	–
Combined (Aus.) XI	4	5	1	78	51	19.50	–	1	2
New South Wales	4	5	2	9	5	3.00	–	–	–
Queensland	3	4	0	59	30	14.75	–	–	1
South Australia	1	1	0	0	0	0.00	–	–	–
Tasmania	1	1	0	35	35	35.00	–	–	1
Victoria	2	3	0	38	22	12.66	–	–	3
Western Australia	1	1	0	42	42	42.00	–	–	2
Bengal Chief Minister's XI	1	2	0	10	10	5.00	–	–	–
Cricket Club of India President's XI	1	1	1	0	0★	–	–	–	2
Auckland	1	1	0	0	0	0.00	–	–	–
Otago	1	2	1	31	25	31.00	–	–	–
Wellington	1	1	0	11	11	11.00	–	–	1
Rhodesia	3	5	2	66	42★	22.00	–	–	1
Cape Province	1	1	0	33	33	33.00	–	–	1
Natal	2	3	1	26	24	13.00	–	–	1
A Natal XI	1	1	0	0	0	0.00	–	–	1
Orange Free State	1	1	1	77	77★	–	–	1	1
Transvaal	2	2	0	32	32	16.00	–	–	–
Western Province	1	–	–	–	–	–	–	–	–

Summary

	M	I	NO	Runs	HS	Avge	100	50	Ct
Against British Teams	374	428	146	4168	126	14.78	1	10	227
Against Overseas Teams	60	77	20	853	77★	14.96	–	2	36
Test Matches	51	71	15	714	79	12.75	–	1	26
Total	485	576	181	5735	126	14.51	1	13	289

On each ground (including Test matches)

In United Kingdom (listed by county)

	M	I	NO	Runs	HS	Avge	100	50	Ct
Chesterfield	2	3	1	34	25★	17.00	–	–	3
Derby	5	7	1	37	16	6.16	–	–	2
In Derbyshire	7	10	2	71	25★	8.88	–	–	5
Brentwood	1	1	0	3	3	3.00	–	–	1
Chelmsford	1	2	2	46	42★	–	–	–	1
Clacton-on-Sea	2	2	0	0	0	0.00	–	–	–
Ilford	3	3	0	5	3	1.66	–	–	–
Leyton	1	2	0	0	0	0.00	–	–	–
Romford	1	2	1	10	10	10.00	–	–	–
Southend-on-Sea	2	2	1	36	36★	36.00	–	–	1
In Essex	11	14	4	100	42★	100.00	–	–	3

	M	I	NO	Runs	HS	Avge	100	50	Ct
Cardiff	5	8	3	143	73	28.60	–	1	1
Llanelli	1	1	0	0	0	0.00	–	–	–
Swansea	2	2	1	26	19★	26.00	–	–	2
In Glamorgan	8	11	4	169	73	24.14	–	1	3
Bristol	2	3	3	22	17★	–	–	–	1
Cheltenham	4	7	1	48	25	8.00	–	–	4
Gloucester	2	4	3	15	11	15.00	–	–	4
Stroud	1	1	0	0	0	0.00	–	–	2
In Gloucester	9	15	7	85	25	10.63	–	–	11
Bournemouth	3	3	2	13	11	13.00	–	–	2
Portsmouth	5	7	1	81	35	13.50	–	–	3
Southampton	3	2	1	12	12★	12.00	–	–	2
In Hampshire	11	12	4	106	35	13.25	–	–	7
Blackheath	9	9	4	82	23★	16.40	–	–	6
Canterbury	1	2	1	0	0★	0.00	–	–	–
In Kent	10	11	5	82	23★	13.66	–	–	6
Old Trafford	16	19	5	215	37	15.35	–	–	8
Leicester	11	10	3	92	25	13.14	–	–	7
Loughborough	1	1	1	4	4★	–	–	–	1
In Leicestershire	12	11	4	96	25	13.71	–	–	8
Lord's	42	57	16	610	59	14.87	–	1	26
Kettering	2	3	1	34	25	17.00	–	–	2
Northampton	4	4	4	19	18★	–	–	–	–
Peterborough	1	–	–	–	–	–	–	–	1
Rushden	1	2	0	24	20	12.00	–	–	–
In Northamptonshire	8	9	5	77	25	19.25	–	–	3
Trent Bridge	20	21	7	108	22	7.71	–	–	8
Bath	1	–	–	–	–	–	–	–	1
Taunton	3	1	0	126	126	126.00	1	–	1
Wells	1	1	0	5	5	5.00	–	–	–
Weston-super-Mare	3	3	1	11	8	5.50	–	–	–
In Somerset	8	5	1	142	126	35.50	1	–	2
Guildford	20	18	5	221	87★	12.00	–	1	16
Kingston-upon-Thames	1	2	0	7	6	3.50	–	–	1
The Oval	181	206	74	1902	66	14.40	–	4	112
In Surrey	202	226	79	2130	87★	14.49	–	5	129
Hastings	4	7	3	90	57	22.50	–	1	3
Hove	6	10	3	63	22	9.00	–	–	1
In Sussex	10	17	6	153	57	13.91	–	1	4
Coventry	2	3	0	68	66	22.66	–	1	2
Edgbaston	6	5	1	36	20	9.00	–	–	5
In Warwickshire	8	8	1	104	66	14.86	–	1	7

	M	I	NO	Runs	HS	Avge	100	50	Ct
Dudley	1	2	0	33	33	16.50	–	–	3
Kidderminster	1	1	0	4	4	4.00	–	–	–
Worcester	9	11	2	136	58	15.11	–	1	5
In Worcestershire	11	14	2	173	58	14.42	–	1	8
Bradford	4	4	2	15	13★	7.50	–	–	3
Headingley	7	11	4	171	79	24.43	–	1	5
Scarborough	19	18	5	243	43★	18.69	–	–	7
Sheffield (Bramall Lane)	5	8	0	23	7	2.88	–	–	1
In Yorkshire	35	41	11	452	79	15.07	–	1	16
Fenner's	4	2	2	6	6★	–	–	–	3

Overseas (listed by country)

	M	I	NO	Runs	HS	Avge	100	50	Ct
Adelaide	3	5	0	12	7	2.40	–	–	3
Brisbane	6	9	0	87	30	9.66	–	–	4
Hobart	3	4	0	110	51	27.50	–	1	2
Launceston	1	1	1	2	2★	–	–	–	1
Melbourne	6	9	3	127	27★	21.16	–	–	4
Perth	2	2	0	43	42	21.50	–	–	2
Sydney	8	12	4	54	14	6.75	–	–	2
In Australia	29	42	8	435	51	12.79	–	1	18
Bombay	1	1	1	0	0★	–	–	–	2
Calcutta	1	2	0	10	10	5.00	–	–	–
In India	2	3	1	10	10	5.00	–	–	2
Auckland	1	1	0	0	0	0.00	–	–	–
Christchurch	2	2	1	13	8★	13.00	–	–	1
Dunedin	1	2	1	31	25	31.00	–	–	–
Wellington	2	2	0	39	28	19.50	–	–	2
In New Zealand	6	7	2	83	28	16.60	–	–	3
Bloemfontein	1	1	1	77	77★	–	–	1	1
Bulawayo	1	2	1	47	42★	47.00	–	–	1
Cape Town	3	2	0	49	33	24.50	–	–	2
Durban	3	5	2	38	24	12.66	–	–	2
Johannesburg (Ellis Park)	4	5	0	64	32	12.80	–	–	–
Pietermaritzburg	1	1	0	0	0	0.00	–	–	1
Port Elizabeth	1	2	0	34	33	17.00	–	–	1
Salisbury	1	1	0	9	9	9.00	–	–	1
Salisbury (Police 'A')	1	2	1	10	10★	10.00	–	–	–
In Rhodesia and South Africa	16	21	5	328	77★	20.50	–	1	9

Summary

	M	I	NO	Runs	HS	Avge	100	50	Ct
In United Kingdom	432	503	165	4879	126	14.43	1	11	257
Overseas	53	73	16	856	77*	15.02	–	2	32
Total	485	576	181	5735	126	14.51	1	13	289

BOWLING

Season by season

	O	M	R	W	Avge	5wi	10wm	BB
1939	†18	2	59	0	–	–	–	–
1946	1030.1	202	2577	128	20.13	10	3	7-46
1946/7	140.3	31	1667	47	35.47	–	–	4-21
	†392.3	58						
1947	1220.4	268	3175	130	24.42	6	1	6-53
1948	1138	282	2632	115	22.89	6	1	6-44
1948/9	†475.1	97	1273	45	28.29	1	–	6-17
1949	1005.2	251	2344	110	21.31	5	–	8-42
1950	1242.4	341	2797	122	22.93	6	1	8-53
1950/1	84	26	1148	53	21.66	3	1	5-46
	†350.3	58						
1951	1100	338	2024	130	15.57	9	2	7-58
1952	1185.4	296	2530	154	16.43	10	1	8-18
1953	1253	340	2702	162	16.68	12	2	8-18
1954	958.1	300	1828	121	15.11	5	1	7-38
1954/5	†206.7	33	659	24	27.46	1	–	5-57
1955	1146.3	295	2752	144	19.11	6	–	6-36
1956	900.5	250	1950	96	20.31	4	1	7-28
1956/7	49	10	119	2	59.50	–	–	2-66
1957	1032.4	264	2170	131	16.56	4	1	6-49
1958	457	169	816	48	17.00	2	–	7-53
1959	963	256	2208	91	24.26	3	–	5-29
1959/60	54.2	13	120	4	30.00	–	–	2-50
1960	786.4	230	1729	67	25.80	3	1	6-27
Total	15748.1	4162	39279	1924	20.42	96	16	8-18
	†1442.6	248						

† 8-ball overs

For each team

	O	M	R	W	Avge	5wi	10wm	BB
Surrey (County Championship)	10812.5	2889	23753	1241	19.14	62	10	8-18
Surrey (other matches)	1944.4 †18	539 2	4165	218	19.11	10	1	6-14
England (Tests)	1740.3 †685	461 113	5876	236	24.89	15	5	7-44
An England XI	106.4	24	242	17	14.24	1	–	6-78
The Rest	74	17	176	4	44.00	–	–	2-83
MCC	19 †739.6	43 133	2686	108	24.87	3	–	6-17
MCC South African XI	42	4	119	3	39.66	–	–	3-84
South	81	15	291	5	58.20	–	–	3-80
Players	451.1	97	1152	56	20.57	2	–	5-34
T.N. Pearce's XI	188.2	53	462	25	18.48	2	–	5-44
C.G. Howard's XI	49	10	119	2	59.50	–	–	2-66
H.D.G. Leveson-Gower's XI	67	10	238	9	26.44	1	–	5-101
Total	15748.1 †1442.6	4162 248	39279	1924	20.42	96	16	8-18

Summary

	O	M	R	W	Avge	5wi	10wm	BB
Surrey	12757.3 †18	3428 2	27918	1459	19.14	72	11	8-18
England (Tests)	1740.3 †685	461 113	5876	236	24.89	15	5	7-44
Other Teams	1250.1 †739.6	273 133	5485	229	23.95	9	–	6-17
Total	15748.1 †1442.6	4162 248	39279	1924	20.42	96	16	8-18

Against each opponent (excluding Test matches)

In United Kingdom

	O	M	R	W	Avge	5wi	10wm	BB
Derbyshire	717.3	177	1568	101	15.52	8	2	6-25
Essex	798.3	198	1781	103	17.29	6	—	6-53
Glamorgan	609.4	184	1222	75	16.29	5	1	7-28
Gloucestershire	631.5	175	1401	68	20.60	2	—	7-53
Hampshire	669.1	197	1316	85	15.48	4	1	7-38
Kent	617.2	150	1412	62	22.77	—	—	4-38
Lancashire	565.2	168	1237	57	21.70	4	1	6-24
Leicestershire	705.5	203	1420	85	16.70	4	2	8-53
Middlesex	861.4	228	1896	81	23.41	2	—	8-42
Northamptonshire	696.2	157	1769	81	21.84	5	1	7-46
Nottinghamshire	953.4	230	2253	106	21.25	7	1	8-18
Somerset	584.3	165	1251	74	16.91	4	—	6-46
Sussex	653.4	176	1487	61	24.38	4	—	6-44
Warwickshire	477	113	1134	63	18.00	3	1	8-18
Worcestershire	601.3	173	1266	72	17.58	2	—	6-25
Yorkshire	840.2	233	1763	86	20.50	3	—	5-38
Cambridge Univ.	238.5	84	433	30	14.43	1	—	5-26
	†12	1						
Oxford Univ.	330.2	101	679	42	16.17	1	1	6-46
	†6	1						
MCC	477.1	134	1019	56	18.20	5	—	6-14
Gentlemen	451.1	97	1152	56	20.57	2	—	5-34
The Rest	209.4	45	517	29	17.83	1	—	6-78
North	81	15	291	5	58.20	—	—	3-80
Combined Services	53.5	13	117	4	29.25	—	—	4-58
H.D.G. Leveson-Gower's XI	42	4	119	3	39.66	—	—	3-84
England XI	37	7	83	2	41.50	—	—	2-83
Australians	142.4	31	388	20	19.40	1	—	5-86
Indians	170	44	358	15	23.87	1	—	5-135
New Zealanders	158.5	45	375	17	22.06	1	—	5-101
Pakistanis	74.4	19	171	7	24.43	—	—	4-53
South Africans	212.3	58	484	26	18.62	2	—	6-65
West Indians	139.2	28	331	10	33.10	—	—	3-75

Note: The figures against the counties are all for matches in the County Championship except for one match for Surrey against each of Essex (44.3-11-115-9) and Middlesex (37-10-93-2). He also played in two matches against Yorkshire for MCC (89.3-17-215-8).

Overseas

	O	M	R	W	Avge	5wi	10wm	BB
Australian XI	†42	7	136	1	136.00	–	–	1-39
Combined (Aus.) XI	†102.7	7	366	14	26.14	1	–	5-57
New South Wales	†120.7	17	474	14	33.86	1	–	5-57
Queensland	†95	23	205	7	29.29	–	–	3-40
South Australia	†25	5	61	5	12.20	–	–	3-20
Tasmania	†23.4	4	86	8	10.75	–	–	4-30
Victoria	†41	7	149	5	29.80	–	–	3-40
Western Australia	†21	3	62	2	31.00	–	–	2-62
Bengal Chief Minister's XI	31	7	74	2	37.00	–	–	2-66
Cricket Club of India President's XI	18	3	45	0	–	–	–	–
Auckland	18	8	26	3	8.66	–	–	3-26
Otago	44.4	6	115	5	23.00	–	–	3-76
Wellington	38.5	12	72	7	10.28	–	–	4-21
Rhodesia	54.2	13	156	11	14.18	1	–	6-17
	†28	14						
Cape Province	†28	4	83	3	27.66	–	–	2-56
Natal	†54	14	120	3	40.00	–	–	2-68
A Natal XI	†37.4	7	114	5	22.80	–	–	4-70
Orange Free State	†42	10	103	1	103.00	–	–	1-33
Transvaal	†50	10	137	4	34.25	–	–	3-67
Western Province	†29	1	126	6	21.00	–	–	4-30

Summary

	O	M	R	W	Avge	5wi	10wm	BB
Against British Teams	12904.5	3427	28586	1487	19.22	73	11	8-18
	†18	2						
Against Overseas Teams	1102.5	274	4817	201	23.97	8	–	6-17
	†739.6	133						
Test Matches	1740.3	461	5876	236	24.89	15	5	7-44
	†685	113						
Total	15748.1	4162	39279	1924	20.42	96	16	8-18
	†1442.6	248						

On each ground (including Test matches)

In United Kingdom (listed by county)

	O	M	R	W	Avge	5wi	10wm	BB
Chesterfield	89.2	27	204	16	12.75	2	1	6-56
Derby	206.4	44	456	23	19.83	2	–	5-22
In Derbyshire	296	71	660	39	16.92	4	1	6-56
Brentwood	17	3	47	1	47.00	–	–	1-47
Chelmsford	30	9	68	5	13.60	1	–	5-30
Clacton-on-Sea	92.3	24	187	11	17.00	1	–	5-49
Ilford	103	21	281	4	70.25	–	–	2-40
Leyton	18	2	48	2	24.00	–	–	2-48
Romford	33	6	93	5	18.60	–	–	3-33
Southend-on-Sea	69.5	12	147	11	13.36	–	–	4-68
In Essex	363.2	77	871	39	22.33	2	–	5-30
Cardiff	181.5	65	339	27	12.55	2	1	7-28
Llanelli	36.4	10	60	2	30.00	–	–	2-60
Swansea	88	18	269	9	29.88	–	–	4-78
In Glamorgan	306.3	93	668	38	17.58	2	1	7-28
Bristol	113	31	281	13	21.62	1	–	7-53
Cheltenham	165.2	36	404	25	16.16	–	–	4-42
Gloucester	26.5	6	57	3	19.00	–	–	2-42
Stroud	43	16	77	4	19.25	–	–	2-27
In Gloucestershire	348.1	89	819	45	18.20	1	–	7-53
Bournemouth	87.3	22	179	9	19.88	–	–	4-40
Portsmouth	206	60	467	20	23.50	1	–	5-68
Southampton	99	32	167	8	20.87	–	–	4-26
In Hampshire	392.3	114	813	37	21.97	1	–	5-68
Blackheath	279.5	67	642	32	20.06	–	–	4-38
Canterbury	36.5	9	100	7	14.29	1	–	6-78
In Kent	316.4	76	742	39	19.03	1	–	6-78
Old Trafford	626.5	171	1494	85	17.58	8	3	7-52
Leicester	398	118	741	46	16.10	3	1	6-27
Loughborough	47	15	124	6	20.66	–	–	4-48
In Leicestershire	445	133	865	52	16.63	3	1	6-27
Lord's	1633	425	3680	160	23.00	9	1	8-42
Kettering	67	20	139	11	12.64	1	–	7-46
Northampton	135	34	341	14	24.36	–	–	4-43
Peterborough	12	4	24	2	12.00	–	–	2-24
Rushden	40.4	6	95	8	11.88	1	–	5-49
In Northamptonshire	254.4	64	599	35	17.11	2	–	7-46
Trent Bridge	838.1	222	1904	82	23.22	6	1	7-44

	O	M	R	W	Avge	5wi	10wm	BB
Bath	37	10	89	4	22.25	–	–	4-73
Taunton	85	23	205	6	34.17	–	–	4-27
Wells	44	7	123	6	20.50	1	–	6-92
Weston-super-Mare	120	40	204	21	9.71	1	–	5-14
In Somerset	286	80	621	37	16.78	2	–	6-92
Guildford	756.3	238	1529	93	16.44	5	1	7-38
Kingston-upon-Thames	21	8	53	0	–	–	–	–
The Oval	6144.3	1613	13354	715	18.68	36	6	8-18
	†18	2						
In Surrey	6922	1859	14936	808	18.49	41	7	8-18
	†18	2						
Hastings	114.3	21	316	9	35.11	–	–	4-59
Hove	215.2	66	473	22	21.50	–	–	4-15
In Sussex	329.5	87	789	31	25.45	–	–	4-15
Coventry	61.4	7	198	8	24.75	1	–	5-51
Edgbaston	204.2	51	453	21	21.57	–	–	4-41
In Warwickshire	266	58	651	29	22.45	1	–	5-51
Dudley	48	18	87	3	29.00	–	–	2-58
Kidderminster	15.5	3	35	2	17.50	–	–	1-7
Worcester	306.2	90	629	34	18.50	1	–	6-25
In Worcestershire	370.1	111	751	39	19.26	1	–	6-25
Bradford	110.1	37	227	14	16.21	–	–	4-18
Headingley	340.1	81	801	26	30.81	1	–	6-95
Scarborough	679.5	144	1841	78	23.60	4	–	5-44
Sheffield (Bramall Lane)	197.3	60	407	22	18.50	1	–	5-49
In Yorkshire	1327.4	322	3276	140	23.40	6	–	6-95
Fenner's	97.5	30	154	14	11.00	1	–	5-26

Overseas (listed by country)

	O	M	R	W	Avge	5wi	10wm	BB
Adelaide	†121	22	362	11	32.90	–	–	3-20
Brisbane	†196.2	38	549	17	32.29	–	–	4-45
Hobart	†69.4	7	280	14	20.00	–	–	4-30
Launceston	†28.7	2	86	7	12.28	1	–	5-57
Melbourne	†200.1	31	648	28	23.14	2	1	5-46
Perth	†49	5	148	3	49.33	–	–	2-62
Sydney	†284.7	44	955	23	41.52	1	–	5-57
In Australia	†949.5	149	3028	103	29.40	4	1	5-46
Bombay	18	3	45	0	–	–	–	–
Calcutta	31	7	74	2	37.00	–	–	2-66
In India	49	10	119	2	59.50	–	–	2-66
Auckland	18	8	26	3	8.66	–	–	3-26
Christchurch	80	15	178	5	35.60	–	–	4-95
Dunedin	44.4	6	115	5	23.00	–	–	3-76
Wellington	81.5	28	127	8	15.87	–	–	4-21
In New Zealand	224.3	57	446	21	21.24	–	–	4-21
Bloemfontein	†42	10	103	1	103.00	–	–	1-33
Bulawayo	32	8	71	3	23.66	–	–	2-50
Cape Town	†98	10	341	9	37.88	–	–	4-30
Durban	†85.5	21	210	9	23.33	–	–	4-39
Johannesburg (Ellis Park)	†130	23	365	9	40.55	–	–	3-67
Pietermaritzburg	†37.4	7	114	5	22.80	–	–	4-70
Port Elizabeth	†54	12	104	5	20.80	–	–	4-61
Salisbury	†28	14	36	7	5.14	1	–	6-17
Salisbury (Police 'A')	22.2	5	49	1	49.00	–	–	1-39
In Rhodesia and	54.2	13	1393	49	28.43	1	–	6-17
South Africa	†475.1	97						

Summary

	O	M	R	W	Avge	5wi	10wm	BB
In United Kingdom	15420.2	4082	34293	1749	19.61	91	15	8-18
	†18	2						
Overseas	327.5	80	4986	175	28.49	5	1	6-17
	†1424.6	246						
Total	15748.1	4162	39279	1924	20.42	96	16	8-18
	†1442.6	248						

189

BATTING AND FIELDING

Series by series

Date	Opponents	M	I	NO	Runs	HS	Avge	100	50	Ct
1946	India	3	2	0	38	30	19.00	–	–	3
1946/7	Australia	5	10	3	106	27★	15.14	–	–	3
1946/7	New Zealand	1	1	1	8	8★	–	–	–	1
1947	South Africa	2	3	0	9	7	3.00	–	–	1
1948	Australia	5	9	1	176	79	22.00	–	1	1
1948/9	South Africa	5	8	1	94	33	13.43	–	–	3
1949	New Zealand	2	2	0	20	10	10.00	–	–	4
1950	West Indies	3	6	0	20	13	3.33	–	–	–
1950/1	Australia	5	8	2	43	14	7.33	–	–	5
1950/1	New Zealand	2	2	0	33	28	16.50	–	–	1
1951	South Africa	5	6	3	66	30★	22.00	–	–	1
1952	India	4	3	0	27	17	9.00	–	–	1
1953	Australia	5	6	3	38	22	12.66	–	–	1
1954	Pakistan	2	1	1	22	22★	–	–	–	–
1954/5	Australia	1	2	0	10	5	5.00	–	–	1
1955	South Africa	1	2	0	4	3	2.00	–	–	–
Total		51	71	15	714	79	12.75	–	1	26

Against each opponent

	M	I	NO	Runs	HS	Avge	100	50	Ct
Australia	21	35	9	373	79	14.35	–	1	11
India	7	5	0	65	30	13.00	–	–	4
New Zealand	5	5	1	61	28	15.25	–	–	6
Pakistan	2	1	1	22	22★	–	–	–	–
South Africa	13	19	4	173	33	11.53	–	–	5
West Indies	3	6	0	20	13	3.33	–	–	–
Total	51	71	15	714	79	12.75	–	1	26

On each ground (listed by country)

	M	I	NO	Runs	HS	Avge	100	50	Ct
Headingley	5	7	2	134	79	33.50	–	1	4
Lord's	7	9	1	83	30	10.38	–	–	3
Old Trafford	7	8	2	128	37	21.33	–	–	3
The Oval	7	7	1	24	22★	4.00	–	–	2
Trent Bridge	6	9	2	51	22	7.29	–	–	–
In England	32	40	8	420	79	13.55	–	1	12
Adelaide	2	4	0	12	7	3.00	–	–	3
Brisbane	3	5	0	28	18	5.60	–	–	3
Melbourne	3	5	3	81	27★	40.50	–	–	1
Sydney	3	6	2	38	14	9.50	–	–	2
In Australia	11	20	5	159	27★	10.60	–	–	9

	M	I	NO	Runs	HS	Avge	100	50	Ct
Christchurch	2	2	1	13	8*	13.00	–	–	1
Wellington	1	1	0	28	28	28.00	–	–	1
In New Zealand	3	3	1	41	28	20.50	–	–	2
Cape Town	1	1	0	16	16	16.00	–	–	1
Durban	1	2	1	12	11	12.00	–	–	1
Johannesburg	2	3	0	32	19	10.66	–	–	–
Port Elizabeth	1	2	0	34	33	17.00	–	–	1
In South Africa	5	8	1	94	33	13.43	–	–	3
Total Overseas	19	31	7	294	33	12.25	–	–	14
Total	51	71	15	714	79	12.75	–	1	26

Half-century: 79 v Australia, Headingley, 1948

BOWLING

Series by series

Date	Opponents	O	M	R	W	Avge	BpW	5wi	10wm	BB
1946	India	144.2	33	298	24	12.42	36.08	2	2	7-49
1946/7	Australia	†246.3	38	876	16	54.75	123.18	–	–	3-97
1946/7	New Zealand	39	5	95	4	23.75	58.50	–	–	4-95
1947	South Africa	111	24	233	4	58.25	166.75	–	–	3-106
1948	Australia	274.3	75	688	18	38.22	91.50	–	–	4-81
1948/9	South Africa	†206.5	37	554	16	34.63	103.31	–	–	4-39
1949	New Zealand	85	19	215	7	30.71	72.85	–	–	4-74
1950	West Indies	181	49	377	11	34.27	98.72	1	–	5-127
1950/1	Australia	†195	34	482	30	16.07	52.00	2	1	5-46
1950/1	New Zealand	84	26	138	2	69.00	252.00	–	–	1-34
1951	South Africa	275.5	84	517	30	17.23	55.16	3	1	7-58
1952	India	163.5	57	279	20	13.95	49.15	2	–	5-27
1953	Australia	265.1	58	682	39	17.49	40.79	5	1	7-44
1954	Pakistan	74.5	28	158	10	15.80	44.90	–	–	3-9
1954/5	Australia	†37	4	131	1	131.00	296.00	–	–	1-131
1955	South Africa	41	3	153	4	38.25	61.50	–	–	2-61
Total		1740.3	461	5876	236	24.90	67.44	15	5	7-44
		†685			113					

Against each opponent

	O	M	R	W	Avge	BpW	5wi	10wm	BB
Australia	539.4	133	2859	104	27.49	67.93	7	2	7-44
	†478.3	76							
India	308.1	90	577	44	13.11	42.02	4	2	7-49
New Zealand	208	50	448	13	34.46	96.00	–	–	4-74
Pakistan	74.5	28	158	10	15.80	44.90	–	–	3-9
South Africa	428.5	111	1457	54	26.98	78.16	3	1	7-58
	†206.5	37							
West Indies	181	49	377	11	34.27	98.72	1	–	5-127
Total	1740.3	461	5876	236	24.90	67.44	15	5	7-44
	†685	113							

On each ground (listed by country)

	O	M	R	W	Avge	BpW	5wi	10wm	BB
Headingley	245.1	55	578	16	36.13	91.94	1	–	6-95
Lord's	437.5	121	957	34	28.15	77.26	2	1	7-49
Old Trafford	302.4	88	686	51	13.45	35.61	5	2	7-52
The Oval	249.3	55	550	25	22.00	59.88	1	–	5-41
Trent Bridge	382.2	111	829	41	20.22	55.83	4	1	7-44
In England	1617.3	430	3600	167	21.56	58.08	13	4	7-44
Adelaide	†96	17	301	6	50.17	128.00	–	–	3-74
Brisbane	†101.2	15	344	10	34.40	81.00	–	–	4-45
Melbourne	†143.1	22	460	22	20.91	52.05	2	1	5-46
Sydney	†138	22	384	9	42.66	92.00	–	–	4-107
In Australia	†478.3	76	1489	47	31.68	81.43	2	1	5-46
Christchurch	80	15	178	5	35.60	96.00	–	–	4-95
Wellington	43	16	55	1	55.00	258.00	–	–	1-34
In New Zealand	123	31	233	6	38.83	123.00	–	–	4-95
Cape Town	†41	5	132	0	–	–	–	–	–
Durban	†31.5	7	90	6	15.00	42.17	–	–	4-39
Johannesburg	†80	13	228	5	45.60	128.00	–	–	2-81
Port Elizabeth	†54	12	104	5	20.80	86.40	–	–	4-61
In South Africa	†206.5	37	554	16	34.63	103.31	–	–	4-39
Total Overseas	123	31	2276	69	32.99	90.12	2	1	5-46
	†685	113							
Total	1740.3	461	5876	236	24.90	67.44	15	5	7-44
	†685	113							

Five wickets in an innings

7-44 v Australia	Trent Bridge	1953	5-41	v India	The Oval	1952
7-49 v India	Lord's	1946	5-46	v Australia	Melbourne	1950/1
7-52 v India	Old Trafford	1946	5-54	v South Africa	Old Trafford	1951
7-55 v Australia	Trent Bridge	1953	5-59	v Australia	Melbourne	1950/1
7-58 v South Africa	Old Trafford	1951	5-105	v Australia	Lord's	1953
6-37 v South Africa	Trent Bridge	1951	5-115	v Australia	Old Trafford	1953
6-95 v Australia	Headingley	1953	5-127	v West Indies	Trent Bridge	1950
5-27 v India	Old Trafford	1952				

Methods of dismissal

Caught	136	57.63%
Bowled	69	29.24%
Lbw	28	11.86%
Stumped	3	1.27%
Total	236	100.00%

Batsmen most frequently dismissed by Bedser (all Australian unless stated)

18 A.R. Morris
12 R.N. Harvey
10 R.R. Lindwall
 9 A.L. Hassett
 6 D.G. Bradman, J.E. Cheetham (South Africa), G.B. Hole, B. Mitchell (South Africa)

Note: Sir Alec had a higher success ratio against Bradman in Test cricket than almost any other bowler, as the following shows:

Most Test dismissals of Bradman

Bowler (All England)	Tests	Innings	Dismissals	Dismissals per Innings
W.E. Bowes	5	9	5	0.55
A.V. BEDSER	10	17	6	0.35
H. Verity	16	29	8	0.28
H. Larwood	11	20	5	0.20

Note: Five of Bradman's dismissals by Sir Alec came in consecutive innings – an unprecedented feat. The 18 dismissals of Morris by Sir Alec is a world record for Test cricket, as the following shows:

Most dismissals by one bowler against one batsman in Test cricket

Bowler	Batsman	Dismissals	Tests	Innings
A.V. BEDSER (England)	A.R. Morris (Australia)	18	21	37
C.E.L. Ambrose (West Indies)	M.A. Atherton (England)	17	25	48
C.A. Walsh (West Indies)	M.A. Atherton (England)	17	26	50
M.D. Marshall (West Indies)	G.A. Gooch (England)	16	21	40

Note: For the 21 Tests in which Sir Alec and Morris opposed each other the next most successful bowler was J.C. Laker with three dismissals.

Most fielding dismissals from Bedser's bowling (all caught unless otherwise stated)
26 T.G. Evans (24ct, 2st)
16 L. Hutton
12 J.T. Ikin
11 D.C.S. Compton
 6 A.V. BEDSER, T.E. Bailey

Highest Test wicket aggregate (as at 31 August 1955)

	Tests	Balls	Runs	Wkts	Avge	BpW	5wi	10wm	BB
A.V. BEDSER (Eng) 1946–55	51	15918	5876	236	24.90	67.44	15	5	7-44
C.V. Grimmett (Aus) 1924/5–35/6	37	15413	5231	216	24.22	67.19	21	7	7-40
R.R. Lindwall (Aus) 1945/6–55	47	10732	4203	192	21.89	55.90	11	–	7-38
S.F. Barnes (Eng) 1901/02–13/4	27	7873	3106	189	16.43	41.66	24	7	9-103
W.A. Johnstone (Aus) 1947/8–54/5	40	11048	3826	160	23.91	69.06	7	–	6-44

Bowlers holding record Test wicket aggregate for longest period since 1945

			Date record taken (wkts)	Date record lost or equalled (wkts)
F.S. Trueman	England	12 years 322 days	15/03/63 (243)	31/01/76 (307)
A.V. BEDSER	England	9 years 186 days	24/07/53 (217)	26/01/63 (236)
Kapil Dev	India	6 years 48 days	08/02/94 (432)	27/03/00 (434)
R.J. Hadlee	New Zealand	5 years 79 days	12/11/88 (374)	30/01/94 (431)
L.R. Gibbs	West Indies	4 years 331 days	31/01/76 (308)	27/12/81 (309)
D.K. Lillee	Australia	4 years 237 days	27/12/81 (310)	21/08/86 (355)

Highest Test wicket aggregate for England (as at 1 October 2000)

	Tests	Balls	Runs	Wkts	Avge	BpW	Rp100B	WpT	5wi	10wm	BB
I.T. Botham 1977–92	102	21815	10878	383	28.40	56.96	49.86	3.75	27	4	8-34
R.G.D. Willis 1970/1–84	90	17357	8190	325	25.20	53.41	47.19	3.61	16	–	8-43
F.S. Trueman 1952–65	67	15178	6625	307	21.57	49.44	43.65	4.58	17	3	8-31
D.L. Underwood 1866–81/2	86	21862	7674	297	25.83	73.61	35.10	3.45	17	6	8-51
J.B. Statham 1950/1–65	70	16056	6261	252	24.84	63.71	38.99	3.60	9	1	7-39
A.V. BEDSER 1946–55	51	15918	5876	236	24.90	67.44	36.91	4.63	15	5	7-44
J.A. Snow 1965–76	49	12021	5387	202	26.66	59.51	44.81	4.12	8	1	7-40

It is also useful to compare these records with those of two bowlers similar in style to Sir Alec:

	Tests	Balls	Runs	Wkts	Avge	BpW	Rp100B	WpT	5wi	10wm	BB
S.F. Barnes 1901/2–13/4	27	7873	3106	189	16.43	41.65	39.45	7.00	24	7	9-103
M.W. Tate 1924–35	39	12523	4055	155	26.16	80.79	32.38	3.97	7	1	6-42

Best bowling figures for England in first innings of début Test

7-46	J.K. Lever	v India	Delhi	1976/7
7-49	A.V. BEDSER	v India	Lord's	1946
7-103	J.C. Laker	v West Indies	Bridgetown	1947/8

Most wickets in a career for England against Australia (up to 1955)

	Tests	Balls	Runs	Wkts	Avge	5wi	10wm	BB
W. Rhodes 1899–1926	41	5796	2616	109	24.00	6	1	8-68
S.F. Barnes 1901/2–12	20	5749	2288	106	21.58	12	1	7-60
A.V. BEDSER 1946/7–54/5	21	7065	2859	104	27.49	7	2	7-44
R. Peel 1884/5–96	20	5216	1715	102	16.81	6	2	7-31

Most balls bowled for England against Australia

	Tests	Balls	Runs	Wkts	Avge	BpW	5wi	10wm	BB
I.T. Botham 1977–89	36	8479	4093	148	27.65	57.29	9	2	6-78
D.L. Underwood 1968–79/80	29	8000	2770	105	26.38	76.19	4	2	7-50
M.W. Tate 1924/5–30	20	7686	2540	83	30.60	92.60	6	1	6-99
R.G.D. Willis 1970/1–82/3	35	7294	3346	128	26.14	56.98	7	–	8-43
A.V. BEDSER 1946/7–54/5	21	7065	2859	104	27.49	67.93	7	2	7-44

Note: Bedser's average of 336.4 balls per Test is exceeded only by Tate's 384.3.

Most wickets in a series for any country against Australia (all for England)

	Venue	Season	T	Balls	Runs	W	Avge	BpW	5wi	10wm	BB
J.C. Laker	Eng	1956	5	1703	442	46	9.60	37.02	4	2	10-53
A.V. BEDSER	Eng	1953	5	1591	682	39	17.48	40.79	5	1	7-44
M.W. Tate	Aust	1924/5	5	2528	881	38	23.18	66.53	5	1	6-99
I.T. Botham	Eng	1981	6	1635	700	34	20.58	48.09	3	1	6-95

Note: Sir Alec took 30 wickets in the 1950/1 series and this makes him the only bowler, from any country, to take at least 30 wickets in a series against Australia, both home and away. Sir Alec also took 30 wickets in the 1951 series against South Africa and this makes him the only English bowler to take 30 wickets in a series three times since 1945.

The 1953 Test series – leading bowling averages (qualification – 5 wickets, average 45)

	O	M	R	W	Avge	BpW	5wi	10wm	BB
A.V. BEDSER (Eng)	265.1	58	682	39	17.48	40.79	5	1	7-44
R.R. Lindwall (Aus)	240.4	62	490	26	18.84	55.54	3	–	5-54
G.A.R. Lock (Eng)	61	21	165	8	20.62	45.75	1	–	5-45
J.C. Hill (Aus)	66	18	158	7	22.57	56.57	–	–	3-35
J.C. Laker (Eng)	58.5	11	212	9	23.55	39.22	–	–	4-75
J.H. Wardle (Eng)	155.3	57	344	13	26.46	71.77	–	–	4-7
A.K. Davidson (Aus)	125	42	212	8	26.50	93.75	–	–	2-22
K.R. Miller (Aus)	186	72	303	10	30.30	111.60	–	–	4-63

Note: Sir Alec took the first Australian wicket to fall in each of the five Tests. Sir Alec bowled 31.7 per cent of England's overs in the five Tests.

Most balls bowled and wickets taken in Ashes Tests 1946/7–1953

	Balls	Runs	Wkts	Avge	BpW	5wi	10wm	BB
A.V. BEDSER (Eng)	6769	2728	103	26.49	65.72	7	2	7-44
R.R. Lindwall (Aus)	4553	1731	86	20.13	52.94	6	–	7-63
W.A. Johnston (Aus)	4131	1395	56	24.91	73.77	2	–	5-35
K.R. Miller (Aus)	3778	1239	56	22.13	67.46	1	–	7-60
D.V.P. Wright (Eng)	3069	1613	36	44.80	85.25	2	–	7-105
I.W. Johnson (Aus)	2990	1044	24	43.50	124.58	1	–	6-42
N.W.D. Yardley (Eng)	1504	576	19	30.32	79.16	–	–	3-67
T.E. Bailey (Eng)	1459	585	22	26.59	66.32	–	–	4-22

Note: Sir Alec bowled more balls than any other bowler in each of the four series between the dates shown, except in 1948 when his 1647 compared with Johnston's 1856. Sir Alec took five wickets in an innings on five consecutive occasions.

English bowlers taking 50 Test wickets on one ground

		T	O	M	R	W	Avge	BpW	5wi	10wm	BB
A.V. BEDSER	Old Trafford	7	302.4	88	686	51	13.45	35.61	5	2	7-52
I.T. Botham	Lord's	15	532.2	125	1693	69	24.54	46.29	8	1	8-34
I.T. Botham	The Oval	11	435.5	90	1379	52	26.52	50.29	2	1	6-125
F.S. Trueman	Lord's	12	514.3	113	1394	63	22.13	49.00	5	1	6-31

Note: Sir Alec was the first bowler from any country to achieve this feat.

Five wickets in an innings in five consecutive Test innings

5-27	v India	Old Trafford	1952
5-41	v India	The Oval	1952
7-55	v Australia	Trent Bridge	1953
7-44	v Australia	Trent Bridge	1953
5-105	v Australia	Lord's	1953

Note: T. Richardson, also a right-arm pace bowler from Surrey, is the only other England player to achieve this feat – in 1894/5–6.

Most wickets for England in first two Tests

	Opponents	Venue	O	M	R	W	Avge	BpW	5wi	10wm	BB
A.V. BEDSER	India	England	112.2	27	238	22	10.82	30.64	2	2	7-49
S.F. Barnes	Australia	Australia	131.2	33	302	19	15.89	41.47	3	1	7-121
N.G.B. Cook	N. Zealand	England	135.2	56	275	17	16.18	47.76	2	–	5-35

Note: Barnes played his first two Tests in 1901/2 and Cook in 1983. A.E. Trott took 17 wickets in his first two Tests for England, in 1898/9, but after previously playing in three Tests for Australia.

Numbers of batsmen dismissed by Sir Alec by batting order

	Australia	India	N. Zealand	Pakistan	S. Africa	W. Indies	Total
1	18	4	1	1	8	1	33
2	17	3	3	1	6	0	30
3	12	3	0	1	4	1	21
4	11	6	3	0	3	2	25
5	5	5	1	1	6	0	18
6	6	5	3	1	7	1	23
7	6	3	1	2	4	3	19
8	7	5	0	2	5	1	20
9	9	4	0	0	5	1	19
10	10	5	1	0	3	1	20
11	3	1	0	1	3	0	8
Total	104	44	13	10	54	11	236

Lowest number of championship matches by English professionals before Test début since 1919

	Matches	Days	Championship Début	Test Début
A.V. BEDSER	7	35	Surrey v Somerset, The Oval, 18/5/46	v India, Lord's, 22/6/46
B.C. Hollioake	10	428	Surrey v Yorkshire, Middlesbrough, 6/6/96	v Australia, Trent Bridge, 7/8/97
C.P. Schofield	13	666	Lancashire v Glamorgan, Colwyn Bay, 22/7/98	v. Zimbabwe, Lord's, 18/5/00
D.B. Close	14	66	Yorkshire v Somerset, Wells, 18/5/49	v New Zealand, Old Trafford, 23/7/49
J.C. Laker	14	231	Surrey v Worcestershire, The Oval, 4/6/47	v West Indies, Bridgetown, 21/1/48
J.B. Statham	14	273	Lancashire v Kent, Old Trafford, 17/6/50	v New Zealand, Christchurch, 17/3/51

Other points of interest in Test cricket

Sir Alec's match figures of 14-99 against Australia in 1953 are the best in any Test match at Trent Bridge.

Only S.F. Barnes (7) and D.L. Underwood (6) have taken ten wickets in a match for England on more occasions than Sir Alec.

Sir Alec opened the bowling with 17 different partners in his 51 Tests; the first was W.E. Bowes and the last F.H. Tyson.

100th Test wicket

R.J. Christiani c A.J. McIntyre b A.V. Bedser   11
England v West Indies, The Oval, 14/8/1950

200th Test wicket

A.K. Davidson c J.B. Statham   b A.V. Bedser   76

England v Australia, Lord's, 26/6/1953

MISCELLANY

BATTING

Century

126   Surrey v Somerset, Taunton, 1947

Century partnerships

197	8th	T. Barling	Surrey v Somerset	Taunton	1947
155	3rd	W.J. EDRICH	England v Australia	Headingley	1948
151	8th	J.C. Laker	Surrey v Glamorgan	Cardiff	1951
143*	8th	M.F. Tremlett	MCC v Orange Free State	Bloemfontein	1948/9
142	7th	A.J. McIntyre	Surrey v Northamptonshire	The Oval	1950
121	8th	D.C.S. COMPTON	England v Australia	Old Trafford	1948
116	9th	J.F. Parker	Surrey v New Zealanders	The Oval	1949
116	8th	H.E. Dollery	Players v Gentlemen	Lord's	1950
114	7th	E.R.T. Holmes	Surrey v Warwickshire	Coventry	1947
102	7th	G.J. Whittaker	Surrey v Derbyshire	The Oval	1950

Pairs

ENGLAND v AUSTRALIA	The Oval	1948
Surrey v Worcestershire	Worcester	1949
Surrey v Leicestershire	Leicester	1950
ENGLAND v WEST INDIES	The Oval	1950
Surrey v Lancashire	The Oval	1951
Surrey v Middlesex	The Oval	1953
Surrey v Hampshire	Portsmouth	1956
Surrey v Essex	Leyton	1958
Surrey v MCC	Lord's	1959

Note: In the instance against Worcestershire, Sir Alec was dismissed in both innings by R.O. Jenkins. In 1950 Sir Alec scored four consecutive ducks, beginning with the pair against West Indies.

BOWLING

Seven wickets in an innings

8-18	Surrey v Warwickshire	The Oval	1953
8-18	Surrey v Nottinghamshire	The Oval	1952
8-42	Surrey v Middlesex	Lord's	1949
8-53	Surrey v Leicestershire	The Oval	1950
7-28	Surrey v Glamorgan	Cardiff	1956
7-38	Surrey v Hampshire	Guildford	1953
7-41	Surrey v Glamorgan	Cardiff	1956
7-44	ENGLAND v AUSTRALIA	Trent Bridge	1953
7-46	Surrey v Northamptonshire	Kettering	1946
7-49	ENGLAND v INDIA	Lord's	1946
7-52	ENGLAND v INDIA	Old Trafford	1946
7-53	Surrey v Gloucestershire	Bristol	1958
7-55	ENGLAND v AUSTRALIA	Trent Bridge	1953
7-58	ENGLAND v SOUTH AFRICA	Old Trafford	1951

Ten wickets in a match

14-69	Surrey v Glamorgan	Cardiff	1956
14-99	ENGLAND v AUSTRALIA	Trent Bridge	1953
13-46	Surrey v Nottinghamshire	The Oval	1952
12-35	Surrey v Warwickshire	The Oval	1953
12-106	Surrey v Leicestershire	The Oval	1950
12-112	ENGLAND v SOUTH AFRICA	Old Trafford	1951
11-89	Surrey v Lancashire	Old Trafford	1946
11-91	Surrey v Derbyshire	Chesterfield	1948
11-93	ENGLAND v INDIA	Old Trafford	1946
11-102	Surrey v Derbyshire	The Oval	1947
11-145	ENGLAND v INDIA	Lord's	1946
10-45	Surrey v Hampshire	Guildford	1954
10-59	Surrey v Leicestershire	Leicester	1960
10-76	Surrey v Oxford University	The Oval	1951
10-79	Surrey v Northamptonshire	The Oval	1957
10-105	ENGLAND v AUSTRALIA	Melbourne	1950/1

Hat-trick

Surrey v Essex, The Oval, 1953 (second innings) – victims: T.C. Dodds, W.T. Greensmith and R. Horsfall

Economical bowling (conceding less than one run per over)
(a) in an innings (minimum 20 overs)

25-13-24-4	v Nottinghamshire	The Oval	1951
20-8-18-8	v Nottinghamshire	The Oval	1952
21-8-20-1	v Lancashire	The Oval	1954

(b) in a match (minimum 25 overs)

27-16-22-6	v Sussex	Hove	1958

Note: In the 1951 and 1952 seasons, Sir Alec's figures in four matches against Nottinghamshire were: 138.4-44-197-29 – avge 6.79

1000th first-class wicket
H.J. Butler c J.F. Parker b A.V. Bedser 0 (2nd innings)
Surrey v Nottinghamshire, The Oval, 5/8/1952

Best position in national averages
4th–1951   5th–1952

Best position in national aggregates
3rd–1952, 1953

Best position in Surrey's championship averages
1st–1948, 1951, 1952, 1954   2nd–1949

Best position in Surrey's championship aggregates
2nd–1946, 1947, 1949, 1950, 1952, 1953, 1955, 1957

Methods of dismissal

Caught	1177	61.17%
Bowled	526	27.34%
Lbw	176	9.15%
Stumped	43	2.23%
Hit wicket	2	0.22%
Total	1924	100.00%

Batsmen most frequently dismissed by Sir Alec

22	A.R. Morris (New South Wales and Australia)
19	R.T. Simpson (Nottinghamshire)
17	D.J. Insole (Essex)
16	T.C. Dodds (Essex)
14	W.J. Edrich, J.D. Robertson (both Middlesex), R.N. Harvey (Australia)
13	D.C.S. Compton (Middlesex)
12	F.W. Stocks (Nottinghamshire)

Note: Sir Alec dismissed Bradman eight times in first-class cricket in 19 innings (a ratio of 0.42). This compares most favourably with the only two bowlers who took his wicket on more occasions: C.V. Grimmett (10 dismissals, 27 innings, ratio 0.37) and H. Verity (10,

41, 0.24). Sir Alec dismissed Bradman in six consecutive innings in which they opposed each other – an unprecedented feat.

Most fielding dismissals from Sir Alec's bowling

167	A.J.W. McIntyre (143 ct, 24 st)
108	G.A.R. Lock
69	W.S. Surridge
61	J.C. Laker
60	T.G. Evans (51 ct, 9 st)
55	J.F. Parker
52	A.V. BEDSER
49	M.J. Stewart
42	K.F. Barrington
39	D.G.W. Fletcher
33	E.A. Bedser
31	P.B.H. May

Fifty wickets in a season in Australia by English tourists since 1919

		Balls	Runs	Wkts	Avge	5wi	10wm	BB
M.W. Tate	1924/5	4018	1464	77	19.01	7	2	7-74
J.C. White	1928/9	5213	1471	65	22.63	5	1	8-126
A.V. BEDSER	1950/1	2819	1010	51	19.80	3	1	5-46
F.H. Tyson	1954/5	2368	1002	51	19.64	4	1	7-27
D.V.P. Wright	1946/7	3164	1699	51	33.31	3	1	7-105

CAPTAINCY

The results of matches in which Sir Alec was captain are as follows:

		Total			Totals as percentages			
	P	W	L	D	P	W	L	D
Surrey in Championship	60	22	15	23	81.1	29.7	20.3	31.1
Surrey in other matches	13	6	1	6	17.6	8.1	1.4	8.1
Players	1	1	0	0	1.4	1.4	0.0	0.0
Total	74	29	16	29	100.0	39.2	21.6	39.2

Note: Sir Alec led Surrey 18 times (out of 28 matches) in the Championship in 1959, when Surrey finished third, and 25 times (also out of 28) in 1960 when they finished seventh.

TEST SELECTION

England Test selectors involved in choosing most teams

		M	W	D	L	%
A.V. BEDSER	1962–85	124	48	48	28	58.1
P.B.H. May	1965–68, '82–88	61	20	20	21	49.2
D.J. Insole	1959–68	52	24	17	11	62.5
A.C. Smith	1863–73, '82–86	51	18	17	16	52.0
D. Kenyon	1965–72	39	17	14	8	61.5
L.E.G. Ames	1950–56	37	18	11	8	63.5

Note: The percentage table is arrived at by allocating two points for a win and one for a draw then dividing this total by the number of points possible. Sir Alec was a selector from 1962 to 1985 (23 seasons excluding the 1970 series against the Rest of the World); the next longest serving was May with 11 seasons but in two stints (1965–68 and 1982–88).

Longest-serving chairmen of England Test selectors

		Seasons	Series	W	D	L	%
A.V. BEDSER	1969–81	12	18	10	3	5	63.9
P.B.H. May	1982–88	7	11	5	1	5	50.0
G.O. Allen	1955–61	7	7	6	0	1	85.7
P.F. Warner	1926, '31–2, '35–8	7	7	5	1	1	78.6
Lord Hawke	1899–1909, '33	6	6	3	0	3	50.0
E.R. Dexter	1989–93	5	7	3	1	3	50.0

Note: Sir Alec was chairman for four series against Australia, the results being won two, drew one and lost one. His record in four series against West Indies was won one, lost three.

ERIC ARTHUR BEDSER

BATTING AND FIELDING

Season by season

	M	I	NO	Runs	HS	Avge	100	50	Ct
1939	2	2	0	15	14	7.50	–	–	1
1946	26	41	2	832	101	21.33	1	3	17
1947	30	48	2	1272	92*	27.65	–	8	20
1948	22	34	3	496	128	16.00	1	1	13
1949	33	56	5	1740	163	34.12	2	6	34
1950	29	52	5	1321	160	28.11	2	3	20
1950/1	1	1	0	2	2	2.00	–	–	–
1951	26	44	1	1236	95	28.74	–	8	17
1952	31	54	5	1723	116	35.16	3	8	18
1953	28	44	6	1039	135	27.34	1	5	18
1954	24	36	4	746	86	23.31	–	4	8
1955	23	36	4	776	79	24.25	–	4	12
1956	32	50	10	804	55	20.10	–	3	17
1957	33	41	5	717	65	19.92	–	3	15
1958	29	36	5	426	56	13.74	–	1	3
1959	24	34	2	456	65	14.25	–	2	2
1959/60	2	4	1	24	13	8.00	–	–	2
1960	30	38	4	622	67*	18.29	–	2	7
1961	31	39	15	434	37	18.08	–	–	11
1962	1	2	0	35	22	17.50	–	–	1
Total	457	692	79	14716	163	24.01	10	61	236

For each team

	M	I	NO	Runs	HS	Avge	100	50	Ct
Surrey (County Championship)	363	552	66	11821	163	24.32	6	50	175
Surrey (other matches)	80	117	12	2327	113*	22.16	3	10	51
A Surrey XI	1	2	0	55	30	27.50	–	–	3
MCC	5	7	0	243	160	34.71	1	–	2
South	4	7	0	208	54	29.71	–	1	2
Players	2	3	0	16	12	5.33	–	–	1
Rest of England	1	2	0	33	30	16.50	–	–	–
Surrey & Kent	1	2	1	13	13	6.50	–	–	2
Total	457	692	79	14716	163	24.01	10	61	236

Against each opponent

	M	I	NO	Runs	HS	Avge	100	50	Ct
Derbyshire	21	35	5	480	76	16.00	–	3	11
Essex	20	30	3	530	116	19.63	1	–	12
Glamorgan	22	33	2	609	61	19.65	–	2	9
Gloucestershire	24	41	6	997	88	28.49	–	5	11
Hampshire	19	28	3	599	101	23.96	1	3	14
Kent	29	40	6	766	62	22.53	–	2	12
Lancashire	20	31	2	464	59	16.00	–	1	10
Leicestershire	23	32	9	841	135	36.57	2	3	17
Middlesex	24	42	3	806	79	20.66	–	5	16
Northamptonshire	24	36	1	870	95	24.86	–	4	6
Nottinghamshire	23	30	7	784	163	34.09	1	3	8
Somerset	20	27	2	832	154	33.28	1	3	9
Sussex	23	37	7	811	75	27.03	–	7	13
Warwickshire	23	33	2	636	65	20.52	–	2	12
Worcestershire	24	36	6	881	74	29.37	–	4	9
Yorkshire	25	42	2	921	89	23.03	–	3	8
Cambridge Univ.	22	26	2	661	113★	27.54	1	4	9
Oxford Univ.	14	19	3	816	160	51.00	3	2	14
MCC	14	24	1	373	96	16.22	–	2	5
Gentlemen	2	3	0	16	12	5.33	–	–	1
Combined Services	5	6	0	90	24	15.00	–	–	3
North	4	7	0	208	54	29.71	–	1	2
Rest of England	4	8	1	149	30★	21.29	–	–	10
England	1	2	0	33	30	16.50	–	–	–
Middlesex & Essex	1	2	1	13	13	6.50	–	–	2
Australians	6	10	1	75	19	8.33	–	–	3
Indians	4	7	1	91	40	15.17	–	–	–
New Zealanders	4	5	1	96	65	24.00	–	1	3
South Africans	4	6	1	100	67★	20.00	–	1	4
West Indians	5	9	0	142	37	15.77	–	–	1
Rhodesia	2	4	1	24	13	8.00	–	–	2
Tasmania	1	1	0	2	2	2.00	–	–	–
Total	457	692	79	14716	163	24.01	10	61	236

Note: The figures against the counties are all for matches in the County Championship except for one match for Surrey against Essex (6, two catches).

On each ground (listed by county and country)

	M	I	NO	Runs	HS	Avge	100	50	Ct
Chesterfield	4	7	2	155	76	31.00	–	2	–
Derby	5	9	1	122	55	15.25	–	1	4
In Derbyshire	9	16	3	277	76	21.31	–	3	4
Brentwood	2	2	0	9	6	4.50	–	–	–
Chelmsford	2	3	0	80	38	26.66	–	–	–
Clacton	2	4	1	40	15	13.33	–	–	–
Ilford	3	6	1	165	116	33.00	1	–	3
Leyton	1	2	1	20	11	20.00	–	–	–
Southend	1	1	0	13	13	13.00	–	–	2
In Essex	11	18	3	327	116	21.80	1	–	5
Cardiff	6	11	0	252	60	22.91	–	1	5
Ebbw Vale	1	1	0	27	27	27.00	–	–	1
Llanelli	1	2	0	17	11	8.50	–	–	–
Pontypridd	1	1	0	20	20	20.00	–	–	–
Swansea	3	4	0	101	61	25.25	–	1	6
In Glamorgan	12	19	0	417	61	21.95	–	2	6
Bristol	4	6	1	101	40	20.20	–	–	2
Cheltenham	5	9	0	131	46	14.55	–	–	2
Gloucester	3	6	1	179	51	35.80	–	1	3
Stroud	1	2	0	31	31	15.50	–	–	–
In Gloucestershire	13	23	2	442	51	21.05	–	1	7
Bournemouth	2	4	1	58	20	19.33	–	–	–
Portsmouth	3	6	1	105	51	21.00	–	1	3
Southampton	2	3	0	92	81	30.66	–	1	2
In Hampshire	7	13	2	255	81	23.18	–	2	5
Blackheath	13	17	3	332	52	23.71	–	1	1
Old Trafford	10	16	2	254	59	18.14	–	1	8
Ashby-de-la-Zouch	1	2	0	0	0	0.00	–	–	1
Leicester	10	16	5	367	97	33.36	–	2	11
Loughborough	1	1	0	135	135	135.00	1	–	–
In Leicestershire	12	19	5	502	135	35.86	1	2	12
Lord's	30	52	1	1078	160	21.14	1	6	15
Kettering	2	3	0	107	95	35.66	–	1	1
Northampton	7	10	0	181	52	18.10	–	1	–
Peterborough	2	2	0	32	30	16.00	–	–	1
Rushden	1	2	0	51	48	25.50	–	–	–
In Northamptonshire	12	17	0	371	95	21.82	–	2	2
Trent Bridge	12	14	1	314	56	24.15	–	1	4

	M	I	NO	Runs	HS	Avge	100	50	Ct
Taunton	7	7	0	303	86	43.29	–	3	3
Wells	1	2	1	11	11*	11.00	–	–	–
Weston-super-Mare	3	5	1	114	43	28.50	–	–	–
In Somerset	11	14	2	428	86	35.66	–	3	3
Guildford	30	39	8	1061	128	34.23	2	6	21
Kingston-upon-Thames	7	12	1	295	54	26.82	–	1	7
The Oval	203	303	38	6669	163	25.17	5	24	108
In Surrey	240	354	47	8025	163	26.14	7	31	136
Hastings	3	5	0	51	36	10.20	–	–	1
Hove	8	13	1	359	75	29.92	–	3	6
In Sussex	11	18	1	410	75	24.12	–	3	7
Coventry	3	5	0	81	29	16.20	–	–	2
Edgbaston	9	13	2	215	65	19.55	–	1	3
In Warwickshire	12	18	2	296	65	18.50	–	1	5
Dudley	1	2	0	44	30	22.00	–	–	2
Kidderminster	1	2	1	35	35	35.00	–	–	1
Worcester	11	16	2	310	48	22.14	–	–	5
In Worcestershire	14	20	3	389	48	22.88	–	–	8
Bradford	5	9	1	129	34	16.13	–	–	1
Headingley	4	6	0	162	73	27.00	–	1	–
Scarborough	3	5	0	30	14	6.00	–	–	4
Sheffield (Bramall Lane)	5	9	0	111	48	12.33	–	–	–
In Yorkshire	17	29	1	432	73	15.43	–	1	5
Fenner's	8	10	0	141	52	14.10	–	1	1
Hobart	1	1	0	2	2	2.00	–	–	–
Bulawayo	1	2	1	11	7*	11.00	–	–	2
Salisbury	1	2	0	13	13	6.50	–	–	–
Total	457	692	79	14716	163	24.01	10	61	236

BOWLING

Season by season

	O	M	R	W	Avge	5wi	10wm	BB
1939	†18	1	67	1	67.00	–	–	1-48
1946	370.3	65	968	25	38.72	–	–	3-79
1947	579	109	1682	50	33.64	–	–	4-15
1948	391.5	100	927	33	28.39	1	–	5-75
1949	847.3	251	2116	88	24.05	4	–	7-99
1950	263.4	53	890	14	63.57	–	–	2-9
1950/1	†12	1	39	0	–	–	–	–
1951	658	180	1430	61	23.44	4	2	7-142
1952	716.4	229	1530	70	21.86	2	–	5-40
1953	408.5	134	784	27	29.04	–	–	4-43
1954	246.1	82	578	22	26.27	–	–	4-39
1955	367.2	104	893	42	21.26	1	–	7-33
1956	794.3	236	1668	92	18.13	2	–	6-63
1957	548.5	178	1188	77	15.43	5	1	7-53
1958	552.2	205	1015	46	22.07	1	–	5-55
1959	438.3	124	1075	44	24.43	1	–	5-57
1959/60	56	14	131	4	32.75	–	–	2-46
1960	583.2	187	1265	53	23.87	–	–	4-46
1961	968.3	276	2505	84	29.82	3	1	5-58
1962	12	2	33	0	–	–	–	–
Total	8803.3	2529	20784	833	24.95	24	4	7-33
	†30	2						

† 8-ball overs

For each team

	O	M	R	W	Avge	5wi	10wm	BB
Surrey (County Championship)	7009.5	2083	15935	660	24.14	19	4	7-33
Surrey (other matches)	1506	400	3896	137	28.44	5	–	6-38
	†18	1						
A Surrey XI	16	0	64	2	32.00	–	–	2-44
MCC	97	23	251	6	41.83	–	–	3-46
	†12	1						
South	113.2	19	378	18	21.00	–	–	4-50
Players	20.5	1	89	6	14.83	–	–	3-40
Rest of England	13	0	60	0	–	–	–	–
Surrey & Kent	27.3	3	111	4	27.75	–	–	4-75
Total	8803.3	2529	20784	833	24.95	24	4	7-33
	†30	2						

Against each opponent

	O	M	R	W	Avge	5wi	10wm	BB
Derbyshire	271.2	75	587	25	23.48	1	—	5-55
Essex	355.4	88	864	31	27.87	1	—	5-32
Glamorgan	431.4	136	1025	32	32.03	1	—	6-56
Gloucestershire	534.2	146	1230	47	26.17	1	1	7-142
Hampshire	397.5	103	993	40	24.83	—	—	4-30
Kent	599.4	192	1281	66	19.41	2	—	5-55
Lancashire	351.5	94	840	34	24.71	1	—	5-75
Leicestershire	501.5	176	977	54	18.09	1	—	7-33
Middlesex	432.4	124	1043	47	22.19	4	1	7-99
Northamptonshire	527.3	163	1083	41	26.41	2	1	5-62
Nottinghamshire	369.4	114	858	34	25.24	—	—	4-49
Somerset	310.5	83	778	23	33.83	—	—	3-18
Sussex	451.2	119	1152	41	28.10	—	—	4-26
Warwickshire	483.3	142	1125	58	19.40	3	1	7-53
Worcestershire	428	152	872	41	21.27	—	—	4-29
Yorkshire	570.1	177	1254	48	26.13	2	—	5-27
Cambridge Univ.	496	154	1115	33	33.79	1	—	5-57
	†10	0						
Oxford Univ.	345.3	91	837	39	21.46	3	—	6-38
	†8	1						
MCC	222.2	44	672	23	29.22	1	—	5-116
Gentlemen	20.5	1	89	6	14.83	—	—	3-40
Combined Services	71.3	15	192	8	24.00	—	—	2-8
North	113.2	19	378	18	21.00	—	—	4-50
Rest of England	72	15	194	6	32.33	—	—	3-48
England	13	0	60	0	—	—	—	—
Middlesex & Essex	27.3	3	111	4	27.75	—	—	4-75
Australians	98.3	21	286	9	31.77	—	—	4-44
Indians	29	8	75	3	25.00	—	—	3-13
New Zealanders	38	8	127	4	31.75	—	—	3-21
South Africans	90	32	195	6	32.50	—	—	3-46
West Indians	92.1	20	321	8	40.13	—	—	4-50
Rhodesia	56	14	131	4	32.75	—	—	2-46
Tasmania	†12	1	39	0	—	—	—	—
Total	8803.3	2529	20784	833	24.95	24	4	7-33
	†30	2						

Note: The figures against the counties are all for matches in the County Championship except for one match for Surrey against Essex (8-1-27-2).

On each ground (listed by county and country)

	O	M	R	W	Avge	5wi	10wm	BB
Chesterfield	26	10	36	1	36.00	–	–	1-11
Derby	109	25	216	13	16.62	1	–	5-55
In Derbyshire	135	35	252	14	18.00	1	–	5-55
Brentwood	14	5	23	0	–	–	–	–
Chelmsford	21	2	60	2	30.00	–	–	1-9
Clacton	41	12	74	2	37.00	–	–	2-36
Ilford	44	10	143	1	143.00	–	–	1-40
Leyton	–	–	–	–	–	–	–	–
Southend	24	6	88	3	29.33	–	–	2-47
In Essex	144	35	388	8	48.50	–	–	2-36
Cardiff	168.4	49	407	17	23.94	1	–	6-56
Ebbw Vale	50	19	125	3	41.66	–	–	2-73
Llanelli	17	8	21	0	–	–	–	–
Pontypridd	1	1	0	0	–	–	–	–
Swansea	62	21	158	3	52.66	–	–	2-36
In Glamorgan	298.4	98	711	23	30.91	1	–	6-56
Bristol	149.3	35	375	10	37.50	–	–	4-42
Cheltenham	77	29	144	5	28.80	–	–	3-79
Gloucester	43	12	87	7	12.43	–	–	4-44
Stroud	14	3	26	1	26.00	–	–	1-26
In Gloucestershire	283.3	79	632	23	27.48	–	–	4-42
Bournemouth	76.5	10	252	7	36.00	–	–	4-30
Portsmouth	75	17	207	5	41.40	–	–	3-86
Southampton	12	3	30	3	10.00	–	–	2-25
In Hampshire	163.5	30	489	15	32.60	–	–	4-30
Blackheath	321	119	647	34	19.03	1	–	5-59
Old Trafford	173.1	59	355	14	25.36	–	–	3-19
Ashby-de-la-Zouch	51	21	83	3	27.66	–	–	3-83
Leicester	189	51	430	20	21.50	–	–	3-5
Loughborough	12	3	23	0	–	–	–	–
In Leicestershire	252	75	536	23	23.30	–	–	3-5
Lord's	609.4	144	1586	65	24.40	5	1	7-99
Kettering	77.2	29	156	12	13.00	2	1	5-62
Northampton	156.1	43	322	17	18.94	–	–	4-4
Peterborough	16	5	29	2	14.50	–	–	–
Rushden	–	–	–	–	–	–	–	–
In Northamptonshire	249.3	77	507	31	16.35	2	1	5-62
Trent Bridge	237.1	74	540	22	24.55	–	–	4-49

	O	M	R	W	Avge	5wi	10wm	BB
Taunton	128.3	30	372	7	53.14	–	–	2-65
Wells	18	5	45	2	22.50	–	–	1-15
Weston-super-Mare	33	5	99	2	49.50	–	–	1-13
In Somerset	177.3	40	516	11	46.91	–	–	2-65
Guildford	635.3	186	1516	66	22.97	2	–	5-48
Kingston-upon-Thames	156.5	22	553	24	23.04	–	–	4-50
The Oval	3560.5	1036	8355	328	25.47	8	1	7-33
	†18	1						
In Surrey	4353.1	1244	10424	418	24.94	10	1	7-33
	†18	1						
Hastings	66	19	174	6	29.00	–	–	4-64
Hove	152	45	376	11	34.18	–	–	4-63
In Sussex	218	64	550	17	32.35	–	–	4-63
Coventry	91	34	215	12	17.92	–	–	4-84
Edgbaston	250.5	70	554	35	15.83	3	1	7-53
In Warwickshire	341.5	104	769	47	16.36	3	1	7-53
Dudley	19	4	42	3	14.00	–	–	3-42
Kidderminster	27	8	60	2	30.00	–	–	2-44
Worcester	234	77	506	20	25.30	–	–	4-29
In Worcestershire	280	89	608	25	24.32	–	–	4-29
Bradford	132.3	42	302	14	21.57	1	–	5-63
Headingley	109.4	24	299	4	74.75	–	–	2-116
Scarborough	41.5	7	125	7	17.86	–	–	3-40
Sheffield (Bramall Lane)	59.1	13	116	5	23.20	–	–	2-26
In Yorkshire	343.1	86	842	30	28.07	1	–	5-63
Fenner's	164.2	63	262	9	29.11	–	–	2-37
Hobart	†12	1	39	0	–	–	–	–
Bulawayo	11	3	23	1	23.00	–	–	1-23
Salisbury	45	11	108	3	36.00	–	–	2-46
Total	8803.3	2529	20784	833	24.95	24	4	7-33
	†30	2						

BATTING

Centuries

101	Surrey v Hampshire	Kingston-upon-Thames	1946
128	Surrey v Oxford University	Guildford	1948
163	Surrey v Nottinghamshire	The Oval	1949
154	Surrey v Somerset	The Oval	1949
160	MCC v Oxford University	Lord's	1950
113★	Surrey v Cambridge University	The Oval	1950
116	Surrey v Essex	Ilford	1952
108	Surrey v Oxford University	Guildford	1952
103★	Surrey v Leicestershire	The Oval	1952
135	Surrey v Leicestershire	Loughborough	1953

Double-century partnerships

260	1st	L.B. Fishlock	Surrey v Somerset	The Oval	1949
226	1st	D.G.W. Fletcher	Surrey v Oxford University	Guildford	1948
221	2nd	L.B. Fishlock	Surrey v Hampshire	The Oval	1949
205	1st	D.G.W. Fletcher	Surrey v Essex	Ilford	1952

Eric took part in 35 century partnerships, as follows:
31 for Surrey
2 for South
1 for MCC

16 for the first wicket
5 for the second and fifth wickets
4 for the fourth wicket
2 for the third wicket
1 for the sixth, seventh and eighth wickets

9 with D.G.W. Fletcher
6 with L.B.Fishlock
3 with P.B.H. May and J.F. Parker
2 with K.F. Barrington, T.H. Clark and A.J. McIntyre
1 with M.R. Barton, N.H. Bennett, S.M. Brown, B. Constable, A.E. Fagg, H.S. Squires, R. Subba Row and W.H.H. Sutcliffe

15 at The Oval
5 at Guildford and Lord's
2 at Chesterfield and Kingston-upon-Thames
1 at Derby, Edgbaston, Hove, Ilford, Loughborough and Southampton

Pairs

Surrey v Leicestershire	Ashby-de-la-Zouch	1951
Surrey v Derbyshire	The Oval	1953
Surrey v Yorkshire	The Oval	1956

Methods of dismissal

Caught	345	56.28%
Bowled	162	26.43%
Lbw	71	11.58%
Run out	19	3.10%
Stumped	14	2.28%
Hit wicket	2	0.33%
Total	613	100.00%

Bowlers who most frequently dismissed Eric

11   C. Gladwin (Derbyshire), D.V.P. Wright (Kent)

10   T.E. Bailey (Essex), J.A. Young (Middlesex)

9   J.J. Warr (Middlesex)

8   W.E. Hollies (Warwickshire), R. Illingworth (Yorkshire), R.T.D. Perks (Worcestershire), D.J. Shepherd (Glamorgan), R. Tattersall (Lancashire)

Best position in national averages

45th–1952

Best position in national aggregates

26th–1952

Best position in Surrey's Championship averages

5th–1949, 1951, 1952

Best position in Surrey's Championship aggregates

2nd–1952   3rd–1949

BOWLING

Seven wickets in an innings

7-33	Surrey v Leicestershire	The Oval	1955
7-53	Surrey v Warwickshire	Edgbaston	1957
7-99	Surrey v Middlesex	Lord's	1949
7-142	Surrey v Gloucestershire	The Oval	1951

Ten wickets in a match

11-111	Surrey v Warwickshire	Edgbaston	1957
10-129	Surrey v Middlesex	Lord's	1961
10-139	Surrey v Northamptonshire	Kettering	1951
10-231	Surrey v Gloucestershire	The Oval	1951

Methods of dismissal

Caught	496	59.54%
Bowled	246	29.53%
Lbw	63	7.56%
Stumped	27	3.24%
Hit wicket	1	0.12%
Total	833	100.00%

Batsmen most frequently dismissed by Eric

8   V.S. Munden (Leicestershire)

7   D.W. Barrick (Northamptonshire), D.B. Close (Yorkshire)

6   T.E. Bailey (Essex), W.J. Edrich (Middlesex), C.J. Poole (Nottinghamshire), R.T. Spooner (Warwickshire)

Most fielding dismissals from Eric's bowling

48   A.J.W. McIntyre (32 ct, 16 st)

44   M.J. Stewart

43   W.S. Surridge

42   G.A.R. Lock

35   E.A. BEDSER

29   J.F. Parker

26   A.V. Bedser

24   R. Swetman (18 ct, 6 st)

20   K.F. Barrington

Best position in national averages
5th–1957

Best position in national aggregates
26th–1956

Best position in Surrey's Championship averages
3rd–1948, 1949, 1956, 1957, 1959, 1960

Best position in Surrey's Championship aggregates
3rd–1949 4th–1947, 1951, 1956, 1958, 1961

Eric compared with Laker

(in matches for Surrey in which Eric played with, or without, Laker)

	Overs	Runs	Wickets	Avge
1946–52				
Eric without Laker	1444.1	3359	136	24.70
Eric with Laker	1774.1	4478	150	29.85
Laker with Eric	4674.4	9796	552	17.75
1953–55				
Eric without Laker	330.1	688	20	34.40
Eric with Laker	671.2	1478	65	22.74
Laker with Eric	2022.3	4315	248	17.40
1956–59				
Eric without Laker	1412.2	2792	161	17.34
Eric with Laker	922.5	2154	98	21.98
Laker with Eric	2195.2	4599	271	16.97

Interesting to note that Laker's career average was 16.60; therefore his average is slightly worse than normal when bowling with Eric.

Eric's best seasons (when he took 50 wickets at an average of fewer than 25) when Laker was also in the Surrey side are now detailed separately.

Eric v Laker in certain seasons

	Overs	Runs	Wkts	Avge	Runs per Over	Balls per Wkt
1949						
Eric without Laker	199.3	474	27	17.55	2.38	44.33
Eric with Laker	607.3	1471	55	26.74	2.42	66.27
Laker with Eric	1120.1	2276	117	19.45	2.03	57.44
1951						
Eric without Laker	343.1	756	32	23.63	2.20	64.34
Eric with Laker	293	617	25	24.68	2.11	70.32
Laker with Eric	807.1	1747	87	20.08	2.16	55.66
1952						
Eric without Laker	440	925	44	21.02	2.10	60.00
Eric with Laker	246.4	533	19	28.05	2.16	77.89
Laker with Eric	784.1	1584	98	16.16	2.02	48.01
1956						
Eric without Laker	498.5	991	60	16.52	1.99	49.88
Eric with Laker	295.4	677	32	21.16	2.29	55.44
Laker with Eric	511	1166	61	19.11	2.28	50.26
1957						
Eric without Laker	369.3	775	53	14.62	2.10	41.83
Eric with Laker	179.2	413	24	17.21	2.30	44.83
Laker with Eric	695.3	1227	100	12.27	1.76	41.73

All of which appears to show that:

(a) Eric bowled better when Laker was not playing;

(b) Laker bowled better, overall, than Eric when both were in the same matches.

It is also worth pointing out that two of Eric's best seasons (1960 and 1961) came after Laker had left Surrey.

However, it was not always the case that Laker's figures were better than Eric's. Taking just the innings when both bowlers bowled at least ten overs, over the same seasons, Eric out-bowled Laker in 1951 and 1956 (!!!).

Eric v Laker in innings when both bowled a minimum of ten overs

	Overs	Runs	Wkts	Avge	Runs per Over	Balls per Wkt
1949						
Eric	488	1201	46	26.11	2.46	63.65
Laker	713	1425	60	23.75	2.00	71.30
1951						
Eric	253	535	22	24.32	2.11	69.00
Laker	449.3	944	26	36.32	2.10	103.73
1952						
Eric	126	257	6	42.83	2.04	126.00
Laker	279.4	568	32	17.75	2.03	52.44
1956						
Eric	232.2	527	29	18.17	2.27	48.07
Laker	276	620	25	24.80	2.25	66.25
1957						
Eric	87	204	11	18.55	2.34	47.45
Laker	126.3	178	11	16.18	1.41	69.00
Totals						
Eric	1186	2724	114	23.89	2.30	62.42
Laker	1844.4	3735	154	24.25	2.02	71.87

All of which seems to show that the difference between them, on certain occasions, was not so marked.

ALL-ROUND ACHIEVEMENTS

100 runs and ten wickets in a match for Surrey in County Championship

E.A. BEDSER	71 & 30	7-142 & 3-89	Gloucestershire	The Oval	1951
J.N. Crawford	148	7-85 & 4-63	Gloucestershire	Bristol	1906
P.G.H. Fender	104	3-48 & 7-76	Essex	Leyton	1926
R.J. Gregory	171	5-36 & 5-66	Middlesex	Lord's	1930
W.H. Lockwood	63 & 37	6-48 & 6-48	Lancashire	The Oval	1902

10,000 runs and 600 wickets for Surrey

		Matches	Runs	Avge	Wkts	Avge
E.A. BEDSER	1939–61	444	14148	23.94	797	24.88
P.G.H. Fender	1914–35	414	14117	28.01	1586	24.07

THE BEDSER TWINS – APPEARANCES IN SAME MATCH

The Bedser twins played in 303 first-class matches together as team-mates, as follows:

1939	2	1948	10	1950/1	1	1953	18	1956	25	1959	20
1946	16	1949	22	1951	13	1954	18	1957	32	1950/60	2
1947	24	1950	21	1952	21	1955	20	1958	13	1960	25

For Surrey in County Championship	247
For Surrey in other matches	52
For Players v Gentlemen	2
For South v North	1
For MCC v Tasmania	1

They also played on opposite sides in the match England (Sir Alec) v The Rest (Eric) at Bradford in 1950. This was the first time in the history of first-class cricket that twins had been in opposition.

ACKNOWLEDGEMENTS

The staff of the City of York Central Library
Jeff Hancock, Librarian, Surrey CCC, The Oval
Stephen Green, Curator, MCC, Lord's
Glenys Williams, Assistant Curator, MCC, Lord's
Peter Wynne-Thomas, Librarian, Nottinghamshire CCC, Trent Bridge
Brian Cowley

BIBLIOGRAPHY

PUBLICATIONS CONSULTED BY THE AUTHOR

Arlott, J., *Indian Summer* (Longmans, Green, 1947)

— *Fred: Portrait of a Fast Bowler* (Eyre & Spottiswoode, 1971)

Bannister, A., *Cricket Heroes* (Phoenix Sports Books, 1959)

Bedser, A., *Bowling* (Hodder & Stoughton, 1952)

— *Cricket Choice* (Pelham, 1981)

— *Twin Ambitions* (Stanley Paul, 1986)

Bradman, Sir Donald, *Farewell to Cricket* (Hodder & Stoughton, 1950)

Brodribb, G., *Maurice Tate* (London Magazine Editions, 1976)

Cardus, Sir Neville, *Playfair Cardus* (Dickens Press, 1963)

— *Cricket All the Year* (Collins, 1952)

Fingleton, J.H., *Brown & Company* (Collins, 1951)

— *Brightly Fades the Don* (Collins, 1949)

Gover, A., *The Long Run* (Pelham, 1991)

Hill, A., *The Family Fortune: A Saga of Sussex Cricket* (Scan Books, 1978)

— *Bill Edrich* (Andre Deutsch, 1994)

— *Jim Laker* (Andre Deutsch, 1998)

Holding, M., *Whispering Death* (Andre Deutsch, 1993)

Howat, G., *Walter Hammond* (George Allen & Unwin, 1984)

Hutton, Sir Leonard, *Fifty Years in Cricket* (Stanley Paul, 1984)

Jenkinson, N., *C.P. Mead: Hampshire's Greatest Run-maker* (Paul Cave, 1993)

Lodge, J., *Sir Alec V. Bedser* (ADS Publications, 1999)

McHarg, J., *Arthur Morris: An Elegant Genius* (ABC Books, Sydney, 1995)

May, P.B.H., *Peter May's Book of Cricket* (Cassell, 1956)

Moyes, A.G., *The Fight for the Ashes: 1950–51* (Hodder & Stoughton, 1951)

Norrie, D. (ed.), *The Bedsers at 80: commemorative brochure* (SportsPlus Ltd, 1998)

Robinson, R., *From the Boundary* (Collins, 1951)

— *The Glad Season* (Phoenix House, 1956)

— *Between Wickets* (Fontana, 1958)

— *On Top Down Under* (Cassell Australia, 1975)

Ross, G., *The Surrey Story* (SBC, 1958)
— *Surrey* (Arthur Barker, 1971)
Swanton, E.W., *Elusive Victory: with F.R. Brown's Team in Australia* (Hodder & Stoughton, 1951)
— *The Test Matches of 1953* (Daily Telegraph)
— *Swanton in Australia: with MCC, 1946–1975* (Collins, 1975)
Wellings, E.M., *Vintage Cricketers* (Allen & Urwin, 1983)
White, W.S., *Sydney Barnes* (E.F. Hudson, 1937)

Newspaper and magazine reports from the *The Cricketer, Daily Herald, Daily Telegraph, London Evening News, Manchester Guardian, News Chronicle, The Times, Surrey Advertiser, Sydney Morning Herald, Yorkshire Post* and various editions of *Wisden Cricketers' Almanack* and *Surrey Year Book*s have provided the nucleus of contemporary printed sources.

PUBLICATIONS CONSULTED BY THE STATISTICIANS

Bailey, P., Thorn, P., and Wynne-Thomas, P., *Who's Who of Cricketers* (Hamlyn, 1993)
Bedser, A.V., *Twin Ambitions* (Stanley Paul, 1986)
Botham, I.T., *My Autobiography* (HarperCollins, 1994)
Brooke, R., *The Collins Who's Who of English First-class Cricket* (Collins, 1985)
— *A History of the County Championship* (Guinness, 1991)
Dawson, M., *Cricket Extras* (Blandford, 1993)
Frindall, W., *England Test Cricketers* (Collins, 1989)
— *The Wisden Book of Test Cricket* (Headline, 2000)
— *The Wisden Book of Cricket Records* (Headline, 1998)
Frith, D., *England v Australia Test Match Records 1877–1985* (Collins, 1986)
Griffiths, P., *Complete First-class Match List* vol. 3: 1945–1962/63 (ACSH, 1999)
Hill, A., *Jim Laker* (Andre Deutsch, 1998)
Lodge, J., *Sir Alec Bedser CBE, His Record Innings by Innings* (ACSH, 1999)
Lynch, S., *The Lord's Test 1884–1989* (Spellmount, 1990)
Martin-Jenkins, C.M.J., *The Wisden Book of County Cricket* (Queen Anne Press, 1981)
— *World Cricketers* (Oxford University Press, 1996)
Ross, G., *Surrey Cricketers, 1839–1980* (ACSH, 1981)
Synge, A., *Sins of Omission* (Pelham, 1990)
Wat, C., *Australian First-class Cricket* (Five Mile Press, 1993)
Woolgar, J., *England's Test Cricketers* (Robert Hale, 1997)
Wynne-Thomas, P., *The Complete History of Cricket Tours* (Guild Publishing, 1989)

Also various editions of the *Cricket Statistician, The Cricketer, The Newsletter of The Cricket Society, Playfair Cricket Monthly* and *Wisden Cricketers' Almanack*.

INDEX

Cox, Group Captain, 35
Cox, D.F., 96
Cox, G., 105
Coxon, A., 60
Cranston, K. 60
Crapp, J.F., 60, 171

Dalton, H., 120
Davidson, A.K., 120, 151
Dempster, C.S., 37
Dewes, J.G., 69, 72, 78
Dexter, E.R., 151–6, 165, 170
Dixon, F., 79
Doggart, G.H.G., 66
Dooland, B., 115
Dovey, R.R., 103
Duckworth, G., 123
Duleepsinhji, K.S., 47

Edrich, W.J., 36, 46, 49, 51, 54–5, 57, 60, 65,
    68–9, 90, 124, 134
Eglington, R., 31
Elliott, C.S., 159, 163
Emmett, G.M., 171
Evans, D., 149
Evans, T.G., 33, 36, 51, 56, 71–3, 75, 86, 97–8,
    102, 112, 117, 121, 124, 133, 138

Fagan, J., 148
Fagan, Mrs F., 148
Falcon, M., 130
Faulkner, G.A., 78
Fender, P.G.H., 28, 67, 129
Ferguson, W., 53
Fingleton, J.H.W., 55, 71–2, 77, 86, 88, 134
Fishlock, L.B., 30, 45, 51, 60–2, 65–6
Fletcher, D.G.W., 26, 60, 101–2
Foster, F.R., 127
Freeman, A.P., 28
Fry, C.B., 32

Gaekward, D.K., 112
Gibb, P.A., 47, 49
Gilligan, A.E.R., 70, 129–30
Gladwin, C., 60, 135–6
Goddard, T.W.J., 60, 64
Gordon, Sir Home, 37
Gover, A.R., 21–2, 25–7, 37, 44–5, 59–60, 95,
    122, 147
Gower, D.I., 82, 161
Graveney, T.W., 113, 118, 122, 124, 151, 159–60
Gregory, R.J., 26, 45, 64
Greig, A.W., 160, 163–5
Griffith, S.C., 57, 141, 151
Grimmett, C.V., 48, 137

Grove, C.W., 105

Hadlee, W.A., 59, 65, 109
Halliday, H., 36
Hammond, W.R., 46, 48–51, 53–6, 82, 89, 99,
    160
Hapgood, E., 18
Harding, N.W., 36
Hardstaff, J., 46, 49, 51, 55
Harvey, B., 86
Harvey, C.E. (Mick), 86
Harvey, Harold, 86
Harvey, Horace, 86
Harvey, M.R., 86
Harvey, R.N., 85–7, 116, 118, 120–2, 156, 175
Harvey, R., 86
Hassett, A.L., 54, 70, 76, 85–6, 115, 117–18,
    161
Hayes, E.G., 22
Hayter, R.J., 128
Hayward, T.W., 27
Hazare, V.S., 47, 111–12
Hendren, E.H. (Patsy), 32
Hill, J.C., 119
Hirst, G.H., 31
Hitchcock, R.E., 104
Hobbs, Sir John Berry, 27, 30–2, 82, 127, 130
Holding, M.A., 116
Hole, G.B., 116, 120
Hollies, W.E., 93, 104
Holmes, E.R.T., 60
Holmes, P., 96
Hooker, J.E.H., 45
Howard, C.G., 64, 123–4, 171, 174
Howard, Major R., 53
Howat, Gerald, 51
Hutton, Sir Leonard, 46, 48, 51, 56, 72–8,
    82–3, 87, 89–92, 95–6, 105, 111–16,
    118–19, 121, 123–6, 159, 163

Illingworth, R., 164, 174
Ikin, J.T., 33, 46, 53, 103
Insole, D.J., 104, 132, 138, 144, 146, 150–2,
    158–60, 162
Iverson, J.B., 75–6

Jackman, R.D., 166
Jackson, A., 84
Jackson, H.L., 68
Jardine, D.R., 64, 78, 126, 128
Jenkins, R.O., 135
Jessop, G.L., 167
Johnson, I.W., 85
Johnston, W.A., 73, 76, 134
Jourdain, Rev. R.T., 18